The Worth Expert Guide to Writing in Psychology: Using APA Style

Randolph A. Smith
Moravian College

Series Editors

R. Eric Landrum
Boise State University

Regan A.R. Gurung
Oregon State University

worth publishers
Macmillan Learning

New York

Senior Vice President, Content Strategy: Charles Linsmeier
Program Director: Shani Fisher
Executive Editor: Christine Cardone
Development Editor: Elaine Epstein
Assistant Editor: Dorothy Tomasini
Associate Media Editor: Stephanie Matamoros
Executive Marketing Manager: Katherine Nurre
Marketing Assistant: Steven Huang
Director, Content Management Enhancement: Tracey Kuehn
Senior Managing Editor: Lisa Kinne
Senior Content Project Manager: Won McIntosh
Media Project Manager: Jason Perkins
Senior Workflow Project Manager: Lisa McDowell
Production Supervisor: Robin Besofsky
Director of Design, Content Management: Diana Blume
Design Services Manager: Natasha Wolfe
Design Manager, Cover: John Callahan
Interior Design: Lumina Datamatics, Inc.
Cover Design: John Callahan
Art Manager: Matthew McAdams
Photo Editor: Cecilia Varas
Permissions Editor: Michael McCarty
Composition: Lumina Datamatics, Inc.
Printing and Binding: LSC Communications
Cover Art: exdez/Getty Images

Library of Congress Control Number: 2019957427

ISBN-13: 978-1-319-02141-2
ISBN-10: 1-319-02141-7

Worth Publishers
One New York Plaza
Suite 4600
New York, NY
10004-1562
www.macmillanlearning.com

To my writing teachers:

Lee Flowers, my 11th-grade English teacher

Phil Marshall, my graduate school mentor

Charles Brewer, my APA-Style and editorial guru

About the Author

Ruth E. Louie

Randolph A. (Randy) Smith is an adjunct Professor of Psychology at Moravian College. He previously taught and chaired departments at Ouachita Baptist University, Kennesaw State University, and Lamar University. His professional work centers on the scholarship of teaching and learning. He has written several book chapters and articles and made numerous presentations dealing with varied aspects of teaching, critical thinking, applying social psychology to teaching, and assessment of teaching.

Smith's full-length books include *Challenging Your Preconceptions: Thinking Critically About Psychology* (2002), *The Psychologist as Detective: An Introduction to Conducting Research in Psychology* (2013, with Steve Davis), and *An Introduction to Statistics and Research Methods: Becoming a Psychological Detective* (2005, with Steve Davis). He served as editor of the Society for the Teaching of Psychology's journal *Teaching of Psychology* for 12 years and subsequently served as editor of the *Psi Chi*

Journal of Undergraduate Research. In addition, he developed a comprehensive instructor's resource package for Wayne Weiten's introductory psychology textbook.

Smith received both the American Psychological Foundation's Charles L. Brewer Distinguished Teaching of Psychology Award and the University System of Georgia Regents' Scholarship of Teaching and Learning Award in 2006. He is a Life Member of the American Psychological Association (a Fellow of Divisions 1 and 2 — General Psychology and Teaching) and a Fellow of the Association for Psychological Science.

Brief Contents

Contents

Preface

"We encounter an abundance of complex, scientific information in our world, and such knowledge will only increase in the future" (Keith & Beins, 2017, p. xvii). Clear writing is an essential skill for dealing with complex, scientific information and communicating such information clearly to others. Because humankind faces challenging issues such as climate change, genetic engineering, mental health, and the like, it is critical that scientists who address those issues communicate their knowledge in such a way that politicians, people working in the legal system, members of the media, and laypeople can understand the information and be able to apply it in addressing these complicated issues.

Unfortunately, data from the Nation's Report Card project (National Center for Education Statistics, 2012) indicate that people who will become the scientists; politicians; judges, lawyers, and jury members; media members; and citizens of the future may not be prepared to write in the manner necessary to communicate information clearly. How can the United States expect members of society to adopt scientific advancements if the scientists making those advancements—and the students of science who will join their ranks—cannot communicate them clearly or if their audience cannot understand them?

Technological advances supposedly make it much easier to write and revise a paper using a computer, rather than the pen and paper that your parents and grandparents once used. Finding information to use as sources is also much easier, as you can search for relevant articles from the comfort of your bedroom or workspace rather than hiking to the library as in bygone days. Along these lines, a survey (Purcell et al., 2013) of more than 2400 expert writing teachers found that the teachers believed that technology aided student writing by "facilitating teens' personal expression and creativity, broadening the audience for their written material, and encouraging teens to write more often in more formats than may have been the case in prior generations" (p. 2).

By the same token, evidence suggests that some technological advances have had a negative effect on writing ability. For example, a study of sixth, seventh, and eighth graders (Cingel & Sundar, 2012) showed that the more students texted, the lower they scored on a basic grammar assessment instrument. The survey of writing teachers mentioned earlier (Purcell et al., 2013) found that more than two thirds of the teachers believed that using digital tools such as cell phones and social networking sites led students to take shortcuts and not put forth effort in their writing (only 10% disagreed). Also, 46% of the teachers believed that using technologies led students to write too fast or be careless (only 19% disagreed). Finally, teachers were almost evenly divided (40% to 38%) about whether using technology led to students using poor spelling and grammar, an oft-heard belief about texting and emailing.

Thus, as a writer today, you have it both better and worse than your parents and grandparents did when they were learning to write. It is incumbent on you to use the positive benefits of technology while also staying vigilant to avoid the downside of technology's influences on writing. You will find that the chapters in this book are full of technology-related information to help you travel along the pathway toward more successful, accomplished writing.

About the Book

The aim of this book is to help you learn more about scientific writing, especially in psychology and other research-based disciplines. Specific chapters cover the following key writing assignments that students and professionals often encounter in psychology and related fields:

- Annotated bibliographies (Chapter 5)
- Term papers and literature reviews (Chapter 6)
- Research proposals (Chapter 7)
- Write-ups of research findings (Chapter 8)
- Oral presentations, posters, and journal submissions (Chapter 9)

Becoming familiar with the framework of this book will help you determine which chapters you should focus on given the particular type of writing assignment you are facing. The chapters cover both general writing principles and writing in the latest American Psychological Association (APA) Style (7th ed., 2020). APA Style is important for writing various types of assignments in psychology courses, as well as in other disciplines that use APA Style.

Chapter Organization

The first four chapters prepare you for writing for all types of psychology assignments (and other disciplines using APA Style), whereas the last five chapters cover requirements for specific assignments. Chapter 1 takes a look at the writing process and why writing well is important. In this chapter, you will find questions that help you analyze your approach to writing and plan your writing accordingly, as well as a list of behaviors that will help you write more effectively and easily.

Chapter 2 introduces APA Style and contrasts that style with others you may have used previously in your writing assignments. You will learn a little about the history and evolution of APA Style. Most importantly, you will read about values that are inherent in APA Style and how they differ from other writing styles you have used in the past. Because they are new to you, it is important for you to understand and master these unique values as you learn to write in APA Style. Toward the end of this chapter, you will learn about the mechanics used in APA Style — items such as font style, spacing, margins, and so on.

Chapter 3 focuses on grammar, which is just as important in APA-Style writing as it is in writing you have done for English classes. This chapter contains a good amount of helpful grammar review. In addition, it provides important pointers about specific grammatical emphases used in APA Style.

Chapter 4 guides you about how to read a psychology journal article — or any other journal article written in APA Style. Journal articles are the primary source of scientific information in a wide variety of disciplines, so it is important for you to know what type of information you will find in such articles and where you will find it. The writing assignments covered in this book depend on your ability to read journal articles and extract information from them. It is also logical that reading articles written in APA Style will acquaint you with and prepare you for writing in APA Style in your own assignments. This chapter ends the preliminary chapters about general writing pointers.

Chapter 5 addresses the first of four possible writing assignments you might face: an annotated bibliography. In an annotated bibliography, your task is to find a set of journal articles related to a particular topic, write annotations about those articles, format those sources as APA-Style references, and compile the references and their annotations into a complete bibliography. You will learn how to search PsycINFO to find relevant journal articles, which is a critical skill for completing *all* of the writing assignments you will encounter. The reference format used in

APA Style differs significantly from other reference formats you may have used in the past, so it is an important skill to master.

Chapter 6 covers writing a term paper or a literature review. These writing products are so similar as to be almost synonymous, at least from an APA-Style perspective. You will learn some important behaviors to help reduce the stress you might feel in writing such a paper. The chapter also includes tips regarding important activities both before and while writing your paper. You will learn how to use APA Style to cite the sources that you include in your paper. In addition, you will find out how to type your paper in APA Style, with formatting information dealing with matters such as the title page, running heads, and headers.

Chapter 7 explores the assignment of writing a research proposal. If your major requires you to complete an experimental research project, you will likely need to write and submit a research proposal ahead of time, which will involve selecting and narrowing a researchable topic. You will learn about writing an introduction, Method section, and reference list, as well as important APA-Style elements of a proposal.

Chapter 8 shows you how to write a research report after you have conducted an experiment, including the new components of an abstract, Results section, and Discussion section to add to the introduction, Method section, and reference list that you learned about in Chapter 7. The chapter includes extensive coverage of writing statistical information for your results. Importantly, you will encounter all the APA-Style pointers you need to complete your experimental write-up.

Finally, Chapter 9 presents alternatives for you to consider for disseminating your work after you have completed your research report or other type of paper. Scientists typically communicate the results of their research with their peers. You will learn about the possibility of presenting your work in either oral or poster format at a meeting designed to showcase research projects, as well as various possibilities for publishing your research — including actually writing a journal article such as the ones you originally read to plan your project. You will learn about the many steps involved in the publication process.

Pedagogical Features

Each chapter begins with a **"Do You Know?"** feature that highlights important questions that the chapter will address. You can use these questions as organizing features and learning objectives that guide you through the chapter when you are looking for the relevant answers. However, I also encourage you to return to these questions *after* you have completed each chapter, making sure that you can then answer each one in sufficient detail.

Each chapter ends with a set of **"Critical Thinking Writing Assignments."** Regardless of whether your instructor has you tackle these writing assignments, I encourage you to address them on your own. You should not simply look at the assignments and think about them, but rather actually write an answer as the instructions indicate. Why? Even unassigned and ungraded writing can improve your writing skills in the long run—practice *does* help!

Within chapters, you will find two features designed to help you with the material. **"A Closer Look"** provides more in-depth coverage of some of the critical points from the chapters. **"In Practice"** offers detailed pointers that you can use to make your writing in or learning about APA Style more efficient and, perhaps, easier. Also, the Glossary in the back matter of the book contains the book's boldfaced key terms with their definitions.

To help you learn about APA-Style writing and formatting, **Appendix A** contains an actual journal article published by a student. I use that article to explain how to read journal articles *and* how to write research reports (which could be published later). **Appendix B** shows that journal article annotated with differences between the original article and current APA Style (7th ed., 2020). **Appendix C** shows the published article in manuscript format—the same APA Style and format that you will need to use when you write your research report. **Appendix D** presents a table

I developed of common student writing problems (from my experience) and solutions for those problems. Sprinkled throughout the book, tables and figures highlight specific points about APA Style from the text, so that you have both a verbal description and a visual picture to help make the information more memorable. In addition, these tables and figures will serve as quick-reference guides in the future as you actually write APA-Style papers. Other tables provide you with step-by-step instructions about how to format an APA-Style paper in Word or how to make a graph in Excel, in both PC and Mac versions. As much as possible, the book mirrors APA Style in formatting, down to the headers.

I have tried to capture reader interest throughout the book by using a writing style and tone that reflects a conversation. At various points in the book, you will encounter writing samples from students who wrote papers in various classes; again, these are students just like you. If they can do this type of writing, so can you. Several chapters include testimonials from former students of mine about how writing has been important to them *after* they graduated. I firmly believe that writing well is a skill that will help you not just during college and classes, but also in your life and work after college. I hope you use the book to help guide and assist you on your quest to become a better writer. Good luck in your future writing projects!

Acknowledgments

I thank Executive Editor Christine Cardone for her unfailing support, encouragement, and advice, not just for this book but also for other writing endeavors over many years. I also thank my developmental editor Elaine Epstein, Assistant Editor Dorothy Tomasini, Senior Content Project Manager Won McIntosh, and copy editor Jill Hobbs for their numerous helpful suggestions. Elaine and Won saved my life on many occasions! I thank Pamela Ansburg (Metropolitan State University of Denver), Charles L. Brewer (Furman University), William Buskist (Auburn University), Andrew Christopher (Albion College), Carrie Cuttler (Washington State

University), Christopher Hakala (Springfield College), Jane S. Halonen (University of West Florida), Kenneth Keith (University of San Diego), Marina Sorochinski (CUNY John Jay College of Criminal Justice), Chrysalis Wright (University of Central Florida), and Kevin Zabel (Western New England University) for many helpful suggestions on earlier versions of the manuscript.

I appreciate Paul W. Anderson (Murray State U.), Rebekah Benjamin (Huntington U.), Fabiana DesRosiers (Keiser U.), Ingrid Farreras (Hood College), Amanda R. Hemmesch (St. Cloud State U.), Carolyn B. Kramer (U. of Nebraska-Lincoln), Molly Metz (Miami U.), Lindsay A. Phillips (Albright College), Courtney A. Rocheleau (Metropolitan State U. of Denver), Diane M. Ryan (U.S. Military Academy), Ron Sheese (York U.), and Joanne Zinger (U. of California, Irvine) for their helpful insights into annotated bibliographies (Chapter 5). I owe a deep debt of gratitude to Eugenio A. Peluso, PhD (The Neuroscience Center at NNA; Akron, Ohio) for allowing me to reprint the research article (Appendix A and Appendix B) he published while he was a student at Creighton University.

Finally, I express deep gratitude to my spouse Ruth Louie for her love and support over many years, including as I worked on this book project. I appreciate you more than you can know.

References

American Psychological Association. (2020). *Publication manual of the American Psychological Association* (7th ed.). https://doi.org/10.1037/0000165-000

Cingel, D. P., & Sundar, S. S. (2012). Texting, techspeak, and tweens: The relationship between text messaging and English grammar skills. *New Media & Society, 14*(8), 1304–1320. https://doi.org/10.1177/1461444812442927

Keith, K. D., & Beins, B. C. (2017). *The Worth expert guide to scientific literacy: Thinking like a psychological scientist.* Worth Publishers.

National Center for Education Statistics. (2012). *The nation's report card: Writing 2011* (NCES 2012-470). Institute of Education Sciences, U.S. Department of Education. https://nces.ed.gov/nationsreportcard/pdf/main2011/2012470.pdf

Purcell, K., Buchanan, J., & Friedrich, L. (2013). *The impact of digital tools on student writing and how writing is taught in schools* (National Writing Project/ Pew Research Center). https://www.nwp.org/afnews/PIP_NWP_Writing_and_Tech.pdf

1

I Have to Write a Paper for a Psychology Class

Do You Know?

How can writing well help you in situations other than college classes?

How can analyzing your writing habits make you a more efficient writer?

How can you obtain copies of articles that are not available online or in your library?

What is plagiarism, and how can you avoid it?

What should you do when editing and revising a paper beyond simply proofreading it?

"You fail only if you stop writing."

—Ray Bradbury

I f you are like most students, finding out on the first day of class that you are required to write a paper is an experience that makes your throat tighten or your palms sweat (or both!). Writing is often not a favorite experience for students. There is no reason to feel guilty about your possible dislike of writing—even professional writers have a love/hate affair with the writing process. For example, Ernest Hemingway said, "We are all apprentices in a craft where no one ever becomes a master." I have written this book in an attempt to make the writing process simpler and more pleasant for you.

Writing Is Not a Simple or Easy Process

According to Theodore Roosevelt (26th president of the United States), "Nothing in the world is worth having or worth doing unless it means effort, pain, difficulty." If you reflect on your progress through your school career, and perhaps life in general, you will probably find yourself agreeing with Roosevelt. The times that you have accomplished the most and been the most proud of those accomplishments have probably required hard work and effort. Writing is no different—you must work hard at becoming a practiced and good writer.

So, let's take a realistic look at writing. It can be a difficult process, but also a valuable and rewarding experience. With demonstrable benefits related to both college and job success, it is reasonable for you to decide to work at becoming a better writer. This book is designed to help you in that quest, and this chapter will provide you with some general writing ideas and guidelines that will help you as you attempt to improve your writing. The remainder of the chapters will be more specific in nature, addressing writing in psychology style and for specific types of assignments.

Before moving on, let me provide two overall tips that can help you before you even begin to work on your psychology papers. First, if you do have a negative view about writing, do your best to change that mindset. As you probably know from previous experience, having negative expectations tends to create negative outcomes. If you expect writing to be a miserable experience, it will probably end up being miserable. Look for the positive aspects of writing as you approach the task and while you write.

Second, to get better at writing, plan to practice your writing. One of the most common pieces of advice I have encountered in reading about improving writing is to practice, practice, practice (e.g., Calkins, 1994; Farris & Smith, 1992). Research shows that students can learn about course material through writing about content (writing to learn) even if the writing is not graded (Drabick et al., 2007; Nevid et al., 2012). Thus, writing about material that you are learning will give you both practice at writing *and* help you learn course content. The notion that practicing writing (even ungraded) will improve students' actual writing is an assumption of the "writing across the curriculum" movement because, as McLeod (1992) pointed out, such practice helps students "think on paper" (p. 3).

So, my overarching advice is to adopt a positive attitude about writing and to practice your writing. It's even possible that writing more will help your attitude about writing become more positive.

Why Is Writing Well Important?

Why is it worthwhile to become a good writer? One important reason is linked to success in college. Researchers found that scores on the writing section of the Scholastic Aptitude Test (SAT) showed higher correlations with both high school grades and first-year college grades than scores on either the critical reading or math SAT sections (Kobrin et al., 2008). Garrett et al. (2017) examined all first-year courses at one university and found that writing courses were most critically related to later graduation. Students who failed a remedial writing course had only a 17% chance of eventual graduation. Failing one of two standard first-year writing courses reduced students' chances of graduating by 38%, more than any other first-year course.

If you plan to go to graduate school, you'll find that writing as a graduate student is perhaps even more important than it is as an undergraduate. According to Ondrusek (2012, p. 179), "Writing is the vehicle that most graduate programs embrace as the means for reviewing how well students are able to assimilate knowledge and integrate that knowledge into new ideas." Wadsworth et al. (2002) maintained that developing good writing skills helped graduate students in rehabilitation counselor training programs become discriminating readers of professional literature. According to these authors, "Rehabilitation counselors have the obligation to be able to communicate accurately and effectively to clients and providers of rehabilitation services" (p. 296). It should be obvious that the necessity of writing skills is not important just to graduate students in rehabilitation counseling. In an interview about graduate school (gradlogic.org/stabio/), University of Colorado Medical School faculty member Maureen Stabio listed "learning to write well" as one of the three keys to succeeding in graduate school. She also noted that she spent more time in graduate school writing than in any other activity other than research.

Another reason to work at becoming a good writer is linked to job success. In a survey of 120 major American corporations that employed almost 8 million people (National Commission on Writing for America's Families, Schools, and Colleges, 2004), half of the companies said that they considered writing skill when hiring professional employees. Also, at least 80% of companies in finance, real estate, and insurance sectors (companies with the greatest employment growth potential) assessed writing during the hiring process. Further, two-thirds of salaried employees in the corporations had some writing responsibility in their jobs.

Half of all companies took writing into consideration when considering employees for promotion. Finally, more than 40% of the companies required remedial training for employees with writing deficiencies. This figure *might* imply that the remaining 60% of companies simply jettisoned employees who could not write well.

For further evidence that writing can be important in your career, I contacted former students of mine (at Ouachita Baptist University [OBU]) and asked if they had any stories that documented this point. I include a couple of their stories here, along with the students' graduation dates and current job. You will read more of these stories at other points in the book.

> *Writing is an essential part of my job. As a university professor, I utilize this skill daily and in a variety of ways. I engage in both formal and informal writing. Examples of the types of things I routinely write include emails, letters of recommendations, lectures, memos, assignments, exams . . . and the list goes on and on. Regardless of what I write, I always remind myself that the purpose of writing is to effectively convey information, ideas, and knowledge to others in a clear and concise manner. When it comes to writing, I have not always been comfortable with my level of proficiency. However, one of my college professors (Dr. Randy Smith) told me that improving the quality of your writing requires practice . . . just like honing any other skill in life. Thanks for the useful tip, Randy!* (Loretta Neal McGregor, PhD; OBU, 1988; Professor of Psychology, Arkansas State University, Jonesboro, AR)

> *I write psych evals/reports, letters of recommendation, treatment summaries, and therapy notes. In my field, one has to be careful how these documents are worded so as not to offend the client you're writing for. I think learning writing skills in my psychology classes helped me tremendously in my career*

by acquiring the ability to be concise and direct without sounding too abrupt, but also providing enough information to assist with transferring pertinent client knowledge for continued care in the mental health and medical community. In fact, people in my office often try to bribe me into writing information for their clients because they say I have a gift for taking hours of information and honing it down into a two-page summary. (Autumne Brunson Hart, MS; OBU, 2001; Licensed Professional Counselor, Mt. Vernon, TX)

Let me leave you with one final thought about why writing well and clearly can be important in a job situation. In a list of items, we use commas to set the items apart—for example, "Apples, peaches, pears, and bananas are types of fruit." The comma before "and" is known as the **Oxford comma** (also known as a serial comma) because Oxford University Press mandated its use (Victor, 2018). In your English classes, you may have learned that many grammarians consider the Oxford comma to be optional. However, proponents maintain that not using the comma sometimes renders sentences with lists somewhat vague and unclear. APA Style requires the Oxford comma (APA, 2020, p. 155).

For instance, a dairy in Maine ended up paying its drivers $5 million in back pay because of a dispute that arose over punctuation. Maine law exempted paying overtime for certain jobs dealing with food shipping and distribution—the law read, "The canning, processing, preserving, freezing, drying, marketing, storing, packing for shipment or distribution of: (1) Agricultural produce; (2) Meat and fish products; and (3) Perishable foods" (Victor, 2018). Because the listing did not use an Oxford comma, it was unclear which jobs the law excluded—was "packing for shipment" separate from "distribution," or did these two words express a single activity? Drivers for the dairy sued for overtime pay because the law was not clear about their exclusion, and they won the $5 million in back overtime pay. Although unclear writing may never cost you that kind of money, this example from Maine highlights the importance of clear writing!

Before You Begin to Write

Given that most college students are relatively inexperienced writers, it makes sense to take some time before you start to write to engage in some self-discovery about your approach to writing. Just as you have (I hope) analyzed your approach to studying so as to make it maximally effective, paying conscious attention to aspects of your writing behavior can help to make it more efficient.

Know Your Audience and Your Requirement

Good writers know that they need to write for a specific audience. You typically will write papers for your professors, so the style you use will likely be formal and scholarly. Faculty often require the use of a standard writing format for psychology — **APA (American Psychological Association) Style** (APA, 2020) — for such papers. However, some writing assignments may be less formal and, therefore, require a less formal style. For example, if you keep a journal for a class, your professor may expect you to write more personal entries. When you receive a writing assignment for a class, determining the audience for whom you are writing is crucial. Going hand-in-hand with knowing your audience is determining the specific format of your writing assignment. You may write several different types of papers. This book addresses five types of writing assignments: annotated bibliography (Chapter 5), term paper and literature review (Chapter 6), research proposal (Chapter 7), and research report (Chapter 8).

Plan Your Writing Ahead of Time

Many writers will tell you that some of their most productive time is time *away from the keyboard!* This statement seems counterintuitive, but it will likely make more sense as you write more and more. When you first began writing papers in school, your teacher probably required you to develop an outline for your paper before you actually wrote the paper. An outline is a formal system of organizing your thoughts and direction before you write.

Another way of planning your writing is to think about it during your nonwriting time. In so doing, you will often find that ideas about your writing pop into your head. Be sure to take advantage of these ideas. I am old fashioned, so I write ideas on a notecard or piece of paper and carry them in my pocket. However, when these ideas occur, I have also sent emails or texts to myself or written them in the Notes app on my phone. The important message here is NOT to lose these ideas—they may be invaluable as you work on your writing. Even famous authors use this technique: "The best time for planning a book is while you're doing the dishes," said mystery writer Agatha Christie. If you're not a fan of doing dishes, don't worry. The activity of "doing dishes" is not particularly important; the idea is to capitalize on thinking about writing no matter what you are doing.

Another key idea in this section is the phrase "ahead of time." Procrastinating and waiting until the last minute to begin writing will not help you produce your best work. Good writing takes time. If you know you have a paper to write for class, begin thinking and planning your writing from the beginning of the semester. Writing against a looming deadline is a miserable experience, as even seasoned writers will tell you. Procrastination can even prove detrimental to your grade. Researchers at the University of Warwick (2014) found that students who turned in online writing assignments from 24 hours ahead of deadline until the last minute showed a steady decline in grades on the assignment over that time period. Students who turned in their assignment at the absolute last minute earned grades that were 5% lower than all other students, which could cost them a letter grade.

Analyze Your Approach to Writing

Davis (2010) advised prospective authors to think about their writing and conduct a *personal writing habits inventory* before even turning on the computer to write. Davis suggested that you consider the following four questions before you begin.

Why Are You Writing?

Most likely, you will answer that you are writing to satisfy some class requirement. However, with a more positive response, you may feel more motivated to write. For example, if you are about to write a term paper, I hope you have been able to choose the topic — I always tell students to choose a topic that interests them or about which they want to learn more. Thus, your answer (and motivation) would be "To learn more about <u>paranoid schizophrenia</u>" or "I want to know more about <u>the biochemical basis of learning</u>" (fill in the blank with your specific topic, of course!). Notice how much more rewarding writing will be with this type of mindset and motivation.

Where Do You Write?

It is important to find your optimal location for writing. Although your writing location *might* be the same as your study location, it doesn't have to be. In fact, I would even suggest that, if possible, you find a writing location that is different from the place where you study. You want your writing location to be a signal or cue to you that it is time to write and do nothing else. If you attempt to write in a location where you often nap or watch TV, you will be giving yourself mixed signals about what to do in that spot. (You probably understand this point quite well if you have ever tried to study on your bed — the urge to nap may quickly overwhelm you!) One of the beauties of having a dedicated place to write is that you can probably be more efficient in the use of your time (see an upcoming question on the next page about writing blocks for my rationale).

When Do You Write?

Finding an optimal time to write is also critical to your success as a writer. More than likely, the optimal time is when you are well rested and full of energy. However, you must face reality: You are a college student—when are you ever well rested and full of energy? Swensen (2011), an author of fantasy novels, noted on his blog that ideal writing conditions rarely, if ever, occur; if you wait until conditions are ideal, you may never write. Thus, you must train yourself to write even when the inclination to do so doesn't strike you.

Develop a writing schedule for yourself and *stick to it*. Draw up a calendar and record your projected writing times on it. Committing to an activity ahead of time increases the odds that you will maintain your commitment. The IN PRACTICE: Plan Your Writing Schedule box provides you with a blank schedule on which you can plan your writing. As you develop your schedule, consider the final question.

What Is the Length of Your Writing Block?

How long do you like to spend writing at one time? How long do you need in a writing session to get started, actually do some writing, and then shut things down? Many people think of a writing session as involving only the middle stage of the three (actual writing) that I just listed. Depending on your habits, you might spend 15–20 minutes getting started and 5–10 minutes shutting down. Thus, you might lose half an hour doing things that are not actually productive.

Having a dedicated writing location can increase your efficiency by cutting down the "getting started" stage. Rather than having to locate your sources, your laptop and saved files, and your favorite writing chair, they will be waiting for you in your writing spot. I know of no actual data, but I would venture to guess that most professional writers have a room or office that is dedicated to their writing. Such an arrangement might be difficult for you as a college student to create, but any steps you can take in this direction will help increase your productive time during your writing block.

IN PRACTICE

Plan Your Writing Schedule

Use this grid to develop your writing schedule. Begin by filling in your regular time commitments — classes, work, sleep, meals, and the like. As you fill in time for writing, be realistic, based on your answers from your personal writing habits inventory and typical behaviors. If you watch a favorite TV show or play an intramural sport, don't act like a martyr and replace those activities with writing — that will simply make you resent writing and lead to you not sticking to your schedule. Make a copy of your completed schedule and post it at your desk or some other prominent place. Be sure to monitor and reinforce your writing — treat yourself to something you enjoy when you actually stick to the schedule and write on that basis.

	Sunday	Monday	Tuesday	Wednesday	Thursday	Friday	Saturday
Midnight							
1:00							
2:00							
3:00							
4:00							
5:00							
6:00							
7:00							
8:00							
9:00							
10:00							
11:00							
Noon							
1:00							
2:00							
3:00							
4:00							
5:00							
6:00							
7:00							
8:00							
9:00							
10:00							
11:00							

Resist the temptation to insist on having only extremely long blocks of time for writing ("I'll wait until Saturday and then spend the whole day writing my paper that's due on Monday"). Postponing your writing only increases the pressure when you finally sit down at the computer. Also, as with physical exercise, writing is more likely to become habitual when you practice daily.

Another thing that will help you speed up the "getting started" process is being efficient during the "shutting down" process. You may have wondered why I mentioned taking 5–10 minutes to shut down — obviously, it takes much less time than that to save your file and turn off your computer. However, rather than simply turning off your computer, take a few minutes to type some notes to yourself at the end of the file; I actually highlight these notes in yellow so that they jump out at me when I return to the file. What ideas do you have for what you will write next? Being able to look at these notes will help you get going on the writing process much more quickly the next time you sit down to write.

As You Write

There are several behaviors you should adopt as you write because they will make the process easier. Some of these behaviors make the actual writing easier; some will save you time after you have written. All are valuable.

Monitor and Reinforce Your Writing

This behavior may be one that you have developed on your own for studying, but it is based on the writing behavior of one of psychology's famous figures. Students usually learn about B.F. Skinner in their introductory psychology courses. He taught rats how to press bars in operant chambers to get food pellets, also known as positive reinforcers. Skinner believed strongly in the power of *reinforcement* to control human behavior as well.

He used operant conditioning and reinforcement principles as he wrote. Skinner set an alarm to awaken at midnight and wrote until an alarm at 1:00 a.m. signaled him to stop. He awoke to another alarm at 5:00 a.m. and wrote until 7:00 a.m. . . . seven days a week, 365 days a year. He referred to those three hours of writing as "the most reinforcing part of my day" (Bjork, 1997, p. 217).

My advice to you is to put Skinner's principles to work in your own writing behavior. Set up a *contingency* that you must meet to obtain reinforcement. For example, you could set up a contingency that you must write for 30 minutes or until you have written two pages before allowing yourself a snack, something to drink, a walk around the block, time to check email or texts, or whatever you find reinforcing. In this manner, you will ensure that you make a certain amount of writing progress every day. If you allow interruptions (particularly emails or texts) to derail your writing, you will find that your progress will likely be painfully slow!

Be Meticulous and Thorough

Although obsessive–compulsive disorder (OCD) is listed as an abnormal behavior in the *Diagnostic and Statistical Manual of Mental Disorders* (American Psychiatric Association, 2013), being a little obsessive and compulsive can be a good thing for a writer. For example, setting up a writing schedule and rigidly adhering to it, as previously mentioned, will serve you well in getting your writing done. Likewise, it is good to be driven when researching background sources for your papers. Imagine getting this critique of a paper you have written: "The writer's review of the literature was weak — several important articles were not included." This comment should send a chill down your spine, because it says that you didn't do your background work very well.

Given the ease and convenience of conducting an **electronic literature search** (also known as **online search**), there is little excuse for not surveying the existing literature thoroughly. To avoid this problem, resist the temptation to read only articles for which you can find PDFs or other full-text copies online. Just because an article does not have a full-text version on the web does not mean that it is not an important article to use. It is possible that your school's library subscribes to a journal (i.e., receives a physical paper copy) that you cannot find available online.

In addition, you can get a copy of virtually any published article through a mechanism known as **interlibrary loan**—your library can obtain a copy for you from another library, typically at low or no cost. You should learn early on how interlibrary loan works at your institution so that you can order copies of articles that you cannot access directly through an electronic search (we will cover electronic searching in Chapter 5). Be aware that using interlibrary loan usually takes some time for an article to arrive—so being meticulous and thorough also means that you should begin to search the literature for sources for your paper much earlier than most students start. Giving yourself adequate time to find good articles that are relevant to your topic and obtain copies of them will pay off. The box feature titled A CLOSER LOOK … at Interlibrary Loan gives you a preview of the interlibrary loan process in case you are unfamiliar with it.

Document, Document, Document

This point follows naturally from the previous one. As you are doing your library work to find relevant sources for your paper, *be certain* to fully document your searches and the articles you find. When I was a student, I remember trying to take some shortcuts in the library—perhaps not writing down some sources I found or copying only some pages of an article rather than the piece in its entirety. I was quite confident that I would remember the details later or that I would be able to find the articles again later if I needed to. After a few times of

A CLOSER LOOK
at Interlibrary Loan

To make certain that you take advantage of your library's interlibrary loan option, find the library's homepage on your school's website, and try to locate a link for interlibrary loan (if it is not obvious, search the library homepage for it). You will probably have to complete a form to order a journal article or book. Find out whether you can submit the form electronically, or whether you have to complete a hard copy.

On my college library's Interlibrary Loan page, I can click on a link to request an article, and a form similar to the one you see on the next page pops up. Students and faculty can fill out the form and submit it online, which is convenient if you like to search for articles after the library has closed. If you find a record for an article that is not available in full text, you might be able to click on a link that allows for the form to be autofilled for you.

Using interlibrary loan makes the holdings of your college's library competitive with the best research libraries in the world. Be sure to check your college library's webpage and take advantage of this excellent resource!

Request an article

This interlibrary service is solely for students, faculty, and staff of the College.

Please provide the information in the boxes below.

This journal is not available in full text at the library according to my search.

○ Yes ○ No

Your Name [ ]

Phone Number [ ]

Your Email Address [ ]

Student ID Number [ ]

Name the article you are requesting. Please include full article information:

Title of Article [ ]

Author(s) of Article [ ]

Journal/Magazine/Newspaper Complete Title

[ ]

Volume number [ ]

Issue number [ ]

Issue Date [ ]

Pages of the article [ ]

Requested by (date you would like to receive it) [ ]

[Submit]

making these mistakes, I learned that my "savings" was actually false economy. I remember cursing myself as I trudged back to the library to spend an hour or more locating a reference I had once held in my hand. It is possible that you may not have to trek back to your library to redo a search because of the ease of online searching. However, if you do not save copies of your searches or "hits" from those searches, it is likely that you will find yourself redoing searches and hunting for that article that you previously found. Avoiding this type of frustration will make you happy that you heeded my admonition to "document, document, document"!

You will discover one additional benefit of documenting your searches and articles conscientiously when it comes time to compile a **reference list** (similar to what you know as a bibliography) for your paper. Most of the articles you find while searching will likely have their full bibliographic information printed at the top or bottom of the first page, as highlighted in Figure 1.1. This information gives you all the details you

Figure 1.1 First page of a published article showing bibliographic information.

Journal of Experimental Psychology:
Learning, Memory, and Cognition
2017, Vol. 43, No. 1, 1–22

© 2016 American Psychological Association
0278-7393/17/$12.00   http://dx.doi.org/10.1037/xlm000036

The Role of Long-Term Memory in a Test of Visual Working Memory:
Proactive Facilitation but No Proactive Interference

Klaus Oberauer
University of Zurich

Edward Awh and David W. Sutterer
University of Chicago

We report 4 experiments examining whether associations in visual working memory are subject to proactive interference from long-term memory (LTM). Following a long-term learning phase in which participants learned the colors of 120 unique objects, a working memory (WM) test was administered in which participants recalled the precise colors of 3 concrete objects in an array. Each array in the WM test consisted of 1 old (previously learned) object with a new color (old-mismatch), 1 old object with its old color (old-match), and 1 new object. Experiments 1 to 3 showed that WM performance was better in the old-match condition than in the new condition, reflecting a beneficial contribution from LTM. In the old-mismatch condition, participants sometimes reported colors associated with the relevant shape in LTM, but the probability of successful recall was equivalent to that in the new condition. Thus, information from LTM only intruded in the absence of reportable information in WM. Experiment 4 tested for, and failed to find, proactive interference from the preceding trial in the WM test: Performance in the old-mismatch condition, presenting an object from the preceding trial with a new color, was equal to performance with new objects. Experiment 5 showed that long-term memory for object-color associations is subject to proactive interference. We conclude that the exchange of information between LTM and WM appears to be controlled by a gating mechanism that protects the contents of WM from proactive interference but admits LTM information when it is useful.

Keywords: working memory, long-term memory, proactive interference

The relation between working memory (WM) and long-term   as a subset of LTM representations that temporarily assume a need for each entry in your list of references. However, you will occasionally find an article from a journal that simply lists the title and author(s) on the first page. If you do not have a copy of the search in which you found that article to obtain its bibliographic information, you will have to redo the search to find the article again so that you will have the detailed information needed to reference that article.

As you document the information about your articles, you should be compulsively obsessive about the accuracy of that information. Double- and triple-check the information that you record about the articles to make sure it is correct. If you make an error in recording the information, then you will create a reference list with errors in it. If your article with that reference list is ever published, it will serve as a lasting reminder about your sloppiness in documenting the references. Let me assure you that this problem does occur: I have attempted to find articles from reference lists in both books and journal articles, only to be thwarted by inaccuracies. This experience has been frustrating for me; do your best to make certain that you do not frustrate your readers in the future.

Avoid Plagiarizing

In case you don't know, **plagiarism** means using someone else's words or thoughts as if they are yours. According to the **American Psychological Association's ethics code** (a code of conduct for psychologists), "Psychologists do not present portions of another's work or data as their own, even if the other work or data source is cited occasionally" (see Standard 8.11, www.apa.org/ethics/code).

Over the years, I have found that many students do know about plagiarism, but that they tend to have a rather narrow view of what this term means. Some students maintain that they learned only not to copy an author's writing on a word-for-word basis; they believe that changing a word here and there means that they are not guilty of plagiarism. However, this view is far from the truth. APA defines plagiarism as using "words, ideas, or images of another as one's own" (APA, 2020, p. 21). Thus, APA's definition of plagiarism goes far beyond mere words and includes using ideas from someone else without attribution. The rule for avoiding plagiarism is fairly simple: Anytime you get any information from any source, give that source credit for that information.

Unfortunately, technology has made plagiarism easier to accomplish, which may increase the temptation to engage in plagiarism. An almost infinite amount of material is available through searching the web, and most of it can be easily copied and pasted into a document that you can call your own. There are even websites where you can purchase a term paper.

One of the easiest ways to avoid plagiarism is to begin your writing well in advance of the due date. A looming deadline increases the temptation and motivation to plagiarize exponentially. Avoid those pressures at all costs if you want to become a good writer. Copying someone else's words and ideas will not improve your writing one bit. In fact, you will probably become a worse writer because you will not get any practice at improving your writing skill. So, as a point of personal pride, do not rely on others' words to help you write, but simply use them as information sources.

If internal motivation is not enough, then perhaps some external fear will suffice to help you avoid plagiarism. Although technology makes it simpler to plagiarize, technology also makes it easier to catch writers who plagiarize. Your teacher may have access to a computer program that helps detect plagiarism. In my teaching career, I have worked with two such programs: Turnitin and SafeAssign (within Blackboard). (A web search for "free plagiarism checker" turned up many more such programs.) By uploading a paper to one of these programs, a faculty member can get feedback about the likelihood of a paper having been plagiarized (complete with highlighted passages and corresponding references). Faculty can even conduct a web search for suspicious-sounding passages in your paper. Thus, although plagiarizing a paper might be a quick and easy way to complete your assignment, it is unlikely that you will get away with the theft of others' work. Plagiarism policies for most colleges include punishment ranging from failing the plagiarized assignment, to failing the class, and possibly even to expulsion from the college.

There is one tricky aspect about the definition of plagiarism that can worry students. If you take the plagiarism warnings seriously, you will avoid using psychologists' words and their *ideas.* However, it is impossible to write a good paper without using information from other researchers. You absolutely must read previous journal articles and book chapters to do the research necessary to compile a paper. *The key point is that you must not pass those ideas off as your own.* When you find and use information or an idea from an author or authors, be proud to give them credit for that information. By doing so, you have just engaged in research. You have found material that is important enough to be relevant to your paper, documented that you read that material and extracted some important information from it, and given credit to the original writer/ researcher. The notion of extracting information from sources is extremely important for your development as both a student and a writer. You need to learn to decode difficult ideas and writing and to express them in your words — this test is the best way to determine whether you truly understand the material. If you cannot understand the material, you may attempt to write a paper by stringing together a long list of quotes. Most teachers will not accept such an attempt as a valid paper.

Proofread and Edit/Revise

The goal of all writers is to write as good a product as they can. This section addresses one way to produce the best possible writing that you can — by *proofreading* and *editing/revising.*

My students have been surprised (and dismayed) many times when they have handed me a paper and I immediately spotted an obvious error on the first page. Mahrer (2004) defined **proofreading** as "finding and correcting mistakes" (p. 1130) such as spelling, punctuation, subject–verb agreement, omitted words, and the like.

You may remember learning about a Gestalt principle of organization called *closure* if you studied perception in an introductory psychology course. This principle is quite helpful in everyday life, as it helps us fill in gaps and still perceive whole units. For example, you have probably had a cell phone conversation in which some words were difficult or impossible to hear. It was closure that allowed you to perceive the speaker's full meaning. However, closure is our enemy when it comes to proofreading. Our brain fills in gaps, which may cause us to skip over misspelled or missing words because we know what the passage is *supposed* to say.

Mahrer (2004) gave several pointers to increase your efficiency at proofing. Take frequent breaks from proofing because it is a dull task and your attention will wander. Slow down when you proof—if you read quickly, you are more likely to miss errors. Both of these behaviors will help you focus more clearly on your paper. Another of Mahrer's suggestions is to read your paper aloud—I have long made this suggestion to students. Reading a paper aloud makes it much harder to skip over errors and will help you detect poorly written sentences and phrases. Mahrer also recommended proofreading from a printed copy of your paper rather than on the computer screen; if you point at individual words or use a piece of paper to reveal only one line at a time, you will slow down and catch more errors. Also, if you read paragraphs at random rather than in their natural order, you will lose some of the context of the writing, which should make it easier to spot errors.

I urge you to become familiar with your tendencies; learn the types of errors that you make most frequently. If you look specifically for those types of errors, you will be more likely to find them.

If your knowledge of grammar and writing fundamentals is weak or rusty, I encourage you to visit your on-campus writing center. These centers are often staffed by student peers who have been recruited because of their writing skills and, sometimes, disciplinary expertise. So, it is possible that you could find a psychology major who writes well to help out with your writing. Such a major may have previously completed the same writing assignment on which you are working.

Another strategy is to find and use an online grammar program. Such programs are plentiful—a web search for "online grammar checker" will turn up quite a few hits. Unfortunately, there is no quality control for such sites, so I would *not* recommend that you rely solely on one of these programs. You could submit a paragraph with obvious errors to several such programs to find out which does the best job of detecting your intentional errors, but using your campus's writing center is probably the better option.

Unfortunately, students tend to focus their editing time only on proofreading and less on actual **editing** and **revising**—that is, reworking a paper after it has been written to make it a better paper. Christiansen (1990) noted that professional writers spend about one-fourth of their time revising their writing, whereas students spend less than 1% of their time in revision. Even when students do engage in revision, they seem to spend time on different activities than what teachers envision. On the one hand, teachers see revision as encompassing substantial change: "Revision can lead to re-seeing, restructuring, even re-conceptualizing the entire discourse" (Flower et al., 1986, p. 16). On the other hand, students tend to focus on rule-driven mechanical elements such as proofreading and correcting (Flower et al., 1986). Thus, it is clear that your work on your writing should go well beyond simple proofing and error correction.

Giving specific advice on editing/revising is somewhat difficult because of the different types of writing assignments that you might encounter. I will provide more specific editing/revision tips in the chapters that address different types of assignments. For general editing and revising tips, I turn to one of the best online writing sources around: **Purdue Online Writing Laboratory (OWL)**. Found at owl.purdue.edu, this site is a great place to go when you have any writing-related questions. OWL has two resources related to editing papers: "Revising for Cohesion" and "Steps for Revising."

"Revising for Cohesion" (owl.purdue.edu) focuses primarily on sentences and paragraphs. An important part of editing/revising is making certain that your writing says what you want and mean for it to say. One of the main points OWL gives about both sentences and paragraphs is to keep them relatively brief and on topic. Avoiding "flowery" language that doesn't communicate any meaning is a good way to write for psychology papers. The *Publication Manual of the American Psychological Association* (APA, 2020, p. 113) is in agreement with OWL: "Say only what needs to be said in your writing.... Short words and short sentences are easier to comprehend than are long ones." In "Revising for Cohesion," OWL provides a Diagnosis, Analysis, Revision exercise. This exercise has you diagnose your sentences in a paragraph and then analyze them to determine if your topic is clear throughout the paragraph. After you have diagnosed and analyzed the paragraph, OWL provides tips to revise the sentences so that they form a more focused, unified paragraph.

Table 1.1 on the next page describes OWL's guide for revising a paper. "Steps for Revising" (owl.purdue.edu) reiterates a key point about the editing/revising process: Step away from your paper for a day or two so that you can look at it with fresh eyes. I am convinced that many students submit papers that are not as good as they could be simply because those students finish the paper at the last minute and turn it in immediately. This "immediate strategy" gives you no time to mull over your paper

TABLE 1.1 OWL Seven Guidelines for Revising

OWL Guideline	Guideline Explanation
1. **Find your main point.**	If the reader cannot identify the main **thesis** or main point in your paper, it is not going to be an effective or well-written paper.
2. **Identify your readers and your purpose.**	It is important to identify the audience and what you are trying to accomplish for/with them. Knowing your readers (and their level of expertise and interest) is critical. One reason that students often find published journal articles difficult to read is that such articles are aimed at researchers in the field.
3. **Evaluate your evidence.**	This step is crucial for psychology papers. Psychology is a scientific, empirical discipline, so readers are familiar with (and expect) research evidence to demonstrate and validate points being made in papers.
4. **Save only the good pieces.**	Although a sentence or a paragraph might have seemed like a good idea when you originally wrote it, if it doesn't fit well or support an important point, either rework or eliminate it.
5. **Tighten and clean up your language.**	Does your writing actually communicate what you are trying to say? Is each sentence and paragraph clear in its message and wording? At this point, reading the paper aloud can help tremendously in spotting problematic areas.
6. **Eliminate mistakes in grammar and usage.**	Even though you have proofread the paper, working on editing/revision can turn up problems that you previously missed … or introduce new problems! Here is another opportunity to avoid embarrassing mistakes.
7. **Switch from writer-centered to reader-centered.**	This step is perhaps the most difficult to accomplish, but also perhaps the most rewarding. Rather than reading your paper as the author, try reading it as a reader who is new to the paper. What works, and what doesn't work? Are there holes, confusing spots, or missing information? If you have a friend in the class, perhaps you can exchange papers and read each other's work. Take this chance to clear up any confusion and make sure your paper communicates exactly what you want it to.

Source: Purdue Online Writing Lab. (n.d.). Steps for revising your paper. Retrieved from http://owl.purdue.edu

or for new ideas to occur to you. "Steps for Revising" provides seven helpful guidelines to help as you work on editing and revising. As you examine the guidelines in Table 1.1, you will see that most focus on editing and revising, but proofreading does creep in.

This information about editing/revising may be new to you. Like most students, you have probably spent a majority of time in the past "polishing" your papers by simply proofing them. Remember Christiansen's (1990) information that professional writers spend about one-fourth of their time in editing and revising. If you adopt this approach and follow the suggestions given, you should find that your papers improve over time. But remember — as with most behaviors, you will get better at editing and revising as you practice them more and more! As Nathaniel Hawthorne wrote, "Easy reading is damn hard writing."

Concluding Thoughts

This opening chapter provides some tips that I believe will help you as you endeavor to improve your writing. But I must point out that writing is idiosyncratic — what works for one writer may not work for another. Therefore, I urge you to "try on" these various tips to find out which work best. At the very least, I hope these ideas make you think about your writing. I am convinced that the more you think about your writing, the better your writing will be.

One thread has run throughout this chapter; I hope that you have noticed it. Good writing takes time — time to prepare for writing, time to actually write, and time to edit and revise. As I mentioned earlier, one of the major shortcomings of student writers is waiting until the last minute to attempt to write a paper. If you take to heart only one piece of advice from this chapter, make it this one: Start working on your paper as soon as you know you have a paper to write. Think about your topic, think about how you want to approach the topic, think about where you can find information about the topic. Spend time digging up that information — it is much easier to write a good paper when you have good information with which to work. (I will cover strategies for digging up that information in future chapters.) Most obviously, spend time in the writing of your paper; spread out your writing time and continue to think about your topic as you write. Finally, spend time in the editing/revision process. Bronson Alcott (1872, p. 51), an American writer, teacher, and philosopher (and father of the American novelist Louisa May Alcott), gave us good advice about editing and revising.

> Sleep on your writing; take a walk over it; scrutinize it of a morning; review it of an afternoon; digest it after a meal; let it sleep in your drawer a twelvemonth.

Critical Thinking Writing Assignments

Look through the chapter and find three pieces of writing advice that were new to you. If everything you read in the chapter was familiar, choose three pieces of advice that you think would be most helpful for other students. Afterward, you can complete the three writing assignments.

Assignment 1
Based on one piece of writing advice that you chose, write a paragraph detailing how that piece of advice will change your approach to writing or writing behavior in meaningful way(s). Why do you believe that this change will be of benefit to you in your writing?

Assignment 2
For a different piece of writing advice you chose, write a paragraph in which you explain that piece of advice. For the second

part of the paragraph, create a written rationale that you would use to convince other students why taking this piece of advice would be a good idea and help improve their writing. Use your own words in writing your rationale—be sure not to plagiarize from this book.

Assignment 3

For the final piece of writing advice you chose, conduct a web search and find two articles (or other published works) that give similar advice. Write a paragraph explaining the similarities and differences among the advice given in the articles and in this book.

References

Alcott, A. B. (1872). *Concord days.* Roberts Brothers.

American Psychiatric Association. (2013). *Diagnostic and statistical manual of mental disorders: DSM-5* (5th ed.). https://doi.org/10.1176/appi.books.9780890425596

American Psychological Association. (2020). *Publication manual of the American Psychological Association* (7th ed.). https://doi.org/10.1037/0000165-000

Bjork, D. W. (1997). *B. F. Skinner: A life.* American Psychological Association. https://doi.org/10.1037/10130-000

Calkins, L. M. (1994). *The art of teaching writing* (2nd ed.). Heinemann.

Christiansen, M. (1990). The importance of revision in writing composition. *Education Digest, 56*(2), 70–72.

Davis, S. F. (2010, April). Conduct a personal writing habits inventory. In R. A. Smith (Chair), *How to publish your manuscript* [Symposium]. Southwestern Psychological Association 56th Annual Meeting, Dallas, TX, United States.

Drabick, D. A. G., Weisberg, R., Paul, L., & Bubier, J. L. (2007). Keeping it short and sweet: Brief, ungraded writing assignments facilitate learning. *Teaching of Psychology, 34*(3), 172–176. https://doi.org/10.1080/00986280701498558

Farris, C., & Smith, R. (1992). Writing-intensive courses: Tools for curricular change. In S. H. McLeod & M. Soven (Eds.), *Writing across the curriculum: A guide to developing programs* (pp. 52–62). Sage.

Flower, L., Hayes, J. R., Carey, L., Schriver, K., & Stratman, J. (1986). Detection, diagnosis, and the strategies of revision. *College Composition and Communication, 37*(1), 16–55. https://doi.org/10.2307/357381

Garrett, N., Bridgewater, M., & Feinstein, B. (2017). How student performance in first-year composition predicts retention and overall student success. In T. Ruecker, D. Shepherd, H. Estrem, & B. Brunk-Chavez (Eds.), *Retention, persistence, and writing programs* (pp. 93–113). Utah State University Press. https://doi.org/10.7330/9781607326021.c006

Kobrin, J. L., Patterson, B. F., Shaw, E. J., Mattern, K. D., & Barbuti, S. M. (2008). *Validity of the SAT for predicting first-year college grade point average*

(College Board Research Report No. 2008-5). College Board. https://www.researchgate.net/publication/267954770

Mahrer, K. D. (2004). Proofreading your own writing? Forget it! *The Leading Edge, 23*(11), 1130–1131. https://doi.org/10.1190/1.1825945

McLeod, S. H. (1992). Writing across the curriculum. In S. H. McLeod & M. Soven (Eds.), *Writing across the curriculum: A guide to developing programs* (p. 1–8). Sage.

National Commission on Writing for America's Families, Schools, and Colleges. (2004). *Writing: A ticket to work . . . Or a ticket out. A survey of business leaders.* College Entrance Examination Board. https://www.nwp.org/cs/public/print/resource/2540

Nevid, J. S., Pastva, A., & McClelland, N. (2012). Writing-to-learn assignments in introductory psychology: Is there a learning benefit? *Teaching of Psychology, 39*(4), 272–275. https://doi.org/10.1177/0098628312456622

Ondrusek, A. L. (2012). What the research reveals about graduate students' writing skills: A literature review. *Journal of Education for Library and Information Science, 53*(3), 176–188.

Swensen, D. (2011, November 9). Writing when you're sick, tired, or just hate the world. *Surlymuse.* http://surlymuse.com/writing-when-youre-sick-tired-or-just-hate-the-world/

University of Warwick. (2014, September 9). Students take note: Evidence that leaving essays to the last minute ruins your grades. *ScienceDaily.* www.sciencedaily.com/releases/2014/09/140909144542.htm

Victor, D. (2018, February 9). Oxford comma dispute is settled as Maine drivers get $5 million. *The New York Times.* https://www.nytimes.com

Wadsworth, J., Halfman, A. H., & Upton, T. (2002). Strategies to improve the writing of graduate students. *Rehabilitation Education, 16*(3), 295–305.

What Does "APA Style" Actually Mean?

Do You Know?

What are the major differences and similarities among APA, MLA, and Chicago formats?

How do reference lists and bibliographies differ?

How can you write to avoid passive voice?

How do you write to avoid sexist language?

"When style works best, ideas flow logically, sources are credited appropriately, and papers are organized predictably and consistently."

— American Psychological Association (APA), 2020, p. xvii

If you are like most college students, you will have written a term paper or research paper in an English class before you need to write a psychology paper. Most academic disciplines have a standardized style or format for authors to use as they write papers in that discipline. Three styles cut across several academic disciplines and are probably used more often than specialized styles that pertain primarily to one subject matter. American Psychological Association Style (known as APA Style; APA, 2020) is used in psychology, business, nursing, criminology, economics, sociology, linguistics (https://owl.purdue.edu), and communication disorders (https://pubs.asha.org). Modern Language Association style (known as **MLA style**; MLA, 2016) is used in language arts, cultural studies, and other humanities (https://owl.purdue.edu). Finally, **Chicago style** (also known as **Turabian style**; Turabian, 2018; University of Chicago Press, 2017) is used in literature, history, and the arts (https://owl .purdue.edu).

In this chapter, you will learn about the official writing style for psychology papers as found in the ***Publication Manual of the American Psychological Association*** (APA, 2020) — also referred to as the ***APA Publication Manual*** or simply the ***APA Manual*** — and discover how to use it in your papers. I will specifically highlight critical aspects of APA Style that may differ from other styles you may have previously used.

You may despair about learning a new set of style guidelines for writing papers. However, there are several good reasons for learning to write in APA Style (Kubista, 2010). First, submitting manuscripts for publication in APA Style is necessary in the field of psychology and some other disciplines. Although you probably haven't thought about publishing a paper at this stage in your career, it is a prospect you may consider later (see Chapter 9). Second, reading papers formatted in a consistent style makes it easier and faster for professors to grade your papers. Using that style also keeps you from having to wonder about exactly how to format your papers:

The *APA Publication Manual* (APA, 2020) has answers to *all* of your questions. Kubista (2010) noted that using APA Style shows you are capable of following directions from your professors, which is probably similar to following directions from a future boss. Finally, knowing the basics of APA Style will help you when you begin to read psychology journal articles (see Chapter 4).

APA Style and Scientific Thought

Early psychology articles were idiosyncratic in their presentation; there was no standard style for psychology until 1929 (Sigal & Pettit, 2012). Prior to this time, **journals** were often linked to specific universities, and publication of articles was often negotiated between authors and editors, probably because psychology as a discipline was relatively small and informal. However, in the early 1900s, the discipline began to grow rapidly. For example, the American Psychological Association (APA) was founded in 1892 with only 31 members; by 1915, there were almost 300 members of the APA, with an increase to 530 members by 1930 (Fernberger, 1932). This growth led to the need for more journals. Eight APA-endorsed journals began publishing by the end of 1920, in addition to the five created before 1895 (Sigal & Pettit, 2012). Sigal and Pettit also noted that psychology was becoming more of an applied, helping discipline during this time. This development led to an increased number of journal submissions, some of which now dealt with topics less familiar to the editors. The resulting "information overload" (Sigal & Pettit, 2012, p. 357) made editors realize that they needed to develop standards for publication. This sentiment was not unanimous within APA's membership, but after several years of discussion and debate, the first rudimentary step toward today's *APA Publication Manual* (APA, 2020) — a seven-page article ("Instructions in Regard to Preparation of Manuscript") appeared (Bentley et al., 1929). Given that the current *APA Manual* comprises more than

420 pages, you can see that there are *many* more details to APA Style than there were in 1929! This chapter will acquaint you with some of those details.

Although some authors might see the *APA Manual* (APA, 2020) as simply a style guide that they must follow to compile citation and reference information, format pages, and meet journal editors' fussy demands, Madigan et al. (1995, p. 428) argued that APA Style "encapsulates the core values and epistemology of the discipline." Epistemology is a branch of philosophy that is concerned with the nature and scope of knowledge (Hofer, 2002). According to Madigan et al., APA Style reflects values and attitudes held by psychology researchers—in particular, a bias toward empiricism and commitment toward building psychology knowledge. These authors made an important point for you as a student reading this book: You are probably new to psychology writing and are more familiar with essay writing for English classes and using MLA or Turabian style. If you continue to write in a "humanities voice," it will be obvious to psychologists that you are writing as an outsider to the discipline. This point is the precise reason that psychology faculty will probably critique some aspects of your writing that you have practiced and perfected in previous classes.

My advice is not to fight against this feedback: Faculty are trying to help you become acclimated to psychology's style of writing so that you will be seen as "one of us." Although you may make the valid point that "I am *just* a student, not a PhD psychologist—why should I have to learn APA Style?", there is a chance that someday you will have to write for a graduate program or wish to write for publication. Therefore, you should take your professors' feedback as helpful, friendly advice, as it is intended. As Cash (2009) pointed out, evaluators of papers (whether they be journal editors, reviewers, or faculty members) will likely make negative evaluations when they read manuscripts that are unclearly written or contain stylistic errors.

APA Style Values

Before we dive into the nuances and intricacies of APA Style, let me share the major differences that exist between APA Style and humanities-based writing. Incorporating these values into your mindset as you write papers for your psychology classes will make writing easier for you and more acceptable to your psychology professors.

Cite, Cite, Cite

Few, if any, of your psychology professors are interested in papers based solely on your opinion or on conjecture. Although your writing should include an element of originality (more on that later), the main task in writing a psychology paper is to build a case for any and all claims that you make. Psychologists primarily build their cases by referring to previous research that backs the claims they make. If you examine a psychology journal article, particularly the introduction, you will see what are called *citations* throughout. A **citation** gives you the basic information you need—name(s) and date—to find a reference to an article or book or some other type of publication. I have used citations extensively in this book. If you look back a couple of pages, you will find this sentence:

> Early psychology articles were idiosyncratic in their presentation; there was no standard style for psychology until 1929 *(Sigal & Pettit, 2012).*

The italicized material (Sigal & Pettit, 2012) is a citation—you can use it to look in the list of references for this book and find that Sigal and Pettit wrote an article titled "Information Overload, Professionalization, and the Origins of the *Publication Manual of the American Psychological Association*" that was published in the *Review of General Psychology* in 2012. A **reference** is the entire bibliographic record for some published material. As you can see by examining the Sigal and Pettit (2012) reference, it contains (for a journal article) the authors' names, the date of publication, the title of the article, the journal in which the article was published, the volume and issue numbers, and page range of the publication (and a permanent link to the article). This information would enable you to find Sigal and Pettit's article if you wanted to read it. We will cover the basics of APA-Style references later in Chapters 5 and 6.

The basic rules for citation are laid out in the *APA Publication Manual*:

> Cite the work of those individuals whose ideas, theories, or research have directly influenced your work. The works you cite provide key background information, support or dispute your thesis, or offer critical definitions and data. Cite only works that you have read and ideas that you have incorporated into your writing. . . . In addition to crediting the ideas of others that you used to develop your thesis, provide documentation for all facts and figures that are not common knowledge. (APA, 2020, p. 253)

Madigan et al. (1995) pointed out one important implication of this emphasis on citing your sources of information. They analyzed 100 articles from four journals and found that the two psychology journals they studied showed many more citations than an English journal and almost as many as a history journal. However, direct quotes in the psychology journals were almost nonexistent, with the history and English journals showing much higher quotation rates. Thus, it is important not only to derive information from previous publications, but also to put that information in your own words. These characteristics highlight "APA style as a writing genre" (Madigan et al., 1995, p. 428).

Be Creative, But in a Different Sense

As you have just seen, it is not only important, but *expected* that you will consult other authors' works in writing your paper. For some reason, students often seem to believe that it is "cheating" to consult other sources and that they must write papers totally on their own. This belief may represent an important distinction between psychology and English papers. The premium in an English paper may be on creativity; when that is the case, consulting other sources would be viewed as plagiarism, which occurs when you present the work of another person as if it is yours. If your assignment is to compose a creative essay, then borrowing ideas from other authors would be frowned on. However, your assignment in most psychology papers is to build a case for your thesis, which *should* be based on previous research. Don't claim words or ideas from another writer as your own — be sure to give credit to the original author. If you use information from an article without attributing its source, then you are guilty of plagiarism.

Your creativity in a psychology paper is totally different from that in an English paper. Rather than creating ideas totally on your own, as you might in an English class, creativity for psychology papers comes from finding previous research and weaving it together in a convincing manner to lead to and support your ideas. It is then important to give credit to those previous researchers by citing and referencing them.

Write for Clarity and Communication, Not Entertainment Value

If you have taken any English writing classes, you probably know that there are many types of creative writing assignments — genres such as poetry, essays, plays, fiction, and the like. The major emphasis of many of these types of writing is on entertaining or enlightening the audience. The primary goal of APA-Style writing, however, is on clear communication of scientific information to the audience. These two goals lead to two approaches to writing that are quite different.

One major difference between creative writing and APA Style is the use of literary devices. In English composition classes, you probably learned to use devices such as metaphors, similes, alliteration, hyperbole, foreshadowing, and the like. These writing tools are great for creating interesting novels, short stories, plays, and so on. However, they could very well inhibit clear scientific communication. In fact, the *APA Publication Manual*

(APA, 2020, p. 114) specifically warns authors against using such literary devices because they are not appropriate for scientific writing. As Madigan et al. (1995, p. 433) noted, "APA style writing shares with other empirical disciplines a utilitarian view of language in which words are implicitly assumed to function as simple transmitters of information from the writer to the reader." Literary devices used in creative writing could get in the way of straightforward factual communication with the reader, so you should try to rein in this aspect of your creativity when you write in APA Style.

Another premium in APA Style is brevity in one's writing, stressed as the "importance of conciseness" in the *APA Manual* (APA, 2020, p. 113): "Say only what needs to be said in your writing." Because writing in psychology is typically aimed at publishing an article in a journal, writing must be succinct and to the point: Journal pages are in short supply, and editors would like to publish good articles that tell the story of good research projects but do so in as few pages as possible. As you know from reading novels by disparate authors such as Mary Anne Evans (who wrote under the pen name George Eliot) and Stephen King, brevity is not necessarily an important value for literary authors.

Finally, communicating clearly is a major emphasis in APA Style. Rather than making the reader assume or make inferences about what an author is attempting to communicate, the *APA Manual* (APA, 2020, p. 113) specifically instructs authors to "be deliberate in your word choices, making certain that every word means exactly what you intend." In everyday speaking, we often use words in manners that are different from their actual meanings—this is a habit you should avoid when writing in APA Style. For example, the *Manual* (p. 113) specifically mentions that you should avoid using "feel" for "think" or "believe." There are other important word distinctions in APA Style with which you should familiarize yourself.

"Sex" Versus "Gender"

Although we often use these words interchangeably when speaking, psychologists make an important distinction between them.

In APA Style, "sex" refers to one's assigned sex at birth, whereas "gender" refers to a difference based on culture (APA, 2020, p. 138). Thus, sex would be based on genetic differences, and gender would be based on environmental differences. If you are writing about stereotypical differences between men and women, you should use the term "gender roles," because such differences are based in culture, not biology. In contrast, if you write about differences between men and women without reference to society or culture, you would be referring to sex differences.

"While" and "Since"

In APA Style, "while" is a temporal word, and "since" is primarily a temporal word, meaning that they are time-based (APA, 2020, p. 123). In our everyday speech, we often substitute "while" for "although," "despite," "and," or "but" and "since" for "because." In APA Style, you should use "while" only to denote events that are or were simultaneous. For example, "While participants completed the memory test, they heard classical music playing." This sentence makes it clear that the memory test and the music happened at the same time. Now consider this sentence: "While Watson was a behaviorist, Neisser was a cognitive psychologist." These two events did not occur simultaneously; the writer used "while" incorrectly to draw a contrast between Watson and Neisser. Substituting "Although" or "Whereas" for "While" as the first word in the sentence makes this sentence correct in APA Style. Using "although" or "whereas" sets up a contrast or comparison between the two parts of the sentence (i.e., Watson versus Neisser). For a shorthand chart of this APA guideline (and others), see Appendix D concerning common writing problems, explanations, and solutions.

In APA-Style writing, you should typically use "since" to denote that time has passed after a given event. For example, "The data represented errors that subjects had made since they began Phase 2 of the experiment," in order to make clear that only errors after Phase 2 were scored. Contrast that use of "since" with an incorrect usage: "Since Watson was a behaviorist, he was not interested in internal mental processes." "Since" here does not refer to time passage, so its use is incorrect for APA Style. Beginning the sentence with "because," however, makes the sentence acceptable for APA Style. Be aware that using "since" to mean "because" *is* acceptable in APA Style, but only if the meaning is not ambiguous, which can be difficult for less-experienced writers.

If you are like many of my students, you may have just had a knee-jerk reaction to my advice about beginning the sentence with "because": You may have learned never to begin a sentence with this word. However, there seems to be no grammatical rule against beginning a sentence with "because" (conduct a web search on "beginning a sentence with because") other than the fact that many student authors will then write an incomplete sentence due to the fact that they will not follow a dependent clause with an independent clause to make a complete sentence. If you simply wrote "Because Watson was a behaviorist," then you would have written an incomplete sentence and would have made a grammatical error. However, adding "he was not interested in internal mental processes" (an independent clause) makes the sentence grammatically correct. This sentence is simply a different way of writing "Watson was not interested in internal mental processes because he was a behaviorist."

"This," "That," "These," "Those"

"This," "that," "these," and "those" are known as demonstratives in grammar. In much of our everyday conversation and writing, we tend to use demonstratives as pronouns, which means we allow the demonstrative to stand on its own. For example, if you are eating cookies, you might say, "These are good." From the context, the person to whom you are speaking knows that you are referring to the cookies. APA Style allows the use of demonstratives as pronouns but cautions that the referent in the previous sentence *must* be obvious (APA, 2020, p. 112). Thus, rather than writing "This means that . . .," writing "These results mean that . . . " will remove any uncertainty for the reader.

One of my former students ran into a similar situation in her job revolving around using nonspecific words:

> *As an investigator for the Arkansas Attorney General's office, I had to get assistance in writing my responses and letters to our consumers. I was prone to using "they, he, she" when referring to a consumer. When you are going to court, the judge does not know who "they, he or she" is; we are not allowed to use third person. Each narration has to have the name of the person as the reference point. I am very honored to be able to write better with the assistance of the attorneys I assist on building a case, as the investigator.* (Margie Bright Sexton; OBU, 1989; Investigator, Public Protection, Office of Arkansas Attorney General, Little Rock, AR)

Avoid Racism, Sexism, and Other -isms

APA is committed to avoiding bias of any sort in writing and language: To foster fair treatment of individuals and groups, the *APA Publication Manual* says to avoid prejudiced or biased writing against people based on "age, disability, gender, participation in research, racial or ethnic identity, sexual orientation, socioeconomic status, or some combination of these or other personal factors" (APA, 2020, p. 131). Three general guidelines from the *Manual* follow.

Describe at the Appropriate Level of Specificity

The way to follow this guideline (APA, 2020, pp. 132–133) is to "be more specific rather than less" specific (p. 132). You can always combine groups if you have overly specific information, but you cannot "uncombine" them if the information you have is too general. For example, rather than writing about "elderly subjects," you could specify "subjects between 70 and 80 years of age." Similarly, APA Style (2020, p. 135) uses "girl" and "boy" to refer to people who are younger than 12; "young woman/young man, female adolescent/male adolescent" as terms for people 13–17 years old, and "men" and "women" for people 18 years and older.

The *APA Manual* (2020, pp. 138–149) also includes guidelines for avoiding bias based on gender/sex (addressed earlier in this chapter), sexual orientation, racial and ethnic identity, disabilities, age, socioeconomic status, and intersectionality (a combination of contexts or groupings). When you examine these pages, you will find that "homosexual" is an outdated, negatively stereotyped term. APA prefers terms for sexual orientation such as "lesbian, gay, heterosexual, straight, asexual, bisexual, queer, polysexual, and pansexual" (APA, 2020, p. 146). Since the previous edition of the *Manual* was published, terms for sexual orientation such as "transgender," "cisgender," "gender-nonconforming," and "nonbinary" have evolved. APA has provided updated information about the terms you should use in APA Style (https://www.apa.org/pi/lgbt/resources/sexuality-definitions.pdf). Because of the rapid evolution of gender-related categories and terms, this section of the *Manual* is much longer than the previous edition. Also, it is likely that APA will continue to update these categories online in the future at the previous webpage or at https://apastyle.apa.org.

Words to designate racial and ethnic identity are largely determined by the specific group's preferences; be sure to avoid outdated terms (e.g., Afro-American, Oriental). Words used to denote racial and ethnic groups are considered proper nouns, so they should be capitalized (e.g., "Black" and "White" are correct; "black" and "white" are not). Be certain to use parallel terms such as "African Americans, Caucasian Americans" rather than words that are not parallel (e.g., African Americans, Whites; APA, 2020, p. 145). The previous edition of the *Manual* (APA, 2010, p. 76) specified the use of "people-first language" when describing people with disabilities (use "people with disabilities" rather than "the disabled"). The current *Manual* (2020, pp. 136–137), however, allows either "person-first language" (e.g., "people with disabilities") *or* "identity-first language" (e.g., "a disabled person") to respect disabled individuals. Importantly, if you find that a person or group prefers one approach, you should avoid the other type of term.

Be Sensitive to Labels

The main idea of this guideline (APA, 2020, pp. 133–134) is to "respect the language people use to describe themselves; that is, call people what they call themselves" (p. 133). This idea is based on the realization that preferred terms for groups do change over time — just ask your parents or grandparents for verification of this truism. The primary problem occurs when someone who belongs to a majority group uses that group as the standard against which others are compared. For example, you are probably familiar with the problem of using male-oriented terms such as "mankind," "him or his," and "mailman" (and other gendered occupational terms) exclusively: This approach marginalizes women and paints them as second-class citizens. The *APA Manual* (2020, p. 134) even notes that the order in which we present groups (e.g., "men and women," "Whites and Blacks") may create the impression that the group listed first is the dominant group.

Acknowledge Participation

To acknowledge participation (APA, 2020, pp. 141–142), "Write about the people who participated in your work in a way that acknowledges their contributions and agency" (p. 142). In the fourth edition of the *APA Publication Manual* (APA, 1994), this concern first arose; writers were told to "replace the impersonal term *subjects* with a more descriptive term when possible" (p. 49). This restriction has since been somewhat loosened, as the term *subjects* is acceptable due to long-standing tradition, but the spirit of that guideline remains in place. For example, using passive voice makes it seem that participants are objects rather than actors (contrast "the participants completed the forms" with "the forms were administered to subjects").

Some people might dismiss APA's concern with reducing bias as mere political correctness. However, as Nichol (2011) noted, it is probably the case that those people do not belong to the groups who have experienced bias through writing. Social cognition research has amply demonstrated how likely people are to fall victim to cognitive errors and biases (e.g., Carlston, 2010); these errors and biases could occur unconsciously because of the language we hear and use (and even write). Thus, it behooves us to use unbiased language in our writing to avoid perpetuating bias and stereotyping.

Nuts and Bolts of APA Style

Not all of APA Style revolves around values; there are some nitty-gritty rules for formatting as well. Although most of these rules exist for the ease of the publication process — that is, moving a paper in manuscript form to a published article in a psychological journal — many psychology faculty adhere to these rules when they assign papers that are due in "APA Style" or "APA format." I will introduce some of the general APA-Style guidelines here; we will encounter others in later chapters. For an APA-Style checklist concerning common writing problems, explanations, and solutions in your papers, see Appendix D.

Font

Traditionally, serif **fonts** have been used for printed works and sans serif fonts for online works (serifs are the little lines and dots that "decorate" certain fonts, such as the little line at the bottom of "p" or the dot at the top of "f"). Previous editions of the *APA Manual* specified using 12-point Times New Roman font. However, APA Style (2020, p. 44) now allows a variety of fonts due to improved screen resolution. Serif fonts such as 12-point Times New Roman, 11-point Georgia, or 10-point Computer Modern and sans serif fonts such as 11-point Calibri, 11-point Arial, or 10-point Lucida Sans Unicode are all now acceptable. Note that your professor might have a specific preferred font. If you will write psychology papers on a regular basis, you should set one of the APA options as your default font. To learn computer instructions with Word tailored for APA formatting on either a PC or Mac computer — including setting a default font — see the IN PRACTICE: Computer Formatting Instructions for APA Style box in a few pages.

Margins

The *APA Publication Manual* (APA, 2020, p. 45) specifies 1-inch **margins** for all four margins on a page (top, bottom, left, right). In my experience, Microsoft Word often defaults to 1.25-inch margins on the sides of pages. Although this value may be acceptable for APA guidelines, such a margin looks large to me (and, I suspect, to other professors). For this reason, using Word's larger (default) left and right margins may give the impression that you are attempting to make your paper look longer than it actually is. Thus, I recommend that you use 1-inch margins all around. The IN PRACTICE box shows you how to set these margins.

Running Head

There is a minor exception to the "1-inch all around" margin rule. APA-Style papers typically have a **running head** (left aligned) and page number (right aligned) at the top of each page. In the previous edition of the *APA Manual* (APA, 2010), a running head was required for all manuscripts; now it is not required for student papers (APA, 2020, p. 37). However, given that this change is new, your instructor may require you to use a running head. The running head is an abbreviated version of your title: "a maximum of 50 characters, counting letters, punctuation, and spaces between words" (2020, p. 37). It should be a meaningful abbreviated title rather than just the first few words of your title. The running head does not have to fit within the 1-inch margins. Fortunately, Word is set up to allow us to insert running heads fairly easily, as shown in the IN PRACTICE box.

To make certain that you set up the running head correctly in your document (if required), refer to the A CLOSER LOOK . . . at a Running head box on the following page. As that box shows, you do not see the words "Running head:" along with the actual running head. Again, this is a change from

A CLOSER LOOK
at a Running Head

APA Style no longer requires a running head for student papers (APA, 2020, p. 37), but your instructor may require you to have one. To make certain that you understand the section about running heads, I have created examples of pages 1 and 2 below. All subsequent pages should also display the running head.

LEARNING TO BARPRESS   1

Title of the paper goes here . . .

LEARNING TO BARPRESS   2

text of the paper continues here . . .

Note. These pages do not appear to scale for $8\frac{1}{2}$-inch × 11-inch paper. Remember in APA Style that your left and right margins should be 1 inch wide, and the first line of text for each page should be 1 inch from the top of the page. The running head can be outside the 1-inch margin.

the previous edition of the *Manual* (APA, 2010), which did require those words, but only on page 1 of a document.

Typing instructions

Virtually everything in an APA-Style paper should be double-spaced, even your reference list (APA, 2020, p. 45). Within your paper, you should always left justify your text—your paper should have a ragged right margin. If you find that your typing always aligns perfectly on the right margin, you have the "Justify" or "Justify Full" option selected — change it to "Align Text Left" or "Left Justify."

Use the Tab key or automatic paragraph formatting in Word to indent the beginning of paragraphs (0.5 in.) rather than using the spacebar (APA, 2020, p. 45). Do not divide words at the end of the line. APA Style for manuscripts has lines that run short rather than dividing (hyphenating) the word. However, do not be surprised when you see divided words in actual published articles. To learn how to prevent Word from hyphenating words, see the IN PRACTICE box.

After you have a paper that is totally formatted for APA Style (font, margins, running head, hyphenation, spacing), you have two options to make formatting later papers in APA Style easier. The first option is to edit that paper and save it with a new name that you will recognize as your "APA-Style format." You can delete most of the text of the paper, leaving only the formatting commands and enough text to show your title page, the first couple of pages of the paper, and your reference page header. For a subsequent paper, you can replace the remaining text with your new text, change the running head (if required) to fit the new paper, and go from there. This approach will save you the time and effort of redoing APA formatting every time you start a new paper. The second option is to create a Word template for APA Style. At the upper left of Word documents, there is a "Templates" option that allows you to create a template for new documents in APA style. The great news is that you don't have to set up and create a template for APA style — there should be one available from Microsoft (search templates.office.com; look for the 7th edition of APA Style).

This ends our first foray into APA Style. In this chapter, I have provided you with a list of guidelines that will pertain to any APA-Style writing assignment you have. In later chapters, we will explore APA Style as it fits different types of writing assignments. Although APA Style may still seem somewhat arbitrary to you, it exists (just like other writing styles) to ensure consistency throughout manuscripts and various publications (Kubista, 2010).

IN PRACTICE

Computer Formatting Instructions for APA Style

APA-Style Computer Formatting with Word on a PC

Default Font

- Click the small arrow at the lower-right corner of the "Font" area of the Word home page.
- Select Font: Use an acceptable APA-Style font.
- Click the box in the lower-left corner [Set As Default].

Margins

- Click "Page Layout" at the top of the Word document.
- The "Page Setup" section has a "Margins" pull-down arrow.
- Click to open the Margins option list. The "Normal" setting sets 1-inch margins for the entire document.

Running Head*

- Click "Insert" at the top of the Word document.
- Choose "Header & Footer" section—click "Page Number" and rest the cursor on "Top of Page."
- Select "Plain Number 3" so page numbers will appear on the right side of the page.
- A "1" should appear in a gray box with a blinking line in front of the 1.
- Type the running head/short title in ALL CAPS, remembering the 50-character limit.
- Press the Tab key twice; the running head should appear at the left margin and 1 at the right margin.
- Click the red X (labeled "Close Header and Footer") at the right side of the menu. The header will become grayed out and the cursor should be back in the text of the paper.
- You should see "SHORT TITLE" (what you typed as your running head/short title, *not* the words SHORT TITLE) at the upper left of the page and 1 at the upper right.
- You can now type the text of your paper. When you get to page 2, you should see your running head at the left margin and 2 at the right margin.

*If your instructor does not require a running head, use these instructions *only* to insert page numbers in your document.

Word Division

- Turn this feature off through the "Page Layout" menu.
- Click the "Hyphenation" option and select "None."

Note: The steps listed here may vary slightly depending on your specific version of Word.

APA-Style Computer Formatting with Word on a Mac

Default Font

- Click the "Format" menu at the top of the screen.
- Select the Font option; use an acceptable APA-Style font.
- Click the box in the lower-left corner [Default], and choose "Yes."

Margins

- Click the "Format" menu at the top of the screen.
- Select "Document. . . " and click "Margins."
- Set 1-inch margins for Top, Bottom, Left, and Right.
- Click the box in the lower-left corner [Default], and choose "Yes."

Running Head*

- Click "Insert" above the Font menu of the Word document.
- Choose "Header & Footer" on the Insert menu.
- Choose "Header" from the dropdown menu.
- From the dropdown menu, select "Blank."
- Your document should show [Type here] above a blue line with "Header | Close" underneath.
- Type your running head/short title (ALL CAPS), and it will appear in the [Type here] location.
- Select the "Page Number" menu at the top left of the document (under "Home" menu).
- Click on the "Page Number" option.
- Because you are in the Header, the "Position" should automatically read "Top of page (Header)." If "Alignment" is not set to "Right," choose that option. Make sure the "Show number on first page" box is checked. Click the OK button.
- Click "Close" under your running head.
- You can now type the text of your paper. When you get to page 2, you should see your running head at the left margin and 2 at the right margin.

*If your instructor does not require a running head, use these instructions *only* to insert page numbers in your document.

Word Division

- Select the "Tools" menu at the top of the page.
- Select "Hyphenation. . . ."
- Uncheck the "Automatically hyphenate document" box.

Note: The steps listed here may vary slightly depending on your specific version of Word.

Concluding Thoughts

This chapter has served as an introduction to APA Style — a style of writing that is probably new to you but that will become quite important as you continue in your psychology major (or whatever major you are pursuing that uses APA Style). APA Style represents a scientific way of approaching evidence-based writing, as opposed to more creative writing styles you may have used in English (and other) classes. When you make statements in your APA-Style writing, you must support them with evidence. Subsequent chapters will continue your introduction to APA Style in the context of various types of writing assignments you might encounter in various classes. With some practice, APA Style will become more familiar to you and, thus, easier to accomplish.

Critical Thinking Writing Assignments

For each assignment, write a paragraph aimed at first-year college students who need to address the assignment question.

Assignment 1
Why do different disciplines adopt different writing styles? What are two key differences between APA Style and the styles used by the humanities?

Assignment 2
Why is the use of citations a key value in APA-Style writing? Why is this value important for scientific disciplines?

Assignment 3
Why is it important to use unbiased language as you write? Provide an example of biased language that might be applied to someone you know well and how it should be written in an unbiased manner.

References

American Psychological Association. (1994). *Publication manual of the American Psychological Association* (4th ed.).

American Psychological Association. (2010). *Publication manual of the American Psychological Association* (6th ed.).

American Psychological Association. (2020). *Publication manual of the American Psychological Association* (7th ed.). https://doi.org/10.1037/0000165-000

Bentley, M., Peerenboom, C. A., Hodge, F. W., Passano, E. B., Warren, H. C., & Washburn, M. F. (1929). Instructions in regard to preparation of manuscript. *Psychological Bulletin, 26*(2), 57–63. https://doi.org/10.1037/h0071487

Carlston, D. (2010). Social cognition. In R. F. Baumeister & E. J. Finkel (Eds.), *Advanced social psychology: The state of the science* (pp. 63–99). Oxford University Press.

Cash, T. F. (2009). Caveats in the proficient production of an APA-Style research manuscript for publication. *Body Image, 6*(1), 1–6. https://doi.org/10.1016/j.bodyim.2008.10.003

Fernberger, S. W. (1932). The American Psychological Association: A historical summary, 1892–1930. *Psychological Bulletin, 29*(1), 1–89. https://doi.org/10.1037/h0075733

Hofer, B. K. (2002). Personal epistemology as a psychological and educational construct: An introduction. In B. K. Hofer & P. R. Pintrich (Eds.), *Personal epistemology: The psychology of beliefs about knowledge and knowing* (pp. 3–14). Lawrence Erlbaum Associates.

Kubista, A. (2010, September 15). What is the point? Walden University Writing Center. http://waldenwritingcenter.blogspot.com/2010/09/what-is-point.html

Madigan, R., Johnson, S., & Linton, P. (1995). The language of psychology: APA Style as epistemology. *American Psychologist, 50*(6), 428–436. https://doi.org/10.1037//0003-066x.50.6.428

Modern Language Association of America. (2016). *MLA handbook* (8th ed.).

Nichol, M. (2011). How to avoid bias in your writing. *Daily Writing Tips.* https://www.dailywritingtips.com/how-to-avoid-bias-in-your-writing/

Sigal, M. J., & Pettit, M. (2012). Information overload, professionalization, and the origins of the *Publication Manual of the American Psychological Association. Review of General Psychology, 16*(4), 357–363. https://doi.org/10.1037/a0028531

Turabian, K. L. (2018). *A manual for writers of research papers, theses, and dissertations* (9th ed.; revised by W. C. Booth, G. C. Colomb, J. M. Williams, J. Bizup, W. T. Fitzgerald, & University of Chicago Press Editorial Staff). University of Chicago Press.

University of Chicago Press. (2017). *The Chicago manual of style* (17th ed.). https://doi.org/10.7208/cmos17

3

Grammar Also Counts in APA Style

Do You Know?

Can you distinguish between active and passive voice?

Why can writing with pronouns be confusing to readers (and how can you correct this problem)?

How can you avoid expressing bias in written language?

How can you ensure that subjects and verbs agree in number?

Is using "they" as a singular pronoun acceptable in writing?

"The active voice is usually more direct and vigorous than the passive."

—Strunk & White, 2000, p. 18

In Chapter 2, you learned about some important distinctions between writing in psychology using APA Style (American Psychological Association [APA], 2020) and writing in the humanities and other disciplines using either MLA or Turabian style. This chapter clarifies an assumption that you might have made (erroneously) while reading the previous chapter: Before you begin celebrating the idea that you do not need to be concerned about grammatical issues when writing in APA Style, let me warn you that nothing could be further from the truth!

Grammar Counts

Yes, it is true that you are not writing a paper for an English class, but grammar is still quite important when writing psychology papers. The *Publication Manual of the American Psychological Association* (APA, 2020, pp. 117–125) devotes nine pages to grammar and usage within a chapter titled "Writing Style and Grammar," so it should be clear that you also need to bring your A-game to the writing process when writing psychology papers. Based on my experience, students often have particular trouble with three grammar guidelines that APA provides. Mastering these principles will help you write better and more clearly.

Write in Active Voice

We often talk using passive voice, so that habit tends to bleed over into our writing. In **passive voice**, the writer uses the object of a sentence as the subject, which results in wordy, indirect writing. "A memory test was given to the subjects" is an example of a passive voice construction. "Memory test" is the subject of the sentence, although the test certainly was not active; it did not do anything. The use of a "be" verb ("was" in this example) as a helping verb makes this verb construction passive rather than active. "The subjects completed a memory test" is an **active voice** construction—it is direct, clearer, and even shorter. Although both voices are acceptable in APA Style, the *Publication Manual* (2020, p. 118) notes that many writers tend to use passive voice too much. "Use the active voice as much as possible to create direct, clear, and concise sentences" (APA, 2020, p. 118).

Many people (even psychology professors and researchers) write in passive voice in an attempt to avoid using first-person pronouns (I, we) because they believe that using first person is incorrect in scientific writing. The *APA Publication Manual* encourages the use of first-person pronouns when describing what you did in your experiment and when expressing your opinion (APA, 2020, p. 120). Using first-person constructions will often help you avoid writing in passive voice.

Most of the time when you use a "be" verb as a helping verb, you are writing in passive voice. Note that a "be" verb used alone is perfectly fine. "The subjects were first-year college students" and "The sound volume was 80 decibels" are both fine in APA Style—passive voice and past tense are not the same thing. The IN PRACTICE: Active and Passive Voice box shows you how to review and apply this information.

IN PRACTICE

Active and Passive Voice

Which of the following sentences uses passive voice?

(a) The experimenter gave the memory test to the participants.

(b) The participants took the personality test after a rest period.

(c) The endurance test was given to the participants.

< *The last sentence uses a "be" verb and is in passive voice.* >

All of these sentences contain passive voice. Rewrite them to remove the passive voice.

(d) An experiment was conducted by Jones (1995).

(e) A significant effect was found.

(f) All instances of passive voice have been removed.

< *Jones (1995) conducted an experiment.* >

< *The effect was significant.* >

< *I have removed all instances of passive voice.* >

Use Verb Tense Correctly

The primary problem that student writers have with verb tense occurs when they are summarizing research results. Any research article that you read covers research that took place in the past. Thus, you should write in **past tense** (note again that past tense is different from passive voice!). "Smith and Jones (2007) wrote that . . ." is correct because "wrote" is past tense, whereas "Smith and Jones (2007) believe that . . ." would be incorrect because "believe" is present tense. Similarly, if you are writing about a research study that you conducted, that research also took place in the past, so you should give details about your experiment in past tense. See Table 4.1 in the *Publication Manual* (2020, p. 118) for an at-a-glance reminder of which verb tense to use in different sections of your APA-Style paper.

"That" Versus "Which"

"That" and "which" are not interchangeable in APA Style, although we typically use them synonymously when we speak. According to APA (2020, pp. 122–123), a clause using "that" is a **restrictive clause** and should be essential to the meaning of the sentence. By contrast, a clause using "which" is a **nonrestrictive clause**, is not necessary to make a sentence meaningful, and is set off with commas. Thus, "The rats that were younger had less training time" is correct—"that were younger" is necessary for the sentence to make sense. Likewise, "The stimulus items, which were shown on a computer screen, were half nouns and half verbs" is correct because "which were shown on a computer screen" is not essential to understand the sentence. If it was important to differentiate the way the stimuli were presented, then you should write "The subjects in Group 1 saw words that appeared on a computer screen, whereas the subjects in Group 2 saw words printed on a sheet of paper." In this case, you would be setting up a contrast between subjects in different groups related to the mode of stimulus presentation—here, the presentation format is essential to the sentence, so you should use "that" rather than "which." The IN PRACTICE: "That" and "Which" box gives you a chance to apply this information about "that" and "which." You can refer to the Common Writing Problems, Explanations, and Solutions listed in Appendix D for reminders of this point and other grammar and APA-Style issues.

IN PRACTICE

"That" and "Which"

Which sentences need editing to be correct in APA Style? Make the appropriate corrections.

(a) The experimenter tested the animals which were older first.
(b) The experimenter tested the animals that were older first.
(c) The experimenter passed out writing instruments that were pencils.
(d) The experimenter passed out writing instruments which were pencils.

Answers: (a) The experimenter tested the animals, which were older, first; (b) correct; (c) correct; (d) The experimenter passed out writing instruments, which were pencils.

Grammar Reminders, Pointers, and Refreshers

Because you are in college, I know that you have learned a great deal about grammar during your years in school. However, I also know from years of experience that many students often forget some of the valuable grammar lessons that they learned. Therefore, the remainder of the chapter will provide you with reminders of some important points of grammar, particularly as they concern APA Style and format.

So that you don't feel too badly about having forgotten some of the grammar essentials that you previously learned, I will share another story from one of my former students who now teaches science in middle school.

> *I teach eighth-grade science in a Title 1 school in Texas. The students are from low socioeconomic conditions, and many of them struggle with reading and writing. In my pod, we are working on writing in complete sentences. I teach my students about capitalizing the first letter, a period being required at the end of sentence to show the reader to pause, and that sentences cannot contain only a clause but must contain a subject and a verb. I use warm-ups and wrap-ups where I require my students to answer with a complete sentence. I have seen growth even in my special education students this year.* (Misty Chafin Garland; OBU, 1991; Texas Middle School, Texarkana, TX)

Parts of Speech

You probably began to learn about parts of speech when you first began to learn English. The good thing about that timing is that you have had a long time to learn about parts of speech; the bad thing about that timing is that, without much rehearsal or subsequent learning, you have had a long time to forget about parts of speech! Traditionally, there are nine defined parts of speech: nouns, pronouns, adjectives, verbs, adverbs, prepositions, articles, conjunctions, and interjections (Hurford, 1994; Sinclair, 2010). Although the *APA Publication Manual* (APA, 2020) does not address each part of speech directly, most are important to good writing, regardless of whether you are writing in APA Style.

Nouns

A noun is "a word that names a person, place, thing, or idea" (Strunk & White, 2000, p. 92). Nouns, of course, are typically the subjects of sentences, something that is particularly important in APA Style because of its emphasis on clear and concise writing (e.g., see Chapter 4 of *APA Manual*; APA, 2020, pp. 113–117). In most APA-Style writing, concrete nouns (person, place, thing; e.g., participant, laboratory, computer) predominate over abstract nouns (ideas; e.g., truth, liberty, beauty). Psychologists tend to make abstract nouns concrete through some type of measurement or definition. For example, "attitude" is an abstract noun, but a psychologist may give research subjects an attitude test to measure a specific attitude (e.g., racism, optimism, happiness, prejudice, or bias), thereby making it more concrete.

With both abstract and concrete nouns, psychologists often use operational definitions to make the noun as specific as possible. An **operational definition** describes a noun in terms of the operations or actions used to either manipulate or measure it. Let's use "hunger" as an example. Hunger is an abstract noun—although people may report that they are "hungry," we cannot see their hunger or measure it directly. If we wish to use hunger as an **independent variable** (a variable that we manipulate) with our subjects, we must define hunger in terms of how we "make it happen." One of the most common operational definitions for hunger as an independent variable in animal research is "23 hours of food deprivation." So, rather than using the vague noun "hunger," we have precisely defined how we manipulated it. If we wanted to measure the variable of hunger (the **dependent variable**, or the variable that we measure), however, simply asking subjects if they were hungry would not be very precise. Instead, we would search the psychology literature for some type of test or scale that measures hunger (e.g., Bennett & Blissett, 2014). By giving all our subjects the same scale to measure their hunger, we can be certain that we are measuring this abstract concept in the same way for everyone.

The *APA Publication Manual* (APA, 2020) does not cover nouns in much depth. You will find information about capitalization (pp. 165–169), gender and noun usage (pp. 139–140), and verbs used with collective nouns (p. 119). One important point in the *Manual* refers to noun strings, which are "several nouns placed one after another to modify a final noun" (APA, 2020, p. 112), such as "commonly used investigative expanded issue control question technique," which may confuse readers. Bellquist (1993, p. 127) referred to this type of construction as "noun plague," giving "novel-solution-presented rats" as an example. A long string of nouns makes it difficult for the reader to interpret the writer's meaning. As Bellquist noted, "rats that were presented with a novel solution" (1993, p. 129) is simpler to decode and understand.

Pronouns

As you probably remember, pronouns are words used to stand for nouns (or noun phrases)—words such as "I," "you," "them," "that," "yourself," "one," and so on. People use pronouns extensively in spoken and written language, but they can cause some difficulty in writing because of a lack of clarity. For example, look at the previous sentence: It includes the pronoun "they." But what is the referent for "they"—is it "people" or "pronouns"? You may remember the rule you learned in school: Pronouns should refer to (and thus replace) the most immediately adjacent noun. Therefore, in the sentence referenced, "they" refers to "pronouns," so it is pronouns that can cause some difficulty in understanding sentences. The alternative interpretation (that people can cause difficulty because of a lack of clarity) is humorous, but certainly not true.

The *APA Publication Manual* (APA, 2020, p. 120) instructs authors to avoid this potential problem when using pronouns: "Each pronoun should refer clearly to its antecedent" (see also Chapter 2). Many writing style guides (Alley, 1987; Sternberg, 2003; Strunk & White, 2000) particularly single out the pronoun "this" as especially troublesome, with Alley (1987, p. 43) labeling scientists' use of the word as "criminal." Similar pronouns "that," "these," and "those" are just as problematic. For clarity in your writing, you should follow those pronouns with a noun to remove any potential ambiguity. For example, you should write "this finding implies" rather than "this implies," or "those studies showed" rather than "those showed."

One other important grammatical consideration about pronouns is that pronouns should agree in number and gender with the nouns they replace (Strunk & White, 2000). The rule concerning number is fairly simple: If you use a pronoun for a plural noun, the pronoun should also be plural. The rule concerning pronouns and gender can be a little tricky, given that APA Style emphasizes using unbiased language in writing (APA, 2020, pp. 131–149; see also Chapter 2). For many years, writers used the generic "he" to refer to people, but that usage is now frowned upon because it is not gender inclusive; APA Style does not allow this usage (APA, 2020, p. 121). To combat the "he problem," some writers prefer to use "she," some mix "she" and "he," and some use a combination such as "he/she." However, these solutions can be distracting to readers and are not favored in APA Style (APA, 2020, p. 140). One of the best solutions is to use plural nouns so that the appropriate substituting pronoun is "they" (APA, 2020, p. 121). So, rather than writing "A person with OCD (obsessive-compulsive disorder) may try to ignore their obsessions," you could write "People with OCD (obsessive-compulsive disorder) may try to ignore their obsessions." A recent solution to this problem is to use the singular "they" (APA, 2020, pp. 120–121), which is becoming an increasingly popular solution to specifying a particular gender or sex. For more on this usage, see the section "More About Number: 'They'" later in this chapter. Pronouns should also match the nouns for which you are substituting: If you are referring to humans, use "who"; if you are referring to nonhuman animals or things, use "that" (APA, 2020, p. 121).

Distinguishing Between "That" and "Which." Finally, APA Style distinguishes between two relative pronouns: "that" and "which." A **relative pronoun** connects a noun and a phrase modifying or describing the noun. In speaking and writing, many people use "that" and "which" interchangeably. APA Style (APA, 2020, pp. 122–123), however, treats them differently. As I mentioned earlier, you should use "that" for restrictive clauses—clauses that are necessary for the meaning of a sentence. For example, in the sentence "We used the stimuli that we used in the first experiment for the second experiment as well," the restrictive clause "that we used in the first experiment" is essential to the sentence's meaning—leaving it out leaves a nonsensical sentence. By contrast, you should use "which" for nonrestrictive clauses—clauses that merely add further information to a sentence. For example, in the sentence "We used the stimuli, which were nouns, from the first experiment in the second experiment as well," the nonrestrictive clause "which were nouns" merely adds information about the stimuli that is not essential to the sentence's meaning. Notice, too, that nonrestrictive clauses have commas to set them off from the rest of the sentence.

Adjectives

Adjectives are words that modify nouns or pronouns by describing some property associated with the noun or pronoun (Hurford, 1994; Sinclair, 2010), such as "the *blue* pencil," where "blue" is an adjective modifying or describing the pencil. The *APA Publication Manual* does not directly address adjectives (APA, 2020), probably because they are not present as frequently in APA writing as they are in humanities writing. If you are contemplating adding an adjective, be sure that it is both relevant and important. Given the previous example, is it really important to specify that the pencil was blue? In most cases, that detail is probably not important. If the color of the pencil *was* a variable in your research, then that detail would be relevant, important, and critical to understanding the research.

The primary use of adjectives in APA Style is to describe research participants and apparatus or materials in adequate detail for readers. As the *APA Manual* (APA, 2020, pp. 82–83) notes, it is important to provide details about participants so that readers can assess scientific aspects of the research study. If you include or exclude human subjects based on any criteria, you should specify those characteristics, which might require the use of adjectives. The example list of demographic characteristics provided in the *APA Manual* (APA, 2020, p. 83) is long and exhaustive. Essentially, you should report any characteristic that distinguishes your participants from the general population, describing the participants in as much detail as possible, with a focus on characteristics that are important to your research variables and results. However, it is important to avoid using biased terms. For example, APA Style says to avoid using adjectives as nouns (e.g., refer to Asian participants, not Asians) or pejorative adjectives, such as outdated terms for racial or ethnic groups (APA, 2020, pp. 133–148). APA Style prefers using "male" and "female" as adjectives rather than nouns (APA, 2020, p. 139), in an attempt to avoid sexism. Thus, you should write "female subjects" rather than simply "females." You should avoid using any adjectives that convey bias of any sort.

Verbs

Verbs are words that express actions or states (Hurford, 1994; Sinclair, 2010), such as "research participants *viewed* images" or "we *administered* a recall test to participants." In an effort to foster clear communication, remember the APA Style preference for active voice discussed earlier in this chapter; "use the active voice to describe the actions of participants and others involved in your study" (APA, 2020, p. 118). Although I briefly mentioned avoiding passive voice earlier in the chapter, we will take a more in-depth look at that issue here. Active voice uses verbs as vigorous, direct communicators rather than using them indirectly. In active voice, the subject of the sentence is the actor; passive voice renders the actor as the object of the sentence. Contrast these three sentences:

"The research participants completed a personality test."

"A personality test was completed by the research participants."

"A personality test was given by the experimenter."

Can you tell which sentence uses active voice and which sentences use passive voice? The first sentence illustrates active voice: The research participants were the people who actually did something (completed a personality test). In the second sentence, although "a personality test" is the subject of the sentence, it was *not* active in any way—it did not do anything. Even worse, the third sentence doesn't even mention the people who actually took the personality test. Although the experimenter was active in the sense of administering the test, the subjects were the ones who completed the test. Writers and speakers use passive voice when they use a "be" verb (am, is, are, was, were, being, been) as an auxiliary or helping verb, adding it to a verb. Notice how uncomplicated active voice is when compared to passive voice:

> **Active Voice:** Subject + verb + object *(The research participants + completed + a personality test.)*
>
> **Passive Voice:** Object used as subject + "be" verb + past participle form of verb + by + actual subject used as an object *(A personality test + was completed + by + the research participants.)*

This type of verb construction is wordy, indirect, and typically longer. It interferes with clear, direct communication, as specified in APA Style. The *APA Publication Manual* (APA, 2020, p. 118) *does* allow for the use of passive voice if focusing on the actor is less important than focusing on the recipient of the action (a person or object). For example, "The speakers were mounted on the ceiling" would be an acceptable use of passive voice ("were mounted") because it is the location of the speakers that is important, not who mounted them on the ceiling.

To reiterate a point made earlier in the chapter, the verb tense that you use is also important in APA-Style writing. Most often, you will use past tense in your writing because you are writing about events that occurred in the past, such as previous research. Thus, "Smith and Jones (2015) *found* that . . ." would be correct. When you report results from your experiment, you should still use past tense because you have completed your research project (APA, 2020, pp. 117–118). (Note that past tense and passive voice are not the same thing!) However, when you discuss your results, you should write in present tense because you want your reader to "join you" in discussing your findings (APA, 2020, p. 118). Thus, "These results imply that . . ." would be correct when you discuss your findings.

Adverbs

According to Sinclair (2010, p. xiii), adverbs modify "a verb or adjective, or other adverb (often ends in -*ly*)"; examples include "fully," "gracefully," "usually," and "very." APA writing tends to use adverbs as introductory or transitional words, although the *APA Publication Manual* advises writers to be careful in using them (APA, 2020, p. 112), ensuring that the adverb is needed to make an introduction or transition. Because of this preferred use, adverbs used often in APA Style include words such as "similarly," "consequently," "interestingly," and "importantly," among other such words.

Strunk and White (2000, p. 48) cautioned against incorrectly using the adverb "hopefully," which actually means "in a hopeful manner," not "I hope." The incorrect usage (*hopefully* as "I hope") is commonplace in spoken (and written) language, but is simply wrong.

Another commonly misused word is "only." Although "only" can serve as an adjective, adverb, or conjunction, it is often misplaced when serving as an adverb (APA, 2020, p. 124). "I only cook on weekends" and "I cook only on weekends" do not have the same meaning. The word "only" should come before the word (or phrase that it modifies). The first sentence means that the person does nothing but cook on weekends, whereas the second sentence says that the person cooks solely on weekends but not during the week. Likewise, "The subject only recalled four words" and "The subject recalled only four words" do not have the same meaning. The first sentence implies that the subject did nothing more than recall, whereas the second sentence means that the subject recalled four words from a larger pool. More than likely, the writer meant to imply that the number of words recalled was small, so the second sentence is the correct way to write that information.

Conjunctions

Conjunctions are words used to join words, phrases, or clauses; the most common conjunctions are "and," "but," and "or" (Hurford, 1994, p. 46). You should use conjunctions to join grammatically equivalent elements (Strunk & White, 2000, p. 91); the *APA Publication Manual* (APA, 2020, p. 125) specifies that the elements should be "parallel in form." For example, if you were writing about several types of stimuli, you should write either "the short, medium, and long tones" or "the short, the medium, and the long tones," but not "the short, the medium, and long tones."

Also notice in the prior examples that APA Style *does* include a comma before the conjunction (the Oxford comma). In English classes, some students apparently learn that the final comma is not necessary, but it should be included in APA Style (APA, 2020, p. 155). In Chapter 1, you saw an example of why the Oxford comma can be critical to the meaning of a sentence.

Likewise, you should separate two independent clauses (clauses that include a noun and verb and are complete sentences) with a comma followed by a conjunction (APA, 2020, p. 155). For example, "The men sat on the left side of the room, and the women sat on the right side of the room" expresses two complete thoughts joined by a conjunction, so a comma is necessary.

APA Style (APA, 2020, p. 123) makes a distinction between some subordinate conjunctions (words such as "although," "because," "since," and "while"), which are conjunctions that introduce a **subordinate clause**. Subordinate clauses are clauses that cannot stand alone as a sentence (Sinclair, 2010, p. 177). APA Style prefers the use of "while" and "since" for temporal (time-related) situations. You should always use "while" for situations in which two or more events occur at the same time, such as "While subjects read the passages, they heard music in the background." This sentence informs you that the reading and music occurred simultaneously. Do not use "while" to substitute for "although," which is an error many people make. Thus, rather than writing "While some people support Freud's ideas, they . . . ," you should write "Although some people support Freud's ideas, they. . . ." When writing the word "since," you should often restrict your usage to denote that one event transpired after a previous one—for example, "Since Freud developed his ideas, many people have endorsed them." Because of this use of "since," it is clear that people's endorsements came after Freud developed his ideas. You should not use "since" to substitute for "because" (see Chapter 2), which is a common usage, unless the meaning is totally clear (APA, 2020, p. 123). Thus, you should write "Data totals differ for various questions because subjects did not answer all questions." Using "since" instead of "because" in this sentence could lead to a misunderstanding about the timeline of the events.

The *APA Manual* (2020) does not address the remaining parts of speech (prepositions, articles, interjections), so we will cover them in less detail. The information that you have previously learned about these parts of speech is mostly applicable in your APA-Style writing.

Prepositions

Prepositions are words that indicate relationships, such as "for," "through," "to," "up," and so on (Sinclair, 2010, p. xiii). Prepositions typically occur before a noun phrase and make a **prepositional phrase** (Hurford, 1994, p. 190), such as "the time period *after* the stimulus presentation." You would most likely use prepositions and prepositional phrases in APA writing to add information clarifying nouns about which you were writing. For example, in summarizing previous research, you might write "Research *before* Skinner's ideas was. . . ." With this prepositional phrase, you would be clarifying the time period of research about which you were writing. In a Method section of an article, you might read "*Before* subjects participated, they completed an informed consent document." This prepositional phrase clarifies when an important aspect of the research process took place. Be careful not to use a prepositional phrase as a sentence because it will result in an incomplete sentence.

Articles

Articles are "special types of adjectives, showing whether the noun is definite or indefinite" (Sinclair, 2010, p. xiii). There are only two examples of articles: "the" and "a/an." "The" refers to a definite noun; "a/an" refers to an indefinite noun. I have seen a specific type of error in student writing regarding articles—using "the" when "a/an" should be used. Specifically, you should not use "the" the first time you refer to a noun, because the noun at that point is indefinite. After you have mentioned the noun, then it is definite, and you can use "the." For example, if you administer a personality test to your subjects, you should write "Subjects took a personality test measuring shyness. The test was. . . ." In contrast, if you wrote "Subjects took the personality test measuring shyness," the sentence would read as if you had previously mentioned that test. The same rule holds true if you are writing about a research study. On your first mention of the study, you should write "Smith and Jones (2012) conducted a study in which. . . ." After that first mention, you can refer to "the Smith and Jones (2012) study."

Interjections

You are unlikely to either read or write interjections in an APA-Style paper. Sinclair (2010, p. xiii) described interjections as "words expressing emotion which is unrelated to the rest of the sentence" (such as "Wow!") and noted that interjections are typically not appropriate in academic writing.

Combining Subjects and Verbs in Sentences

Of course, there is *much* more to grammar than simply knowing the parts of speech. A great deal of grammar "happens" when you begin to combine various parts of speech into sentences. One of the most important guidelines in standard English grammar and in APA Style (APA, 2020, pp. 119–120) is that the subject and the verb in a sentence should agree in number. In other words, singular subjects require singular verbs, and plural subjects require plural verbs. In many cases, subject–verb agreement is fairly simple because the subject and the verb are often adjacent in sentences: "This result implies . . ." and "These results imply. . . ." In other cases, writers insert words between the subject and verb, which may cause difficulty with determining the true subject of the sentence. As an example, consider the sentence "Each of the four sets of stimuli _____ named by one of the four groups of subjects" (Bellquist, 1993, p. 23). Which verb should you insert in the blank: "was" or "were"? The correct answer depends on which word serves as the subject of the sentence. "Sets" and "stimuli" are nouns that are close to the verb phrase "_____ named," and they are both plural. However, neither of those words serves as the subject of the sentence; instead, "Each" is a pronoun serving as the subject. Thus, the verb should match "each" in number, so the correct answer is "was." If a writer loses track and believes "sets" or "stimuli" to be the subject of the sentence, the writer would use "were" and the sentence would be grammatically incorrect: "Each of the four sets of stimuli were named by one of the four groups of subjects." One way to avoid this error is to (mentally) remove the words intervening between the subject and verb and then pick the verb that matches the true subject in number: "Each . . . was named." See the *APA Manual* (2020, pp. 119–120) for helpful hints about subject–verb agreement for collective nouns, compound subjects, and the word "none."

Some words seem particularly tricky to match in number. In my experience with student writing, the prime offender is the word "data." "Data" is the plural of "datum," so it needs a plural verb (APA, 2020, p. 162). Thus, you should write "the data are," not "the data is." This error is commonplace not only in student writing, but also in newspapers, magazines, and news broadcasts. The same rule should apply for words that are plural and end in the letter "a," such as "phenomena" (plural of "phenomenon"), "media" (plural of "medium"), "bacteria" (plural of "bacterium"), and many others. To be fair, some media outlets have given the okay to "data is," such as *The Wall Street Journal* ("Data Is or Data Are?", 2012) and *The Washington Post* (Walsh, 2015), but APA Style still considers "data" to be a plural noun.

More About Number: "They"

In addition to nouns and verbs agreeing in number, so should nouns and pronouns. This issue is a thorny one, in part because of APA's guidelines about avoiding biased language (APA, 2020, pp. 131–149; see also Chapter 2). In an effort to avoid sexism, many speakers and writers will use "they" (or a variant) when the grammar technically would require a singular pronoun (e.g., "he," "she," "it"). Thus, you might read (or hear), "The participant indicated their choice on a blank sheet of paper." The grammatical problem in this sentence is that "the participant" is singular, but "their" is plural. It is admirable both to avoid sexist language (using "his" only) and to avoid awkward constructions (e.g., "his/her"), but mixing number has traditionally been grammatically unacceptable. As mentioned previously, often the simplest solution is to use plural nouns: "The participants indicated their choices on a blank sheet of paper."

The trend of using "they" with singular nouns is also increasing, with one usage that may well become universally acceptable: to avoid biased language. The *Publication Manual* (APA, 2020, p. 120) specifically states that you should "always use the singular 'they' to refer to a person who uses 'they' as their pronoun." Using "they" as a singular pronoun is also acceptable when a person's gender is unknown or irrelevant to the context. The *APA Manual* (2020, p. 121) notes that using "they" as singular may seem awkward and provides alternative suggestions. Also, note that you should use a plural verb even though you are using the singular "they" (Singular "they," 2020). However, using the singular "they" is a special circumstance regarding gender diversity and using "they" singularly when referring to multiple people is grammatically incorrect and not acceptable in APA format.

Concluding Thoughts

Unlike Chapter 2, which introduced APA Style, much of the material in this chapter was a review or a reminder for you. Even if you never write another APA-format paper in your life, good writing skills are important in many settings, including on the job. Kay (2011) listed writing skills as one of the top five skills that employers want in their new employees, with one employer reporting that good writing could be the difference between success and failure in the workplace. A recent survey of more than 300 *Fortune* 1000 executives found that 97% of them rated "ability to write clearly and persuasively" as either "absolutely essential" or "very important" (Markow & Pieters, 2011, p. 21). You should also remember the stories from my former students about the importance of writing in their careers. Thus, attending to grammatical concerns could be important for your future career and livelihood.

> *As a psychology major, I developed writing skills that have been highly valuable and transferable to my graduate education and career. I earned an MEd and EdD in Higher Education, and having significant writing experience was an extremely beneficial asset for graduate school research. For 14 years, I have pursued a career in higher education and student services. Written communication is critical to success in this position, as a major component of any position involved translating complex information between faculty, students, and staff. I have utilized writing experience to provide written reports to presidents of colleges, accreditation agencies, journals, and conference presentations.* (Peggy Sharp, EdD; OBU, 2001;

Senior Advisor, Department of Aerospace Engineering & Engineering Mechanics, University of Texas–Austin)

If the many grammatical concerns listed in this chapter have seemed somewhat overwhelming to you, take heart. You should not only try to learn the material in this book for the class you are currently taking, but you should also keep this book as a reference for your future writing endeavors. After exploring how to read journal articles in the next chapter, the remaining chapters address the various types of APA-Style writing assignments you may encounter during your college career, so the book will be helpful in your upcoming classes. This particular chapter could be useful to you even beyond college as you end up writing for your job. If you would like additional help and reminders about important grammar issues, check out the resources listed in the A CLOSER LOOK . . . at Grammar Resources box.

A CLOSER LOOK
at Grammar Resources

You should remember that grammar is important not only in APA-Style writing, but in all your writing. There are many grammar resources available on the web—when in doubt, consult a source for help. I list two sources here that you might find particularly helpful.

http://www.dailygrammar.com/

Daily Grammar provides you with 440 lessons and 88 quizzes to help you refresh your grammar knowledge or even learn new grammar pointers. If you sign up for its Daily Grammar Blog, you will receive lessons Monday through Friday and a quiz on Saturday. (Posts to the blog are also emailed to you.)

https://www.grammarly.com/

Grammarly offers "a free grammar check you can rely on," according to its website.

Critical Thinking Writing Assignments

Answer each of the following assignments in a paragraph aimed at a parent or grandparent who might not appreciate the importance of grammar.

Assignment 1

Why do grammar rules exist? Why are they important? Why are they important for psychology writing?

Assignment 2

How can the grammar we use when speaking cause us difficulty in using correct grammar when writing?

Assignment 3

Explain the correct usage of "data" and "they." For each word, give an original (i.e., not copied from the book) example of both a correct and an incorrect usage.

References

Alley, M. (1987). *The craft of scientific writing.* Prentice-Hall.

American Psychological Association. (2020). *Publication manual of the American Psychological Association* (7th ed.). https://doi.org/10.1037/0000165-000.

Bellquist, J. E. (1993). *A guide to grammar and usage for psychology and related fields.* Lawrence Erlbaum Associates. https://doi.org/10.4324/9781315806655

Bennett, C., & Blissett, J. (2014). Measuring hunger and satiety in primary school children: Validation of a new picture rating scale. *Appetite, 78,* 40–48. https://doi.org/10.1016/j.appet.2014.03.011

Data is or data are? (2012, July 8). *The Guardian.* https://www.theguardian.com/news/datablog/2010/jul/16/data-plural-singular

Hurford, J. R. (1994). *Grammar: A student's guide.* Cambridge University Press.

Kay, A. (2011, May 30). What employers want: 5 more skills to cultivate. *USA Today.* https://usatoday30.usatoday.com/money/jobcenter/workplace/kay/2011-05-30-skills-employers-want-part-ii_N.htm

Markow, D., & Pieters, A. (2011). *The MetLife survey of the American teacher: Preparing students for college and careers. A survey of teachers, students, parents, and* Fortune *1000 executives.* MetLife. https://files.eric.ed.gov/fulltext/ED519278.pdf

Sinclair, C. (2010). *Grammar: A friendly approach* (2nd ed.). Open University Press/McGraw-Hill.

Singular "they." (2020, October 22). *APA Style.* https://apastyle.apa.org/style-grammar-guidelines/grammar/singular-they

Sternberg, R. J. (2003). *The psychologist's companion: A guide to scientific writing for students and researchers* (4th ed.). Cambridge University Press.

Strunk, W., Jr., & White, E. B. (2000). *The elements of style* (4th ed.). Pearson Education.

Walsh, B. (2015, April 7). Grammar geekery with Bill Walsh. *The Washington Post.* https://live.washingtonpost.com/grammar-geekery-with-bill-walsh-20150407.html

4

How to Read a Psychology Journal Article

Do You Know?

Why is reading journal articles so important to your writing success?

What is the most widely read part of a journal article?

What is an abstract?

What is a literature review?

Where can you find details about how an experiment was conducted?

Where can you find a simplified version of complex statistical results?

"To be successful in college, students need to be able to read and comprehend journal articles. . . . Reading empirical articles is no easy task."

—Sego & Stuart, 2016, p. 38

You might be confused about the title for this chapter: Why do you need to learn about reading journal articles in a book about writing psychology papers? The answer to this question is quite simple. Every writing assignment covered in this book will be based, at least to some extent, on your ability to read journal articles. Chapter 2 contrasted scientific writing with humanities writing. One additional important difference in those two writing styles is their products: Scientists, including psychologists, are more likely to write journal articles, whereas humanities writers are more likely to write books. Don't get me wrong—there are plenty of psychology books out there! It is simply the case that advancements in psychology and other sciences are almost universally published in journal articles. That fact means that you are much more likely to read, cite, and reference journal articles than any other type of source.

At this point, I should give a mild warning: Many students find reading journal articles to be a somewhat difficult task. If you are not used to reading scientific writing, it can seem a little dense or confusing at times. One aspect of scientific writing that students may find particularly challenging is the terminology used—there may be words that you don't know or understand. This problem is a common one for novices in *any* field, because all subjects have their own jargon that is specific to that discipline. Just think of how many new terms you have learned in your psychology courses. The way to overcome this problem is to read articles and learn the terminology specific to your area of interest. Soon you'll feel confident in your understanding as you read new journal articles.

Another problem that students encounter is the organization of a journal article into several different sections—they may not know which section contains which information. The design of this chapter will help you with that problem.

APA-Style writing provides a simple road map for reading journal articles that can help you meet these challenges. As the old saying goes, there is "a place for everything and everything in its place." Once you understand the organization of a journal article, you will know exactly where to go to find the information you need. To make the aspects covered in this chapter more concrete, you can refer to Appendix A, which shows you an actual published journal article. Eugenio Peluso was a student at Creighton University interested in sports psychology and wanted research experience before applying for graduate school. He completed a research project and submitted it for publication consideration. The resulting article (Peluso, 2000) is the article featured in this appendix. He is now Eugenio Peluso, PhD after completing his doctorate in clinical psychology at St. Louis University.

Title

The most widely read component of any journal article is its **title**. The title should describe the subject matter of the article clearly and concisely—sometimes a difficult task. The *Publication Manual of the American Psychological Association* (American Psychological Association [APA], 2020, p. 31) says that your title should alert the reader to your subject and the factors under investigation. Although there is no word limit for a title, authors should keep the title "focused and succinct" (APA, 2020, p. 31). When you search for articles to include in a paper, the title will typically be the first part of the article you examine. Ideally, it will be a title that fits APA-Style guidelines and helps you decide whether to read the article to consider including it in your paper. Peluso's title ("Skilled Motor Performance as a Function of Types of Mental Imagery") clearly indicates the main topic (types of mental imagery) and the investigation of that topic in the area of motor (movement) performance (see the first page of Appendix A).

Author Information

Author information (APA, 2020, pp. 33–35) includes the author's or authors' name(s) and institutional affiliation(s) in close proximity to the article's title. The order of authorship is important: The first author typically is most responsible for the article, and subsequent authors are listed in order of their contributions (APA, 2020, p. 25). As shown in Appendix A, Peluso (2000) was the sole author listed on his article, but he did list his faculty sponsor (Mark E. Ware) in a footnote. At the time he published his article, the journal (*Journal of Psychological Inquiry*) tended to footnote faculty sponsors rather than listing them as authors. Current instructions for that journal stipulate that graduate students or faculty can be coauthors if they served a teaching or mentoring role rather than being an equal collaborator. For two articles that I coauthored with students (Khersonskaya & Smith, 1998; Posey & Smith, 2003), the students were the first authors because the articles derived from their research projects, even though I was their supervisor and helped them with their experiments and article writing.

You will typically find contact information for authors listed in an author note (APA, 2020, pp. 35–37). The most important part of this information is an email address for (at least) the first author. Contacting an author by email to ask about a research study or whether the author has written other articles on the same or similar topics is certainly acceptable—and may help you in searching for relevant literature. One caution is in order here: If the article is an older one, the email contact information for the author could be outdated. If so, a web or PsycINFO search on the author's name may turn up current contact information. Note that Peluso's (2000) article (see first page of Appendix A) did not contain contact information, although it did include his professor's name, which might have enabled contact at the time.

Abstract

An **abstract** is a brief summary of an article. Although it is brief, it should be comprehensive (APA, 2020, p. 38). Abstracts will be invaluable to you—after titles, you are likely to read more abstracts of articles than any other parts of articles. As you will see in Chapter 5, when you search the psychological literature via PsycINFO, the abstract is part of the information that you will find. You will then typically read the title and abstract to decide whether to get the full-text article to read (see an important hint in the IN PRACTICE: Reading Abstracts box). In a printed article, the abstract may be set off by a line, italics, or some other typographical feature to distinguish it from the rest of the article, as shown on the first page of Appendix A. The *APA Publication Manual* (APA, 2020, p. 38) notes that abstracts typically have a maximum of 250 words. Abstract length is flexible because instructors and journals may specify exact word limits.

IN PRACTICE

Reading Abstracts

Let me provide a hint about reading abstracts that might help you as you search for relevant articles: If you find an abstract that looks like it *might* be helpful or relevant to you, you do not have to search for the full-text article immediately. When you are reading an abstract in PsycINFO, you can choose to print, email, or save it. Working in this manner, you could find many abstracts and then look at them all together later to see which articles still seem to be a good fit for your research interest.

What information should you expect to find in an abstract? According to the *APA Manual* (APA, 2020, p. 74), you should expect to find information about the following items when reading an abstract for an experimental study:

- a brief statement of the question or issue under investigation;
- important information about the subjects (e.g., age, sex);
- important methodological details;
- basic statistical results; and
- conclusions, including what they imply and how they can be applied.

Not every detail listed here will always appear in the abstracts that you read. As you might imagine, covering all these details in a brief paragraph is not easy. If a critical detail is missing from the abstract, then you will need to find it in the article. The *APA Manual* (APA, 2020, pp. 74–75) also provides lists of information you should expect to find in abstracts of literature reviews or **meta-analyses**—summaries of many findings based on a statistical technique—as well as theory-oriented papers, methodological papers, and replication articles. I am not presenting information listings for those types of articles in this text because you will most likely be reading journal articles that summarize experimental studies for your writing assignments.

Introduction

The **introduction section** is the first major section of an article and begins (typically) immediately under the abstract, but is not labeled with the word "Introduction." According to the *APA Manual* (APA, 2020, p. 4), the introduction presents "a statement of the purpose of the investigation, a review of the background literature, and an explicit statement of the hypotheses being explored."

Most people who read journal articles would probably describe the introduction as a **literature review** or a summary of previous research. An author who writes a good literature review will typically give a broad context for the experimental question to come, provide an overview of research that is relevant to that question, write in an increasingly narrow and focused nature as the review progresses, and end with an experimental question derived from that literature review.

It is important to provide the reader with relevant background literature so it is clear why the author conducted the experiment that follows the review. In Peluso's introduction (the first two pages of Appendix A), you will see that he began broadly by defining his topic of use of mental imagery to improve performance. Peluso narrowed his focus in each successive paragraph until the last paragraph, in which he featured his experimental question: Would relevant mental imagery improve motor performance compared to irrelevant mental imagery or simply reading about mental imagery?

As you read an introduction, you will find citations to the relevant background literature that the author has included in the literature review (see the IN PRACTICE: Finding New Articles from Introductions box for a helpful pointer as you read introductions). In APA Style, a citation includes the author's or authors' name(s) and date of the publication. An example citation for an article that I cite later in this chapter is "(Godden & Baddeley, 1975)." If the writer uses the authors' names in the text, the citation would take the following form: "Godden and Baddeley (1975) investigated context-dependent memory in their study." You will find full bibliographic information for each citation at the end of the article in a reference list.

IN PRACTICE

Finding New Articles From Introductions

As you read the introduction to a journal article, you might find new citations and references to articles that are relevant to your topic that you did not find in your own searches. If so, you can easily find those articles by conducting a PsycINFO search on either the title or the authors of the articles. In this manner, you can continue to shape your literature searching as you read other research articles.

Authors should consider several issues before writing their introduction: the importance of the problem, the relation of the study to previous research, the hypotheses and goals of the study, the relation of the hypotheses and research design, and the potential applications of the study (APA, 2020, pp. 75–76, 78). A good introduction addresses these issues in a few pages and, by combining the literature review and author's reasoning, informs the reader what the researcher did in the study and why.

Like the list of information that should appear in the abstract, this list for the introduction is long and ambitious. In my experience, most introductions focus primarily on the second and third items listed, which is why I find "introduction" and "literature review" to be terms that are close to synonymous. The final item, in particular, is information that authors may be just as likely, if not more likely, to include in their Discussion section.

The main purpose behind reading introductions of research articles is to determine what researchers have done and found in your area of research interest. As you will see in subsequent chapters, you will need to compile a literature review of your research area. If your assignment is to write a term paper about a research area, you need to know what research exists in that area so that you can write about it. If your assignment is to propose an original experiment to conduct later, it is absolutely vital that you know what other researchers have done in the past so that you can generate an experimental idea from that research. As you read research articles that you have found and printed, it is a good idea to make extensive notes on them so that you can quickly see and remember important points when you return to the articles later. It is also a good idea to sort your copies of articles into stacks or folders that deal with similar topics or have similar findings or ask similar questions—or any groupings that make sense to you. That way, it will again be simpler to organize your thoughts (and thus your writing) when you have finished reading all the articles. Do not be surprised if you print and read articles that, at the time, seem relevant to your area of interest but that later simply do not fit into the direction you want to go. Rather than trying to force them into your introduction, just discard them and move on.

A secondary purpose behind reading introductions to research articles is to discover how they are written. I have mentioned the notion of scientific writing several times — reading these articles will be your introduction to scientific writing. You should note that the primary emphasis in an introduction is the prior research itself. Authors should focus on important details, research findings, and conclusions. You will not find conversational writing in introductions—details such as authors' first names, titles of articles, and location of the research are not details of interest to researchers reading an introduction. I often see student writing in introductions that resembles the following:

"Researchers Ann Jones and Tom Smith from the University of Florida conducted a study 'Encoding in Long-Term Memory' in 2015 in which they studied the way that people encode information in long-term memory." There is much superfluous information in that sentence; APA-Style writing should instead resemble this example: "Jones and Smith (2015) studied the role of encoding in long-term memory." Note how much shorter and simpler the second example is; the reference for Jones and Smith would contain all the other information, so it does not need to appear in the introduction. When it comes time for you to write your introduction (or term paper), you should look back at the research articles you found and mimic their writing style.

Method

The **Method section** (APA, 2020, pp. 4, 78–80) contains the important details of how the researchers conducted their experiment. Much like a blueprint of the experiment, it should provide enough details that another experimenter could replicate (copy exactly) the experiment if desired. It is rare that someone would simply replicate a previous study, but with replicating and extending a previous study, most researchers build on and/or add to the earlier study. As a novice researcher about to propose and conduct your first experiment, the Method sections of existing papers can give you invaluable ideas about how to conduct your study. If you are simply writing a term paper, these sections can still provide valuable information — some findings seem to depend on the specific methodology used to study the topic area.

Method sections are typically divided into three subsections, each of which provides different information for the reader (see the second and third pages of Appendix A for Peluso's methodology details). Depending on what you are looking for in an article, you will likely pay differing amounts of attention to the different subsections. See the IN PRACTICE: Method Section Details box on the next page for hints about reading Method sections.

IN PRACTICE

Method Section Details

Reading a Method section in great detail is usually not necessary the first time you read an article to determine whether it will be helpful in your search. However, a second read at a later date will tell you whether there are any critical methodological details you should include about this article (in your introduction) or whether the methodology is something that you may wish to include in your research proposal.

Participants/Subjects

The **Participants/Subjects subsection** is the first subsection within the Method section. If you read older journal articles dealing with humans, you will see this subsection labeled "Subjects"; APA Style changed to "Participants" in a previous edition of the *APA Manual* (APA, 1994). In the current version of the *APA Manual* (APA, 2020, p. 141), using either term is permissible—to me, "participants" seems a little more respectful than "subjects." If you plan to use animals in your research, "subjects" is the preferred term. Thus, although you may read different labels for this subsection, its purpose remains the same.

This section contains information about the "WHO" aspect—the research subjects who participated in the experiment. You should find out the number of subjects who participated, important characteristics about them, and what (if anything) they received in return for their participation. If you are reading about research with humans, most of the research studies will likely have used students from introductory psychology courses as their subjects. Unless a research study deals with a unique population, this information will likely be of more interest when you are planning your actual study. Peluso (2000) did have intro psych students serve as participants in his study (see the second page of Appendix A).

Apparatus/Materials/Testing Instruments/ Measures

The **Apparatus/Materials/Testing Instruments/Measures subsection** is the second subsection of the Method section. It deals with the "WHAT" aspect — what the experimenter used to conduct the study. As you might guess from the different possible labels, researchers use different types of "stuff" depending on their study. Some research projects involve equipment (apparatus), some involve stimuli presented to subjects (materials), some involve testing participants with psychological inventories (testing instruments), and some involve having participants respond on various tests that experimenters have devised (measures). By paying attention to the label of this subsection, you will get an idea of how researchers manipulated and measured their variables. Simply skimming this section until you actually begin planning your study should be adequate. Note that Peluso (2000) chose "Materials" because he used a variety of "stuff," including jacks and a ball, a mirror-tracing apparatus and star (on paper), and a stopwatch (see the second page of Appendix A). He could have labeled this section "Materials and Apparatus" due to the mix of "stuff," but he chose the simpler label.

Procedure

The **Procedure subsection** is typically the third subsection of the Method section and deals with the "HOW" aspect — it provides details about how the experimenter conducted the experiment. Experimenters will provide a step-by-step look at how they carried out the experiment, from beginning to end. Because of this level of detail, this subsection will often be the longest within the Method section. Given that you probably have never conducted an experiment, details from this subsection could be quite helpful as you plan your procedures. Peluso's (2000) Procedure subsection (see the second and third pages of Appendix A) also contained experimental design information (he used a within-subjects design). Occasionally, you may see a separate Design subsection that describes the experimental design of the research. Note that Peluso's description of his procedures is detailed enough that you could replicate his experiment.

Results

The **Results section** (APA, 2020, pp. 4, 80–81) is typically the third major section of an APA-Style research report (see the third page of Appendix A for Peluso's results). The purpose of this section is relatively straightforward—to present information about the statistical findings of the study. Peluso's (2000) Results section contains three paragraphs because he conducted separate statistical tests to analyze the results of each dependent variable (jacks and mirror-tracing performance), plus he analyzed pre-test time scores. This section is often the most difficult section for students to read because it includes **statistics**—a branch of mathematics that involves analysis of data—and other numerical information. If you have not taken a statistics course, you will probably find this section fairly difficult to decipher. Even if you have taken a statistics course, this section may contain advanced information you did not learn in your course. See the IN PRACTICE: Reading Results Sections box for hints about understanding Results sections.

IN PRACTICE

Reading Results Sections

Fortunately, it is rare that you need to read this section in a word-for-word manner. Instead, you simply need to extract the gist or overall meaning of this section. What did the experimenters find in their study? Were the results significant? Did the independent variable cause a difference in the dependent variable?

Statistical Reasoning

Let me provide a quick refresher about what statistical reasoning entails. Statistical conclusions are based on probability; that is, statistics allow us to measure the probability that our results could have occurred simply by chance. On one hand, if an independent variable (IV—a variable that experimenters manipulate) has *no* effect on the dependent variable (DV—a variable that experimenters measure), two groups in an experiment (where one received the IV and one did not) *should* perform equivalently on the DV. If the two groups do show any difference on their DV scores, that difference should be small and due to chance fluctuation, because the IV (having no effect) could not have caused the difference. In this case, the probability of the results being due to chance should be high. On the other hand, if the IV *did* have an effect on DV scores, the two groups' scores should differ considerably, and the probability of chance causing that difference should be low. When the probability of chance causing the results is less than .05 (5%, or 5 times in 100), researchers are willing to conclude that the difference between groups is **statistically significant** (has a low probability of chance) and is due to the IV.

Most authors will include some kind of information that helps you take a shortcut through the Results section. You may find descriptive statistics such as mean scores for the various groups in the study—this information helps you interpret and understand any significant differences reported. For example, if Group A has a mean score of 23.18 on the DV and Group B has a mean score of 28.49, and if the difference between those means is statistically significant ($p < .05$), you will know that Group B scored significantly higher than Group A and that the researchers attributed that difference to the IV (*not* to chance). Of course, the meaning of that result is based on the DV scores: If a high score indicates good performance, then Group B performed better than Group A. Conversely, if a high score indicates poor performance, then Group A performed better than Group B.

Peluso's (2000) IV was mental imagery (three levels: relevant, irrelevant, reading). He used two DVs: jacks performance and mirror-tracing performance. He found that relevant mental imagery improved performance on both DVs relative to the other two IV conditions because $p < .05$ in both statistical tests.

Statistical Analysis

One reason that Results sections are often difficult to interpret is that researchers may use complex designs and/or statistical procedures — ones with which you might not be familiar. For example, many experimenters use factorial designs, which means that they include two or more IVs and have the possibility of interactions between the IVs (Peluso's design was a factorial design because he used two IVs: mental imagery conditions and trials [to see if performance improved over time]; see the third page of Appendix A). Also, many researchers today use complex regression analyses, a statistical procedure with which you may not be familiar. Again, such complexity reinforces the notion that simply extracting the gist or overall picture of the results is what's important. Complex statistics from such analyses and designs are often accompanied by tables and/or figures to help you interpret the statistical results. Authors often use tables and figures to present their statistical results in a brief and more understandable manner (APA, 2020, p. 195).

Tables

A chart in an article is known as a **table**; tables typically display numbers (such as group means and standard deviations) in rows and columns. (Tables can also contain text, but authors would not typically use such a display for results.) This format usually allows the reader to see relationships more readily than is possible when many numbers are displayed in text. For example, Godden and Baddeley (1975) investigated context-dependent memory, which refers to the phenomenon in which memory is better when a person both studies and remembers information in the same context than when an individual

TABLE 4.1	Mean (*SD*) Number of Words Recalled as a Function of Learning and Recall Environment (Godden & Baddeley, 1975)			
		Recall Environment		
		Land	Underwater	*Total*
Learning Environment	Land	13.5 (5.8)	8.6 (3.0)	22.1
	Underwater	8.4 (3.3)	11.4 (5.0)	19.8
	Total	21.9	20.0	

studies and remembers information in different contexts. Godden and Baddeley took this notion to an interesting extreme when they had subjects learn and remember information either on dry land or underwater using scuba equipment. Table 4.1 displays data from their research. What do their data tell you? An inspection of the means shows that the subjects recalled more words when the learning and remembering conditions were the same, regardless of whether the conditions were on dry land or in water.

Figures

A **figure** is a graphical display of statistical findings. Although figures can take variety of forms, Results sections would most likely contain charts or graphs. You have undoubtedly heard the old saying that a picture is worth a thousand words—figures in experimental reports are good examples of this saying in action. Peluso used two figures, one for each DV statistical analysis (see the third page of Appendix A).

Figure 4.1 on the next page shows Godden and Baddeley's (1975) data converted from a table to a line graph. Can you make sense of this figure? Figure 4.1 tells you that people who learned words on land recalled more words on land than underwater and that people who learned words underwater recalled more words underwater than on land. This example is a good reason for using a figure: It makes the results easier to understand. In this case, the figure demonstrates that it is not correct to say simply that people learn and remember words better on

Figure 4.1 Mean Number of Words Recalled as a Function of Learning and Recall Environment (Data from Godden & Baddeley, 1975)

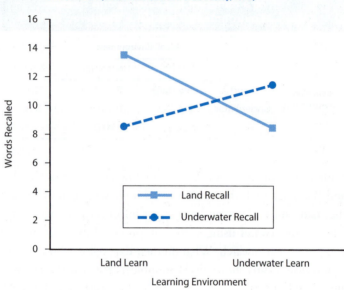

land or underwater; instead, memory was best when subjects learned and remembered in the same context.

Try not to be intimidated when you encounter Results sections as you read journal articles. Instead, focus on determining what the researchers found and how their results were relevant to their question(s). If you try to understand every word in every Results section, you will likely get bogged down and make less than optimal progress on reading your articles. Also, you can get help in interpreting the results by reading the article's Discussion section (see also the next chapter section).

Discussion

The authors' task in the **Discussion section** (the fourth major section of an APA-Style report; APA, 2020, pp. 4, 81) is to pull everything together. This section acts much like a "super-summary" for the experimental report. In this section, authors interpret and evaluate their results and the implications of those results, draw conclusions, point to limitations of their study, and address the importance of those findings. A previous edition of the *APA Manual* (APA, 1994, p. 19) recommended addressing several questions in the Discussion section:

- What contributions does my study make?
- Did my research help answer the original question? If so, how?
- What can I conclude from my study? Does it have any theoretical meaning?
- What knowledge have I added to the psychological literature?
- Do my results shed light on the question I raised?
- What are the outcomes and theoretical applications of my research?

In most cases, authors first summarize the important findings from their study. This account of the results is likely to be simplified compared to the actual Results section. Thus, if you had difficulty reading and understanding the results, you may be able to read the early part of the discussion for clarification.

The remainder of the Discussion section should address the points listed previously. It is difficult to predict the content that you will find in the Discussion section because it has the least specific guidelines in the *APA Manual* (APA, 2020). The introduction, Method, and Results sections have fairly specific roles and well-established formats, which is simply not the case with Discussion sections. You will likely find the greatest variability in writing style and content in Discussion sections in the various articles you read.

Other than a summary of the results, what should you look for in a Discussion section? The main takeaway you should find is the context of the current experiment for the broader area of research. What new findings did this experiment add to the literature? What do you know now about the research area that you did not know beforehand? By determining the new information that the experiment has added, you will have a better idea of questions that still remain unanswered (or have been raised) for your research area. Keeping track of what you know should help you develop a new research question.

Authors might also include another point in their Discussion sections that could help you a great deal. The *APA Manual* (APA, 2020, p. 81) notes that authors might address the implications for future research based on the results of the current research. If you are reading a recent journal article and find this type of information in the Discussion section, it could be quite helpful in your formulation of a new research question that you would like to address (see Chapter 7 on writing research proposals). Peluso's discussion (see the third and fourth pages of Appendix A) covers five paragraphs: one to summarize his findings and compare them to previous research, one to give potential explanations for the findings, one to note limitations of the research, one to mention possible future research, and one to note potential real-life application of the results.

References

In their reference list, authors provide a list of all journal articles (and other sources) that they cited in their article. Every citation in the article should have a corresponding reference (full bibliographic information for an article), and every reference should have a corresponding citation. Thus, because you saw my citation of Godden and Baddeley (1975) earlier in the chapter, you will find a corresponding reference to their article in the reference list both at the end of this chapter and at the end of this book. In a journal article, you will find the reference list at the end of the article. Note that reference lists in older articles will show different formats and elements than you will see in this book because the current edition of the *Publication Manual* (APA, 2020) revised some details about references from previous editions.

Each reference for a journal article includes the author's or authors' name(s), the date of the article, the title of the article, the journal title in which the article appeared, the volume and issue numbers of the journal, the page numbers of the article, and a **digital object identifier (DOI** or **doi)** listing—a unique alphanumeric string used to identify particular content such as a journal article; it is permanent and will not change, unlike many URLs. Articles without DOIs may show URLs, particularly for online articles. Note that Peluso's article (2000) does not display DOIs for journal articles (see the fourth page of Appendix A) because the *APA Manual* in effect at that time did not require them. (There are other aspects of reference formatting that have changed since Peluso's article was published in 2000, as you will find out in Chapters 5 and 6 and Appendixes B and C.) All of this bibliographic information tells you what you need to know to find any cited article or other source that you want to read. As you can imagine, the reference list of journal articles you read becomes vital in your search for articles for your annotated bibliography, term paper/literature review, research proposal, or experiment report. (We will cover how to search for journal articles in Chapter 5.) The IN PRACTICE: Reference Sections Are Important! box gives you an important pointer to avoid becoming frustrated in the future.

IN PRACTICE

Reference Sections Are Important!

In your first reading of a journal article, you may not be certain which references will be relevant to you, so be sure to keep the entire reference section with the journal articles you print or save. I can still remember how stupid I was early in my career as an undergraduate psychology major: To save a few nickels at the copy machine, I didn't copy the reference sections. Later, when I read an article and decided that I wanted to track down some of the citations, I had to find the original article again before I could look for the studies cited in that article that I wanted to find. From this experience, I learned quite well about the problem of false economy.

Footnotes, Appendices, and Supplemental Materials

The vast majority of journal articles you read will not contain any extra material other than tables and figures. Occasionally, however, authors have other material to include that has no spot other than footnotes or an appendix.

Footnotes

It is rare that you will find a **footnote**, an explanatory note at the bottom of a page, in a journal article. The *APA Manual* (APA, 2020, p. 40) mentions only two types of footnotes: content footnotes and copyright attributions. APA Style tends not to use footnotes unless absolutely necessary; there is a strong preference for including important information in the text instead. Thus, content footnotes are rare in APA Style — the *APA Manual* (2020, p. 40) says that they are for supplementing or amplifying information, not for unimportant information. After years of reading APA-Style writing, I often find myself getting bogged down when I read history texts, which frequently include needed footnotes for almost every sentence.

If an author has obtained permission to reproduce or adapt information from a copyrighted source, then a copyright attribution footnote *is* appropriate. It is somewhat unlikely that copyright permission would be needed in a journal article — it would probably be more likely in a book. However, if a researcher used a copyrighted video or written passage as stimulus items or items from a scale for measurement, you might see this type of footnote in an article.

Appendices and Supplemental Materials

Authors may include material that supplements the content of an article in an **appendix** if it is text-based; **supplemental materials** would be made available online (APA, 2020, pp. 41–43). Thus, an appendix would actually appear in print with the article, whereas you would have to access supplemental material online. An appendix might contain stimulus materials, participant instructions, measurement scales, a description of complex equipment used in the experiment, a demographic description of subpopulations in a study, or other detailed items. The most common use of an appendix today is for providing a list of articles compiled (but not cited) in a meta-analysis. Authors would use supplemental material for information that would be more useful if downloaded or that would be difficult to present in the format of a journal article. Examples of such material might include computer code, audio or video clips, data sets, color figures, or oversized tables. An appendix or supplemental material might be invaluable to you if you find one that contains material that you would like to use in your research project. Peluso (2000) did not use footnotes or appendices in his article (see Appendix A).

APA-Style Considerations

Because this chapter is about reading journal articles rather than writing papers, there are no concrete APA-Style issues to cover. Instead, we will cover those points in the subsequent chapters. However, the lack of specific pointers does *not* mean that you shouldn't learn some APA pointers from reading journal articles. Your main focus when reading journal articles, of course, is extracting the important information that you need from them — the information that you need for your specific writing assignment. What you *should* also attend to is how APA-Style writing "looks" and comes across in journal articles. When it comes time for you to write your assignment, you should mimic the style of writing that you saw in the articles you read. Writing in scientific style (rather than in humanities style) may be new to you, but you will have the role models of your journal articles to follow and emulate. If you read the Peluso (2000) article (Appendix A) with sharp eyes, you probably noticed several instances of passive voice. Remember from Chapter 3 that active voice is more preferred in APA Style (APA, 2020, p. 118).

Concluding Thoughts

This chapter has provided an introduction to reading experimental research articles. However, it is important to note that reading about how to read research articles is not as beneficial as actually reading research articles. Reading research articles is a skill you need to master to be a successful psychology major. To get better at this skill, you must practice, practice, practice. So, quit procrastinating—get out there and read some journal articles! To ensure that you are clear about what information you will find and where you will find it in a journal article, complete the exercise in the A CLOSER LOOK ... at Sections of Journal Articles box.

Critical Thinking Writing Assignments

Write one- to two-paragraph answers to the following questions aimed at a student who has an assignment to write a term paper or develop an experimental idea but who has no idea where to begin.

Assignment 1
Why is it likely that you will read many more article titles and abstracts than full articles as you plan your paper or experiment? How can you use information gleaned from these sources to decide whether to read a full article?

Assignment 2
What valuable information will you find in the introduction of a journal article? How can you use this information to plan your paper or experiment?

Assignment 3
Discussion sections can provide valuable information in planning a paper or experiment. What are two types of such information? Describe each type and how you could use it.

A CLOSER LOOK
at Sections of Journal Articles

To make certain that you understand how to read a journal article, match the correct section(s) of a journal article to the information you are seeking.

Information you are looking for	Section(s) where you would look
• Stimuli shown to subjects	_____
• Ideas for future research	_____
• Statistical findings	_____
• Information about subjects in the experiment	_____
• Historical information about the research topic	_____
• Bibliographic information about a study summarized	_____
• The study on which the current experiment was based	_____
• A brief summary of the study	_____
• Summary of how the experiment was conducted	_____
• Other studies relevant to the current experiment	_____

Possible Answers

Abstract	Method (Procedure)
Introduction	Results
Method (Participants)	Discussion
Method (Materials)	References

ANSWERS: Method (Materials), Discussion, Results, Method (Participants), Introduction, References, Introduction, Abstract, Method (Procedure), Introduction & References

References

American Psychological Association. (1994). *Publication manual of the American Psychological Association* (4th ed.).

American Psychological Association. (2020). *Publication manual of the American Psychological Association* (7th ed.). https://doi.org/10.1037/0000165-000.

Godden, D. R., & Baddeley, A. D. (1975). Context-dependent memory in two natural environments: On land and underwater. *British Journal of Psychology, 66*(3), 325–331. https://doi.org/10.1111/j.2044-8295.1975.tb01468.x

Khersonskaya, M. Y., & Smith, R. A. (1998). Cross-cultural differences in perception of physical attractiveness. *Psi Chi Journal of Undergraduate Research, 3*(1), 39–42. https://doi.org/10.24839/1089-4136.jn3.1.39

Peluso, E. A. (2000). Skilled motor performance as a function of type of mental imagery. *Journal of Psychological Inquiry, 5,* 11–14.

Posey, E., & Smith, R. A. (2003). The self-serving bias in children. *Psi Chi Journal of Undergraduate Research, 8*(4), 153–156. https://doi.org/10.24839/1089-4136.jn8.4.153

Sego, A. S., & Stuart, A. E. (2016). Learning to read empirical articles in General Psychology. *Teaching of Psychology, 43*(1), 38–42. https://doi.org/10.1177/0098628315620875

Writing an Annotated Bibliography

Do You Know?

How do you compile an annotated bibliography?

Why might you compile an annotated bibliography?

How do you find relevant research articles by searching PsycINFO?

How do you efficiently narrow a broad PsycINFO search?

How do you write an annotation for a journal article?

How do you format a reference for a journal article?

"Above all, bibliographic research requires the infinite capacity for taking pains."

—Harner, 2000, p. 5

If you are typical of many college students, the term **annotated bibliography** may be new and confusing to you. If you find that you need to write an annotated bibliography for a class assignment, you will compile a list of sources and information about each source. There are only a couple of mentions of an annotated bibliography in the *Publication Manual of the American Psychological Association* (American Psychological Association [APA], 2020, pp. 9, 307–308). The *APA Manual* (2020, p. 307) distinguishes a reference list from a bibliography, pointing out that a bibliography may be used in fields other than psychology. The distinction drawn by the *APA Manual* between the reference list and a bibliography is an important one that you, as a psychology student, should master. In my career, I have read so many student papers that refer to the reference list as a bibliography that I feel as if I want to pull out my hair! APA Style uses reference lists, not bibliographies. It may be this rarity of bibliographies in psychology that makes it difficult to find information about compiling an annotated bibliography. Also, the *APA Manual* (2020, pp. 9, 307) refers to annotated bibliographies as assignments for students, so there is not necessarily a standard or required format.

Interestingly, the *MLA Handbook* (Modern Language Association [MLA], 2016) also does not mention annotated bibliographies. The term "bibliography" does appear in the *MLA Handbook*'s index (p. 302), but only in a list of divisions of a source that you might cite in a paper. MLA did publish a brief book (Harner, 2000; 48 pages—essentially a pamphlet) about annotated bibliographies. However, Harner's approach was geared toward academic professionals who might publish an annotated bibliography dealing with one author's works in an effort to update other professionals; this approach is much less relevant to you as a student for an assignment you might have to complete.

The *Chicago Style Manual* (Turabian, 2013) briefly addresses annotated bibliographies in its general coverage of bibliographies, but not as a solitary work: "Some writers annotate each bibliography entry with a brief description of the work's contents or relevance to their research" (p. 151). Turabian even mentions that a writer might annotate only *some* of the entries in the bibliography, so it is clear that this version of an annotated bibliography is simply an addition to a full paper and would not be relevant to an annotated bibliography that you might tackle as a class project.

As the previous discussion makes clear, the major style manuals will be of little help to you in working on an annotated bibliography. Ideally, this lack of information means that your instructor will provide you with adequate details and requirements so that you can complete the assignment, as the *APA Manual* (2020, p. 307) indicates. This chapter provides some general principles for annotated bibliographies that you can use as starting points. Ideas from psychology instructors who actually use such an assignment in their classes are the basis for many of these general principles.

What Is an Annotated Bibliography?

The most important element of being able to successfully complete any assignment is understanding exactly what the assignment is. Given that the various style manuals offer little standardized information about annotated bibliographies, it is not surprising that there are different ideas about exactly what an annotated bibliography is and how you should compile such an assignment. However, any annotated bibliography should include at least two elements: an alphabetic list of sources (using a particular bibliographic style) and an **annotation** (detailed information) about each source. The typical sources used are journal articles, books, and websites, among others. It is critical that you verify with your instructor the types of resources that are appropriate for your bibliography. Because psychologists predominately write journal articles, your instructor *may* limit your resources to such articles. Given that you are working on an assignment for a psychology course, the appropriate bibliographic style will undoubtedly be APA Style (APA, 2020). Put simply, you can be virtually certain that you will need to provide an APA-Style reference for each source in the annotated bibliography.

Annotations could be summaries, evaluations, or descriptions of how you will use the source (or any combination of these three). Annotations can vary considerably in length depending on which elements your instructor requires. The annotations themselves are the element in which you will likely find the greatest variability in instructor preference, so it is critical to pay attention to any guidelines on this issue that your instructor provides. I will further address annotations shortly.

What Is the Purpose of an Annotated Bibliography Assignment?

The purpose for which you compile an annotated bibliography depends on your instructor. Two typical reasons that you might compile an annotated bibliography are as a stand-alone assignment or as a precursor to (or basis for) a future writing assignment. As you will see from the following descriptions, it is vitally important to know the purpose of your annotated bibliography assignment in order to produce the type of bibliography your instructor wants.

Stand-Alone Annotated Bibliography

In a stand-alone annotated bibliography assignment, you will simply provide a list of resources relevant to a particular subject matter. Thus, you would not be expected to generate a term paper/literature review or an experimental introduction from the bibliography. This type of project is described by the SPARK (Student Papers & Academic Research Kit) resource (York University, n.d.) and by Harner (2000) in his book. According to Harner, annotated bibliographies of this type are "intelligent, accurate, thorough, efficiently organized works that foster scholarship by guiding readers through accumulated studies as well as implicitly or explicitly isolating dominant scholarly concerns, identifying topics that have been overworked, and suggesting needed research" (p. 1). These goals are quite lofty and probably impossible to achieve in a class assignment because you likely would have a specific required number of sources to cite rather than attempting to survey all of the relevant literature.

Annotated Bibliography as a Precursor

In an annotated bibliography constructed as a precursor, you will use the information you compiled in the bibliography to form the basis for a written paper—typically either a term paper/literature review or the introduction section for an experimental proposal or report. Compiling an annotated bibliography helps you find the literature that exists in an area of research and that you can use to develop your thesis. This version of an annotated bibliography seems to be the more common purpose for this type of assignment, particularly in psychology. For an annotated bibliography as a precursor, it is likely that your instructor will specify that the articles you cite in your bibliography should form the basis for your research ideas to come, perhaps for a term paper/literature review (see Chapter 6) or a research proposal (see Chapter 7).

Compiling Your Annotated Bibliography

Compiling an annotated bibliography involves three steps: choosing a topic, finding sources, and writing annotations. These steps are quite similar to processes you will engage in for other types of writing assignments such as term papers/literature reviews (Chapter 6) and research proposals (Chapter 7).

Choosing a Topic for Your Bibliography

The issue of choosing your topic depends, to some extent, on the purpose of your annotated bibliography. If you are compiling a stand-alone bibliography, the options for topics are probably wide open. Most likely, the bibliography assignment would be included in a course such as Psychology of Learning, Abnormal Psychology, Social Psychology, or the like. In this case, an important consideration is to ensure that your topic is relevant to the course's subject matter. Thus, make certain that your topic appears somewhere in the text for the course—you could search the text index.

In addition, you should avoid choosing an overly broad topic. Imagine, for example, how many resources deal with "abnormal psychology" rather than "schizophrenia"—you would be overwhelmed searching on such a broad topic. Even after you believe you have chosen a narrow topic, it is probably wise to narrow it further. A search on "schizophrenia" will be much broader than a search on "schizophrenic symptoms" or "causes of schizophrenia." Although a narrow search will yield fewer hits (a **hit** is an article or book related to your topic), a smaller number of hits will be easier for you to evaluate.

If your annotated bibliography is to serve as a precursor to a later writing project, the process of choosing your topic will follow a somewhat different path. In this case, you must think about not only the bibliography topic, but also the final product that you will create. If you are using your annotated bibliography as the basis for a term paper/literature review, it is essential to understand your articles well enough that you can weave them together into a coherent paper (consult Chapter 6 on writing term papers/literature reviews for helpful pointers). If your annotated bibliography will form the basis for a research proposal, you must be able not only to weave the articles into a coherent introduction, but also to derive a researchable idea from the articles (consult Chapter 7 on writing research proposals for helpful pointers).

Finding Resources for Your Bibliography

Once you have chosen your topic, it is time to locate the resources to cite in your bibliography. For this task, you will use **PsycINFO**, an online database that catalogs psychology (and related disciplines) articles from the 1800s to now, with millions of records archived (www.apa.org). This resource is an incredibly valuable one for *all* the writing you will do in psychology, so let's take a look at how to use it.

Searching PsycINFO

Your college library probably subscribes to PsycINFO, so you will likely access the database through the library's home page. I urge you to access PsycINFO on your computer as you read about using PsycINFO in this chapter. Doing so will give you practice using PsycINFO and allow you to see the pages reproduced here more clearly. Figure 5.1 shows the screen that appears when you access PsycINFO. If you see only one text box with a blinking cursor, click on "Advanced Search" under the box, and then you will see the three text boxes shown in Figure 5.1 displayed. You can type any word(s) into the text box and then click "Search" to find all the stored records that contain the word(s).

Be aware that this approach to bibliographic searching (a **free-text search**) is an inefficient strategy: Use it only if the other approaches covered subsequently do not work. As an example, when I typed the word "learning" and searched for

Figure 5.1 Sample screenshot from PsycINFO.

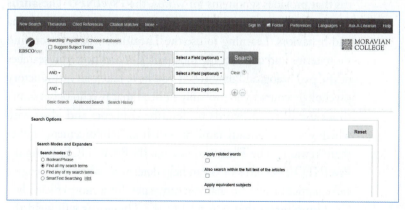

that term, I got more than 460,000 hits! (Please note that the number of hits I have cited in this text will change over time, as new articles are continually added to the database.) This free-text search simply found "learning" *anywhere* in each bibliographic and summary **record**—if an author's last name were Learning, PsycINFO would retrieve that record. Such a record would be of no help in writing a paper about the topic of learning, so I would need to use more efficient search strategies.

To the right of the search box on PsycINFO, notice the box labeled "Select a Field (optional) ▾." When you run a free-text search, you ignore this box. However, this box offers a set of powerful pull-down options. If you click in this box, you will see more than 40 choices from which you can make a selection. Typing "learning" in the search box and then selecting "TI" from the pull-down menu, for example, will search only for records that contain "learning" in their title, resulting in more than 112,000 hits—still quite a few, but many fewer than the free-text search found (more than 460,000). Thus, a bibliographic search of the TI field, known as a **title search**, is better than a free-text search, but still not very efficient.

In Figure 5.1 on the previous page, above the text boxes (in the banner), you will see the word "Thesaurus." Similar to any thesaurus that provides synonyms for words, the **PsycINFO Thesaurus** provides alternative psychological terms for specific phenomena and behaviors. Learning to use the Thesaurus will help you find those terms and conduct the most efficient and powerful searches of the psychological literature. If you have taken an introductory psychology course, you probably noticed that psychologists sometimes use different words to describe concepts and ideas with which you were already familiar—such as "reinforcement" rather than "reward." The Thesaurus (see the IN PRACTICE: Using the PsycINFO Thesaurus box) can help determine what psychologists call a particular term so that you can search for it more efficiently.

Using terms that you find in the Thesaurus will yield the fewest, best-targeted hits in a search—an outcome that is quite

IN PRACTICE

Using the PsycINFO Thesaurus

When you open the Thesaurus, type the word "reward" in the search box, check the "Relevancy Ranked" button, then click the "Browse" button and you will get a long list of terms that are relevant to "reward." Scrolling down, you will find the term "Rewards," which is the closest match. When you click on that term, you will find information about it, including a definition: "Events or objects subjectively deemed to be pleasant to a recipient." This is probably what you had in mind when you thought of the word "reward," so examine the information further. You will notice that a different term listed as a broader term (essentially synonymous) is "Reinforcement." This result lets you know that psychologists are likely to use the term "reinforcement" in place of "reward."

helpful. Assume that you are interested in schedules of reinforcement as a tentative topic for a paper. A free-text search returns more than 13,000 hits, and a title search yields more than 1400. Now let's see how the Thesaurus can help. Open the Thesaurus in PsycINFO, type "reinforcement" in the search box, click the "term contains" button, and click "Browse." This search will find all the terms that contain the word "reinforcement" in PsycINFO; the second one listed is "Reinforcement Schedules." Clicking on that term gives you more information: This term was first used as a specific term in 1967, "Reinforcement" is a broader term, there are several narrower terms (all specific types of reinforcement schedules), and there are several "Used for" terms (essentially synonyms or types of schedules). Now you know that the specific term for your interest area used in PsycINFO is "Reinforcement Schedules."

Back at the search screen, type "Reinforcement Schedules" in the search box and choose "DE Subjects [exact]" from the pull-down Field menu before running your search. "DE Subjects [exact]" specifies a **descriptor term** (also known as a **subject**

term)—a term used to categorize the articles regarding the main subjects they address. Specifying "reinforcement schedules" as a DE Subjects [exact] term (a **descriptor search**) guarantees that any record found will definitely address that topic. Thus, a descriptor search is more precise than either a free-text or title search. In this case (see Figure 5.2), PsycINFO showed more than 6500 hits. This number is less than half of the free-text hits because the search focused on articles that actually address reinforcement schedules; it is considerably higher than the number of hits with a title search simply because authors do not always include all relevant subject terms in their titles. In other words,

Figure 5.2 How to refine results in PsycINFO.

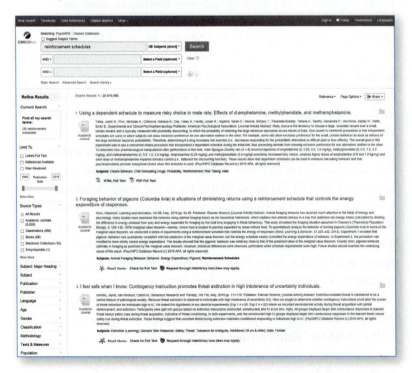

not all articles that concern reinforcement schedules have the words "reinforcement schedules" in their titles.

Clearly, no one wants to read over 6500 articles to compile an annotated bibliography! How can you use PsycINFO to lower the number of hits *and* be more precise in finding articles that interest you? The simple answer is that you should narrow your topic, and thus your search, even more. Take another look at Figure 5.2: PsycINFO allows you to refine your results by making choices about a multitude of options. Notice that PsycINFO displays your search in a box (labeled "Find all my search terms:") above the list of options ("DE reinforcement schedules") on the left side of the screen. Underneath, you could limit your search—for example, to results that have **linked full text** (meaning that a full-text version of the journal article is available by clicking on the link), which would leave only those hits that allow you to read the article in full text. You may miss some good articles by making this selection, however, so I will ignore it for now. (If your time to work on the paper is short and you will not be able to get articles from other libraries sent in time via interlibrary loan [refer to the A CLOSER LOOK box in Chapter 1], you may want to check this box.)

One limiting box you will likely want to check falls under "Source Types." I recommend checking "Academic Journals," which reduced the number of hits in this example to about 5500. The main type of hit you will ignore with this check is **dissertations**, which are long research papers graduate students write to obtain a doctoral degree. Dissertations are almost impossible for you to obtain from the library or via interlibrary loan, so there is no point in including them in the search. Unless you are bilingual or multilingual, another box you should always check is "English" under the "Language" option.

If you click on the "Subject: Major Heading" option, you find that several subjects are covered within Reinforcement Schedules. Given that you began with "operant conditioning" in mind, you could check this box, which reduces the number of hits to about 1000. Clicking on the heading of "Subject," you find that many of the hits pertain to animals (rats, pigeons, monkeys). To exclude animal research and focus solely on humans, you can scroll to the last linked option ("Population") and select "human," which resulted in slightly more than 200 articles. This result is *quite* an improvement over the initial 13,000-plus hits we got using a free-text search!

Once you have narrowed the results to a few hundred hits, quickly scrolling through those records will probably show a good bit of variability in focus, but they all should generally map onto your interest area—in this case, reinforcement schedules used with humans. At this point, tweaking your PsycINFO search further can help you immensely. Until now, we have entered a search topic in only one of the search boxes. If you can come up with a second topic or an area of application for your first topic, running a more narrowed search can focus the records you find much more sharply.

Suppose you have an interest in **industrial/organizational (I/O) psychology**, the branch of psychology that applies psychological findings and theory to business, and you wonder if there is a way to look at the effect of reinforcement schedules in that subject area. You could consult an I/O text or dredge up your memories from an I/O course you may have taken. Let's say that you are interested in how well people perform their jobs, so you want to determine how reinforcement schedules affect such performance. Going back to the Thesaurus, you type "job" in the search box, click "Term Contains," and browse. "Job Performance" shows up several entries down the list, so you select and click that term to explore it. PsycINFO shows that "Employee Efficiency" and "Employee Productivity" are narrower terms within "Job Performance," so you decide to enter them as well so that you will not miss any potential hits. In my search, I went back to the original narrowed search on Reinforcement Schedules and added "Job Performance or Employee Efficiency or Employee Productivity" in the second text box and used the pull-down menu to select "DE Subjects [exact]." See the IN PRACTICE: Boolean Operators box to discover why I linked those three terms with "or."

IN PRACTICE

Boolean Operators

When searching for two terms, be sure that the box that connects the two text boxes shows "AND" (other choices are "OR" and "NOT"; all three terms are known as **Boolean operators**). Using AND tells PsycINFO to find every article that contains both "Reinforcement Schedules" **AND** "Job Performance or Employee Efficiency or Employee Productivity" in the record, which pretty much guarantees that the article will be relevant to your interests. Using "OR" to link all three terms in the second text box would generate a search that links each term with "Reinforcement Schedules."

When I ran the search, I found 41 articles as hits. If you selected "OR," PsycINFO would find all the articles that contain *either* of the two subject terms, which would not help you narrow your search. Using OR resulted in more than 26,000 hits; apparently there are many PsycINFO records related to job performance!

At this point, you should double-check to make sure that all your limiting filters are still applied; when I typed in the terms about job performance and searched, the filters reset. By reapplying the filters for academic journals and human subjects, my number of hits dropped to 26. Eight of those 26 were available to me as full text (look for the symbol and words "PDF Full Text")—this number would vary based on your particular library's holdings. Of course, you could request the articles not available at your library through interlibrary loan.

PsycINFO Records

Now it is time to look at one of our specific hits. In the list of hits, you will notice that the title of each article is hyperlinked. If you click on a title, you will see the full **PsycINFO record** for that particular hit (see Figure 5.3 on the next page). Notice that the record gives you bibliographic information about the article, an abstract, and a list of "Subjects," as well as other information. Recall that *abstract* is an academic name for a summary of the

Figure 5.3 One record from PsycINFO.

article. Reading the abstracts from articles may help you determine which articles are related to your interest.

Yet another PsycINFO trick can narrow your search even further to more related articles. Under the abstract, you will see a field labeled "Subjects." The terms in this field are the ones from the Thesaurus that PsycINFO abstracters chose to represent the article's main topics. The view of Figure 5.3 on your computer screen will show Employee Productivity and Reinforcement Schedules in bold font—the bold terms are ones that I entered into the original search screen and labeled as DE Subjects. Also on your screen, notice that three DE Subjects terms appear that are *not* bold: Monetary Incentives, Salaries, and Working Conditions. Suppose you became interested specifically in monetary incentives (perhaps pay and/or bonuses) in your paper about reinforcement and performance. When you add "Monetary Incentives" as DE Subjects in the third search box, the new PsycINFO search shows only *nine* hits. A quick perusal of those nine titles shows that all appear to be closely related. Thus, you can not only use the Thesaurus to help you find search terms for PsycINFO, but PsycINFO searches themselves may also turn up new and helpful search terms that enable you to narrow your search and find closely related articles. For more information on the DE Subjects field, see the IN PRACTICE: DE Versus SU box.

IN PRACTICE

DE Versus SU

If you examined the options in the pull-down menu for "Select a Field (optional)," you probably noticed "SU Subjects" immediately before "DE Subjects [exact]." You could use either of these terms to add a specific subject search. However, APA indexers created the DE field, whereas EBSCOhost indexers created the SU field (EBSCOhost is the search platform that hosts PsycINFO and many other disciplinary indexes). For this reason, I prefer to use DE rather than SU: I believe that DE may result in higher quality hits given the closer link of its indexers to the discipline of psychology. However, using the SU field will also help you narrow your searches considerably.

At this point, it is clear that an annotated bibliography topic such as "the effects of reinforcement schedules on job performance" would be a viable choice—there are enough articles that you could compile a bibliography on a topic relevant to the course and of interest to you. Notice how narrow this topic is for a course in learning. Your instructor would likely be pleased with a narrow topic as opposed to a broader topic such as reinforcement schedules (something that might have seemed narrow when you began the selection process but actually turned out to be a broad topic).

Your next step would be to get your instructor's approval of this topic. Even if your instructor does not require you to submit a proposed topic for approval, it may be a good idea to check just to be certain that you are on the right track for your particular course.

A Final Word About Using PsycINFO

Your remaining challenge in using PsycINFO is finding approximately the right number of hits (likely specified by your instructor) for your annotated bibliography assignment. In the previous paragraphs, I provided directions for narrowing a search, which you would need to do if your initial search turns up too many hits. If, after the initial narrowing, there are still too many hits, you can simply narrow further. Try searching the PsycINFO Thesaurus to find narrower terms than you are already using. Another possibility for narrowing is to add a third search term—remember that you can use three search boxes to limit the results returned. Adding a third search term will often cut out many broader hits and give you a much more precise (narrow) set of articles to examine. In the example, I added a third search term related to pay to help further narrow my search.

But suppose that you have the opposite problem: Your narrowed search yields only a few (or zero) hits. What should you do in this case? As you might guess, for the opposite problem, you have to adopt the opposite strategy to solve the problem. Instead of narrowing your search, broaden it. There are a couple of good strategies for broadening a search. The simplest solution is to drop one of your search terms from the search boxes. If you have used three search terms, cut back to two. If you have used two search terms, cut back to one. Note, however, that using only one search term typically results in a search that is quite broad and nonspecific. A better strategy when a search with two search terms yields too few hits is to broaden one or both of the search terms. Using the PsycINFO Thesaurus, examine your search terms. The Thesaurus not only provides narrower terms, but also broader terms and related terms. Using a broader or related term may solve your problem of having too few hits.

Writing Your Annotations

After you have found the articles that you plan to include in your annotated bibliography, you need to write an annotation for each article. Given that there is no specific guide to writing annotations in the *APA Manual* (APA, 2020), the style of annotations required by instructors is likely to vary widely. For this reason, it is critical that you understand exactly what your instructor expects in terms of annotations. As a reminder, for each item, your annotations might include a summary, evaluation, and description of use (detailed in the following sections). The lengths of your annotations can vary depending on how many of these three components your instructor requires, how long your summaries should be, and so on.

Summary

The minimum information included in an article annotation is a summary of the article, but instructors often ask for more information. Your instructor might require you to include a variety of elements in your article summary—for example, the article's objective, hypotheses, independent and dependent variables, methods, results, and implications. You might even receive a list of questions to address about the articles. Be sure to take precautions to avoid plagiarism when writing your summaries because it is tempting to copy detailed information from the articles (review the Chapter 1 section "Avoid Plagiarizing"). One suggestion to avoid this risk is to read the article and then put it away while writing your summary. After having drafted the summary, you can review the article again to ensure you made no errors.

Evaluation

If your instructor asks you to evaluate the articles you have cited, you may find this task somewhat intimidating and wonder, "Who am I to critique a published article?" Ideally, your instructor will give you some idea of what to cover in this section. The evaluations might include some or all of the following items:

- your evaluation of the author's arguments and theory,
- what you see as the main importance of this work,
- deficiencies or bias you perceived in the work,
- comparisons of the article with others you cited, and
- a final summary statement (York University, n.d.).

Other possible topics dealing with evaluation could be the strengths, weaknesses, quality, and validity of the articles, with a particular focus on the articles' methodology.

Evaluating research articles may be somewhat simpler if you have taken a course in research methods or experimental psychology. Often, such courses address evaluating the strengths and weaknesses or limitations of published research articles. If you have not taken such a course, you might examine a relevant textbook used at your college or in your college's library (e.g., Davis & Smith, 2005, pp. 423–432; Dunn, 2013, pp. 298–299; Orcher, 2014, pp. 7–8, 25–28; Smith & Davis, 2013, pp. 25–28).

Description of Use

This information might be a requirement if your annotated bibliography serves as a precursor to a follow-up paper. Here, your instructor is interested in how you plan to use each article as background for your term paper/literature review or research project. This information is critical for the future project: It is simple to find research articles that are relevant to your idea, but it requires higher order thinking to see how an article provides actual background information for the project. Because this issue is so important, I will discuss it in future chapters dealing with term papers/literature reviews (Chapter 6) and research proposals (Chapter 7).

Generally, you should discuss what you found to be most informative or useful in the article, state how you plan to use it, and indicate how it will support your paper. Your instructor likely wants you to point out the relevance of the article, how you will use the article in the project, or how the article contributed to the development of your idea.

As noted earlier, the lack of APA guidelines for annotated bibliographies probably means that instructors will vary in the information that they want included or the questions they want answered in article annotations. The ideas I have provided here make it clear why you should consult the guidelines you receive from your instructor about the content of your annotations. If you do not get such guidelines, ask your instructor for guidance.

APA-Style Considerations

Given that an annotated bibliography is the first actual APA-Style paper we have covered, it is important that you become aware of several stylistic issues related to constructing a bibliography or reference list. As a hint for your future APA-Style writing products, these considerations will carry over to the writing products covered in the next three chapters.

References for Journal Articles

An annotated bibliography's closest resemblance to a typical APA-Style section of a paper is to a reference list, but with annotations added. Thus, you need to know how to format the bibliographic information from your articles into APA reference style. Because you will most likely build an annotated bibliography from journal articles, I will concentrate on that information in this chapter (reference formats for books and edited books appear in Chapter 6).

The general format for journal articles uses a specific order for the various bibliographic elements of the article: author(s), date, article title, journal title, volume number and issue number, page numbers, DOI (digital object identifier) or URL (uniform resource locator). Type the first line at the left margin, with subsequent lines indented (use a hanging indent [APA, 2020, p. 40] rather than pressing the tab key). The IN PRACTICE: Hanging Indents box offers guidance to help you format these indents for your references.

. . . .

IN PRACTICE

Hanging Indents

To set a hanging indent for the reference list, you can use the tab stops on the document ruler that you see above the document (make sure this ruler is visible by clicking "Ruler" in the View menu, if necessary). By dragging the bottom pointer to the right, you can set the size of the hanging indent—use the ½ inch mark so that the indent is clearly visible and to meet the APA guideline (APA, 2020, p. 40). The top pointer should be at the left margin, which will turn off the automatic indent function (for paragraphs in text) if you already had that option set.

You can also use a keyboard shortcut to make this task much simpler. First, make sure that both pointers on the ruler are set at the left margin. Then, press the CTRL and T (⌘ and T on Mac) keys simultaneously. You should see the bottom pointer move to the ½ inch mark. These settings are now the opposite of what you use when you are typing the body of your paper: The first line of the reference begins at the left margin, and each subsequent line is indented. The beauty and importance of using a hanging indent rather than a tab stop is that the hanging indent automatically reformats if you edit the reference. In contrast, with tab stops that you insert, you must delete the old ones and add new ones if you edit the reference, which is a big pain in the neck!

. . . .

Here is the proper formatting for a single author journal reference:

Leivo, A. K. (2001). A field study of the effects of gradually terminated public feedback on housekeeping performance. *Journal of Applied Social Psychology, 31*(6), 1184–1203. https://doi.org/10.1111/j.1559-1816.2001.tb02669.x

There are several important items to note. First, use as many initials for the author as there are names and initials listed in the article. If an author has a hyphenated first name, type both initials with a hyphen (e.g., R.-B.). Enclose the publication date (only the year) in parentheses. Capitalize only the first word of an article's title, any proper names, and the first word after a colon. In contrast, capitalize all words in journal titles of four or more letters (APA, 2020, p. 167). Italicize both the journal title and volume number (including the following commas). If the journal uses issue numbers (most do), include the issue number with the journal number in parentheses immediately after the volume number (no space), but do not italicize it or the parentheses and following comma—for example, *New Zealand Journal of Psychology, 44*(3), 4–17. Provide the inclusive page numbers for the journal article (do *not* type "p." or "pp.").

Finally, you must provide the digital object identifier (DOI) for the article, which provides a permanent link to the article to make it easy for readers to access your references. If your article does not show a DOI, you can search for it at https://www.crossref.org. If your search turns up no DOI, provide a URL link to the journal article (rather than the journal) at the end of the reference (e.g., https://www.xxxxxxx.xxxx). Do not end a DOI or URL with a period because it is not part of the address and would cause difficulty in retrieving the article.

Author Variations

The only other factor with variability left to cover for article references is the number of authors for an article. The rules for references are somewhat different than the rules for in-text citations, as you will see in Chapter 6.

- Two authors:
  Smith, R. A., & Davis, S. F. (date)....
- Three to 20 authors:
  Smith, R. A., Davis, S. F., & Buskist, W. F. (date)....

- 21 or more authors: List the first 19 authors' names, insert three ellipsis points, and then list the last author's name. Thus, if the authors of an article were Smith, Davis, Buskist, Beins, Hill, Keith, Jones, White, Black, Brown, Greene, Hays, Cook, Baker, Epstein, Cardone, Garcia, Martinez, Wong, Lee, Kim, Miller, Williams, and Johnson, your entry should look like the following example:

> Smith, R. A., Davis, S. F., Buskist, W. F., Beins, B. C., Hill, G. W., Keith, K., Jones, R., White, W., Black, A., Brown, B., Greene, J., Hays, C., Cook, P., Baker, M., Epstein, E., Cardone, C., Garcia, F., Martinez, G., Wong, K., . . . Johnson, D. E. (date). . . .

Arranging the Annotated Bibliography

When you compile a reference list for any APA-format paper, you arrange the references in alphabetical order by the first author's last name. Typically, this order would also be correct for your annotated bibliography (APA, 2020, p. 307) *unless* your instructor specifies otherwise. One possible exception to alphabetical order might be if your instructor wants the entries listed chronologically from newest to oldest, or vice versa.

As you alphabetize the articles by the authors' last names, *never* change the order of the authors' names within a particular article. This order represents the level of contribution each author has made to the article (APA, 2020, p. 25), so the first author has contributed the most to the article. In other words, do *not* arrange the names alphabetically within a reference, which is a mistake that students sometimes make.

You cannot rely solely on alphabetical order of last names in a few circumstances (APA, 2020, pp. 303–306). For example, you might have two articles whose first authors are both named Smith (different individuals). In this case, you should alphabetize by the authors' first initials (e.g., Smith, A. R. would precede

Smith, R. A.). Often, you may encounter two articles with the same first author. If the articles have only the one author, you should arrange the references chronologically by year, with the earlier year coming first (e.g., R. A. Smith published articles in both 2010 and 2011; list the 2010 article before the 2011 article). If you have multiple articles with the same first author and additional authors, arrange them alphabetically by going to the second author (e.g., Smith, R. A., & Beins, B. C. would precede Smith, R. A., & Buskist, W. F.). If the first two authors of two articles are identical, then proceed to the next author; if all authors are identical, then arrange them chronologically by date. Finally, if all the authors' names *and* the year of publication are identical, arrange the articles in alphabetical order by the first word of the title (excluding "A" or "The"). So that readers can distinguish the articles from each other, use lower-case letters with the dates. This rule would lead to the following entries in a reference list:

Smith, R. A. (2011a). The psychologist as teacher...

Smith, R. A. (2011b). Teaching statistics...

This arrangement would be correct because "psychologist" precedes "teaching" alphabetically (remember to ignore "The" in the first title).

Finally, it is critical that you list all your references without errors. If your instructor finds errors, your grade will suffer. Also, imagine the frustration you would experience if you read a published article, used its reference list to access listed articles, and found errors that made it difficult to track down the articles you wanted (an experience I have had many times). As Bruner (1942, p. 68) wrote many years ago,

> a sin one more degree heinous than an incomplete reference is an inaccurate reference; the former will be caught by the editor or the printer, whereas the latter will stand in print as an annoyance to future investigators and a monument to the writer's carelessness.

Certainly, you do not want to get a reputation for being careless, so be extremely careful as you enter references in your list.

Typing Instructions

Before you begin typing a manuscript, make sure that you have correct settings for APA Style in Word (see the Chapter 2 IN PRACTICE: Computer Formatting Instructions for APA Style box). Chapter 2 instructs that you should use a font acceptable in APA Style (APA, 2020, p. 44). Also, adjust your margins to 1 inch all around. Finally, set the spacing in the paper to double spacing (keep it throughout; do not single space references, a common student mistake). These settings may be different by default in Word, so be sure to check them first. Although an annotated bibliography may not follow strict APA Style (depending on your instructor's preferences), you can refer to the advice near the end of Chapter 2 about using a saved APA-Style file or using Microsoft's APA-Style template (if and when updated for APA, 2020). Another helpful pointer is that the *APA Manual* (APA, 2020, p. 308) contains a page from a sample annotated bibliography to which you can refer if some element of formatting your paper in APA Style is not clear. However, this page may not be compatible with your instructor's guidelines for an annotated bibliography. Your instructor's specific guidelines should clearly carry more weight than this sample page in the *APA Manual*.

Creating a Title Page

This chapter is the first that has actually addressed creating a written assignment. There is not a specific APA format for the text portion of annotated bibliographies (your instructor's guidelines are crucial for this formatting), but there *is* a specific APA Style for title pages.

Professional Title Page

For the first time ever, the *APA Manual* (2020, pp. 30–38) features different title pages for professional papers (traditional; see

Figure 5.4) and student papers (new with this edition; see Figure 5.5 in a few pages). As with annotated bibliographies, however, the *Manual* notes that instructors may require students to use the professional format (something I view as likely in the near future given that the student title page is new). Also, you would use the professional title page if you ever submit a paper for publication (see Chapter 9). The next section outlines the professional title page components, with the following section

Figure 5.4 Sample APA-Style professional title page.

THIS IS MY RUNNING HEAD   1

Title Goes Here

Author S. Student

Department of Psychology, University of Nowhere

Author Note

This research was supportedby a grant from the Student Foundation at

University of Nowhere. Thanks to my faculty advisor for her support.

Address correspondence concerning this article to Author S. Student,

Department of Psychology, University of Nowhere, Nowheresville, AK 00000.

Email: astudent@unowh.edu

showing how to format a student title page. The *APA Manual* (APA, 2020, p. 30) points out that a professional title page has five components: running head, title, author listing, affiliation, and author note.

Running Head. The running head (APA, 2020, p. 37) is a short title that appears at the top of your typed manuscript (and sometimes journal article) pages to help readers identify the manuscript or article. It should be no more than 50 characters, including letters, spaces, and punctuation. Your running head should appear in all caps, left justified, at the top of each page. To set up your running head (if required), follow the instructions in the Chapter 2 section "Running Head." Be sure to follow those instructions while using the Header command in Word rather than typing the header at the top of each page: If you type the header at the top of each page, editing the paper will cause the running head to move up or down the page and cost you time to redo it on each page. Editing your paper will not cause the header to move if you have used the Header command.

Title. After formatting your running head, click below the top margin to enter text on Page 1. Set Word to center the text. Go down three or four lines on Page 1 and type the title for your bibliography (making sure it is centered). As described in Chapter 4, APA Style does not have a word limit for titles but encourages authors to keep them succinct (the previous edition gave a 12-word limit for titles). Type your title in bold and mixed case, capitalizing all words of four letters or more (APA, 2020, p. 167), even though Word may not "like" it when you capitalize some four-letter words.

Author Listing. Type your name, also centered, as the author below your title, leaving a blank double-spaced line after the title before your name. You would typically use your given name(s) and middle initial(s) rather than any nicknames—after all, you are beginning to establish a professional identity when you write papers for your discipline.

If you have a coauthor (or coauthors), arrange the names in order of relative contribution, with the principal contributor listed first (APA, 2020, p. 25). If all authors contributed equally, you could list authors alphabetically.

Affiliation. Immediately below your name, type your institutional affiliation (centered; remember that all lines are double spaced). This listing would be your school's name—where you were when you did the work. If you changed colleges and then published a paper, you would list your new affiliation in an author note.

Author Note. An author note is used primarily for manuscripts submitted for publication and is not listed for a student title page (APA, 2020, pp. 30, 32), so your instructor may not require you to include this element. If you do use an author note, you would type it a few lines below your affiliation, with "Author Note" centered and bolded; each paragraph is left justified with an indented first line.

According to the *APA Manual* (APA, 2020, pp. 35–38), an author note may contain up to four paragraphs. The first paragraph is simply a listing of all authors with their ORCID (Open Researcher and Contributor IDentifier; see https://orcid.org/) IDs. This paragraph does not appear if no authors have an ORCID ID. The second paragraph (if necessary) lists any changes in institutional affiliation since the study or paper—if you conducted a study at one school and submitted it for publication while you were at a second school. The third paragraph contains disclosures and acknowledgments. The primary types of disclosure are studies related to the one being reported (e.g., the data came from a dissertation) or any conflicts of interest, both of which are unlikely for student papers. Acknowledgments are primarily for financial support, although you could include a personal acknowledgment here. The last paragraph provides contact information for the author who would handle any correspondence about the article—both mailing and email addresses. The information in the author note appears in journal articles, so you will have contact information for any article you read, if you wanted to contact the author.

Student Title Page

A student title page (see Figure 5.5), in contrast to a professional title page, has six components: title, author listing, affiliation, course number and name, instructor name, and assignment due date. Again, remember that your instructor may require a professional title page. These instructions summarize the *APA Manual*'s (2020, pp. 30–35) version of a student title page. There is no running head required—only a page number at the right margin. The title, author listing, and affiliation are the same as for a professional title page. Immediately under your affiliation, type (centered) the course number and name for which you are submitting the paper (e.g., PSYC 120: Introduction to Psychology). On the next line, type your instructor's name with title (e.g., Dr., PhD, Professor, RN). On the last line, type the due date for the assignment. No Author Note is required on the student title page.

Page 2

As previously noted (see the Chapter 2 A CLOSER LOOK box), if you use a running head, you should see the all-caps running head at the top left of Page 2 and the number 2 at the right margin. If you do not use a running head, you will only see "2" at the right margin. If your paper does not require an abstract, you will retype your title (centered) on the first line of Page 2 (Page 3 if you have an abstract, which is on Page 2;

Figure 5.5 Sample APA-Style student title page.

1

Title Goes Here

Author S. Student

Department of Psychology, University of Somewhere

PSYC 000: Psychology of Fiction

Dr. Teacher A. Faculty

October 31, 2025

see Chapter 4 section labeled "Abstract"). Be certain that the titles on Pages 1 and 2 are an exact match. On the next line, you would begin your text—probably your first reference (using a hanging indent for second and subsequent lines) and an annotation on a new line under the reference, although the exact appearance will depend on how your instructor wants you to format your bibliography.

Concluding Thoughts

This chapter covers an assignment that is comparatively rare compared to a term paper/literature review, a research proposal, or an experimental report. Although you may never have an assignment to write an annotated bibliography, knowing how to compile one—even on an informal basis—can be quite helpful as you tackle one of the more common writing assignments we will cover subsequently in this text. Many of the topics covered in this chapter (e.g., PsycINFO searching, APA formatting of references) will be awkward and time consuming the first time you tackle them. Although practice may not make perfect (as the old saying suggests), practice *will* help you get better at these tasks.

Critical Thinking Writing Assignments

Write answers of one or two paragraphs to the following questions or requests aimed at a student who has the assignment to compile an annotated bibliography but who has no idea where to begin.

Assignment 1
What is an annotated bibliography? Why would compiling an annotated bibliography be a helpful exercise before writing a term paper/literature review or proposal for an experiment?

Assignment 2
Why is it critical to use a resource such as PsycINFO in compiling an annotated bibliography?

Assignment 3

Why is it important to be slightly "obsessive–compulsive" when compiling your references in an annotated bibliography (or *any* APA writing assignment)?

Assignment 4

Summarize the steps involved in conducting a PsycINFO search for a student. With an actual search as an example, show how to begin with a broad topic and successively narrow it to 20 or fewer hits.

References

American Psychological Association. (2020). *Publication manual of the American Psychological Association* (7th ed.). https://doi.org/10.1037/0000165-000

Bruner, K. F. (1942). Of psychological writing: Being some valedictory remarks on style. *Journal of Abnormal and Social Psychology, 37*(1), 52–70. https://doi.org/10.1037/h0062165

Davis, S. F., & Smith, R. A. (2005). *An introduction to statistics and research methods: Becoming a psychological detective.* Pearson Prentice Hall.

Dunn, D. S. (2013). *Research methods for social psychology* (2nd ed.). Wiley.

Harner, J. L. (2000). *On compiling an annotated bibliography* (2nd ed.). Modern Language Association of America.

Modern Language Association. (2016). *MLA handbook* (8th ed.).

Orcher, L. T. (2014). *Conducting research: Social and behavioral science methods* (2nd ed.). Pyrczak. https://doi.org/10.4324/9781315266626

Smith, R. A., & Davis, S. F. (2013). *The psychologist as detective: An introduction to conducting research in psychology* (6th ed.). Pearson.

Turabian, K. L. (with Booth, W. C., Colomb, G. G., Williams, J. M., & University of Chicago Press Editorial Staff). (2013). *A manual for writers of research papers, theses, and dissertations: Chicago style for students and researchers* (8th ed.). University of Chicago Press.

York University. (n.d.). SPARK: Student papers & academic research kit. Retrieved from https://spark.library.yorku.ca/

6

Writing a Term Paper/ Literature Review

Do You Know?

How can you reduce the stress of writing a term paper/literature review?

How can you develop a good idea for a term paper/literature review?

What should you do to find research articles relevant to your term paper/ literature review topic?

How can you find research articles that are closely related to each other?

Why is it important to link articles in a term paper/literature review?

"The first step toward clarity is to write simply and directly. . . . The second step toward clarity is to organize the manuscript so that it tells a coherent story."

—Bem, 1995, p. 173

I f you are typical of many college students, the idea of writing a term paper is not necessarily a happy thought. However, also like many college students, you often enroll for courses that require a term paper. Thus, you often face completing a task that you may find difficult or distasteful. This chapter will help you navigate through a term paper assignment from beginning to end. Learning the concepts and ideas from this chapter and putting them into practice should make your term paper experience less stressful and more positive.

What Is a Term Paper?

In this chapter, the term "term paper" is synonymous with a library research paper, whereas Chapter 8 focuses on writing a paper based on the results from an experiment. Using the term "research paper" could be confusing in scientific disciplines—in a **term paper**, rather than reporting about original research that you have conducted (see Chapter 8), you are writing about research conducted by other people. Thus, you might also hear a term paper referred to as a literature review (see the Chapter 4 section "Introduction"), so when you see "term paper" throughout this chapter, you can apply the information to a literature review as well.

A term paper is similar to a paper focused on a specific topic, somewhat like papers you may have written in high school. However, rather than using encyclopedias or magazine articles as sources as you probably did in the past, you are much more likely to use journal articles and scholarly books when writing a term paper in college. Also, a college term paper is typically much more narrowly focused than any papers you previously wrote. We will delve into the differences more throughout this chapter.

Reducing the Stress of Writing a Term Paper
The main pointer for reducing the stress you may feel about a term paper assignment is simple: Get started! Actually, you should get started ASAP! What's your first step?

Choosing a Topic for Your Term Paper

Many students take what is perhaps the most critical aspect of writing a term paper for granted—choosing the topic. Assuming that your instructor allows you to choose a topic, selecting that topic for the paper is a step you should take quite seriously.

Relevance to the Course Topic. Relevance to the course is the first consideration in choosing a good topic. Many instructors probably believe that students are familiar with a course's topic upon enrollment—a belief that may be in error. To make my examples in this chapter concrete and specific, I will focus on an upper level (junior/senior) course in social psychology. The specific examples may not be relevant to you and your course, but the general principles of picking and narrowing a topic should generalize to your situation.

I remember telling my students in a social psychology course that their term paper topics should be relevant to the general topic of social behavior. Well, obviously! The problem with that type of statement is that students often come into a course without much knowledge about the course topic—despite the fact that, prior to enrolling in upper level psychology courses, students have typically taken an introductory psychology course. That introductory course usually includes at least some material that is directly relevant to the upper level course. In my case, for my social psychology course, I knew that students had previously read a chapter on social psychology in their introductory course. However, my assumption that they remembered the content from that chapter may have been erroneous.

This situation is possibly where you may find yourself: You enrolled in an upper level psychology course dealing with social psychology (or personality, or abnormal psychology, or cognition, or some other topic) that you studied in an intro course. If that's the case and you still have the text from that introductory course (it is *always* a good idea to keep the textbooks for courses in your major and perhaps even in your minor—you never know when they will come in handy in the future), review the chapter that is relevant to your current course with the term paper requirement. If you don't have an introductory textbook, borrow one from a friend, an instructor, or the library. If you look at a typical introductory psychology text's chapter on social psychology, you can refresh your memory or preview major topics such as attitudes, attraction, conformity/obedience, and group influence, among many others.

You should narrow your topic even more than to simply one of the major topics from the chapter: It is much easier to write a good term paper on a narrow topic rather than a broad one. As an example, imagine that you are taking a course on social psychology and chose group influence as your paper topic—where would you begin? Although group influence is a narrow topic within social psychology, it is still quite broad and, therefore, would make for a challenging paper topic. Each of the major topics in the social psychology chapter of an introductory psychology textbook probably had several subtopics listed—so, for the topic of group influence, you might have seen subtopics such as the bystander effect, social loafing, groupthink, social facilitation, and deindividuation listed under group influence. Ideally, you should begin at least at the level of a subtopic in your quest to find a suitably narrow paper topic. This simple exercise of examining an intro book and looking at narrow topics will probably bring back some memories about social psychology concepts that you might have learned and then forgotten from the introductory course.

What Interests You? As an instructor, I find that student interest in a topic is a prime requisite for a good term paper. Think about this idea for a second: Would you rather look for information about something that interests you or about something that doesn't really push your buttons? Writing a term paper should be like your behavior when surfing the web—I'll bet you click on links that intrigue you and ignore links that don't capture your interest. I have never assigned term paper topics to students because I don't want to undermine their interest in a chosen topic. If you do get a topic assigned, it is possible that you can change your instructor's mind if you follow the steps I lay out and approach that instructor with a good proposal and rationale for a personalized topic.

You should begin by deciding which subtopics from an introductory course that are relevant to your current course particularly interest you. If you find more than one subtopic of interest, read about them in the intro book and choose the one that interests you the most. (Keep the others on the back burner just in case your first choice doesn't pan out.) At this point, you probably believe that you already have an extremely narrow topic for your term paper. However, if you look for your chosen topic in the textbook for your advanced course, you might be surprised to find that this topic from the intro text that you thought was narrow is the subject of an entire chapter (or a large section) in your advanced text! For example, it would not be surprising to find a chapter of 30-plus pages on group influence in a social psychology text. In such a case, you should probably narrow your topic further.

Further Narrowing Your Topic. You can use a variety of strategies to further narrow your topic. I will discuss two of the best strategies for this process.

Consult Your Advanced Textbook. One approach to further narrowing your topic is to read about that topic in your advanced textbook. A subtopic that warranted only a paragraph or a page or two in an intro text may take from several pages up to an entire chapter in your advanced text. Thus, it is obvious that much more information is available about your topic than you read in the intro text. For example, it is likely that your social psychology textbook offers much more information about group influence and its effects on behavior, including interesting concepts such as the social facilitation effect (whereby the presence of others affects—positively or negatively—individuals' behavior) and groupthink (where good decision making can be impaired by the pressure to agree or conform). These are two good examples of narrow topics within group influence.

Use PsycINFO. A second approach to narrowing your topic is to use PsycINFO, the online database for psychology that catalogs psychology articles and books (see Chapter 5). Here's a quick refresher about how to use PsycINFO to narrow a prospective paper topic: Use the "Advanced Search" screen (see Figure 5.1) so that you see three text boxes displayed. Also, use PsycINFO's Thesaurus feature (see Chapter 5) to determine the terminology that psychology researchers use for your topic of interest. For example, by using the Thesaurus and searching for the term "facilitation," I found that "social facilitation" is a subject (DE) term that has been in use since 1973. Given the length of time that this term has been around, I should be able to find an ample number of articles dealing with the topic. Perhaps you remember being intrigued, when reading a social psychology chapter, that even cockroaches (Zajonc et al., 1969) and ants (Chen, 1937) have shown evidence of social facilitation, so you choose this topic as a starting point. (A separate search on my other potential topic of "groupthink" showed it has been a subject term only since 2015 and yielded only about 100 hits, so I worried that I might not be able to find enough good articles for a term paper.)

Searching PsycINFO for "social facilitation" as a subject (DE) term yielded about 2100 hits, so there are certainly plenty of articles from which to choose (remember—if you follow along with your own PsycINFO searches as you read, your numbers will likely differ from mine). Be sure to search using a subject (DE) term to obtain more focused results — a free-text search on "social facilitation" yielded over 5800 hits! As explained in Chapter 5, you can use PsycINFO to further refine and narrow this kind of search. In that chapter, I narrowed my annotated bibliography search by entering an additional search term (or terms) in the search boxes.

In this example, rather than using a second search term, let's focus on the options on the left side of the PsycINFO screen. Suppose you are particularly interested in developmental psychology, but you notice that all the research on social facilitation in your textbook seems to involve college students. You wonder if social facilitation also takes place in young children. To determine if there is any literature on this topic, you begin with social facilitation as a subject (DE) term search, which yields more than 2000 hits. To the left of the article records, you see a column labeled "Refine Results" (see Figure 5.2 in the previous chapter). As you scroll down this column, you see a variety of bolded headers with arrows beside them. If you click an arrow, a drop-down menu will appear. Because of your interest in social facilitation in young children, you decide to click the arrow beside "Age," and the options on the Age menu appear. This menu has many options, so a link to "Show More" appears. When you click on this link, all the age options appear (see Figure 6.1 on the next page). Not only do you see all the age options, but you also see how many hits occur for each age option within your topic search. You see that preschool age, defined as 2–5 years, has 59 hits, so you check that box and click the "Update" button. Under "Refine Results," you see that your current search involves social facilitation as a subject (DE) combined with preschool age. As promised, you now have 59 hits instead of over 2000. To examine only journal articles, click on "Academic Journals"; this reduces the number of hits to 50.

At this point, you have narrowed your search enough that you can begin to look for relevant articles to read. Click the

Figure 6.1 Age Options for a PsycINFO Search

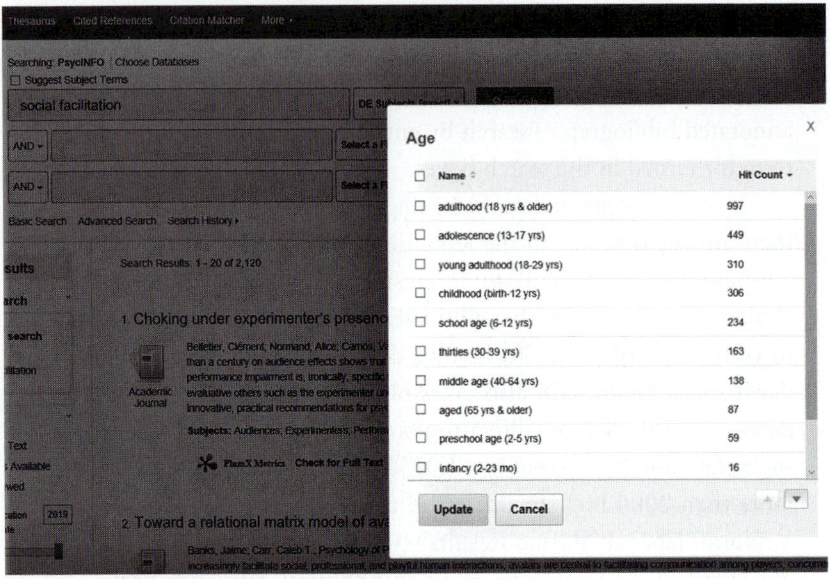

The PsycINFO® Database screenshot is reproduced with permission of the American Psychological Association, publisher of the PsycINFO® Database, all rights reserved. No further reproduction or distribution is permitted without written permission from the American Psychological Association.

"Linked Full Text" box, and PsycINFO indicates that 20 of the 50 articles are available as full text (that's the result for me — your number would vary based on your library's holdings). Remember, however, that you should not limit your search to only the articles available to you in full text — you can order the others on interlibrary loan (see Chapter 1).

Based on the search, it seems clear that a term paper topic such as "social facilitation in preschool children" is a realistic option. At this point, you have used PsycINFO to help find a relatively narrow topic for your term paper; I am convinced you will find it easier to write about a narrow topic than an overly broad one. Your instructor will also likely be pleased with a narrow topic.

From Choosing a Topic to Writing Your Paper

Choosing a narrow topic of interest to you is a large part of the battle of writing a good term paper. Imagine trying to write a paper on a broad topic such as group influence. You might attempt to explain the various types of group influence—social facilitation, social loafing, deindividuation, group polarization, groupthink, and so on—and give examples of each type of influence. In doing so, you would be taking what I call an "encyclopedic approach" to your paper. In the encyclopedic approach, you simply provide definitions and descriptions of your topic and its relevant concepts—much like the encyclopedias you may have read as a child. Most psychology professors do not want an encyclopedic paper; instead, they prefer papers based on research findings that show how an area of research has evolved over time. It is virtually impossible to write a research evolution paper on a broad topic because there is simply too much ground to cover.

How to Begin Your Paper

When you begin with a narrow topic like the one developed in the preceding section ("social facilitation in preschool children"), it is much easier to trace the development of that research line over time. If you have narrowed your topic through PsycINFO searches, you should have a small selection of articles (100 or fewer, in my opinion) to peruse and choose among for inclusion in your paper. This step is where students often run into difficulty—choosing which articles to use for their paper, probably because many students have never written a term paper based on research articles. Actually, the process is not dissimilar to writing a term paper using the typical types of sources you may have used in the past.

Imagine that you were writing a paper on the development of the cell phone. Where would you begin? Would you include information about Alexander Graham Bell inventing the telephone? Certainly, the invention of the phone was necessary before the development of the cell phone could take place, but that information is not critical to knowing about cell phone development. If you would like to begin your paper on a historical note, you could include information about Bell's work, but cover it only briefly.

The same rationale applies to your paper: Should you include the earliest research article that covers your topic? Perhaps you can glean the answer from the assignment your instructor gave you. Should your paper provide a historical overview of your topic, or should it focus on the latest research developments? As you can imagine, the earliest work is more relevant to a historical overview than it is to the latest research developments. Another factor in deciding whether to include the original work is how old that research is. Research dating to the 1960s (or earlier) is probably less relevant than a line of research that began in the 2000s. Based on these factors, you should pick the first article you plan to spotlight in your paper.

Further Developing Your Paper

After choosing the first article, selecting other articles for your paper should come more easily. Given that you are tracing the development or evolution of a research area over time, the most logical arrangement of articles would be in chronological order — from oldest to newest. Because you need to tell a story, choose articles that logically link to each other. Thus, the second article that you include should be tied in some way to the first article. For example, perhaps the authors of the second article directly based their experiment on the research findings of the first article. If you think of my example of writing about the development of the cell phone, inventors typically base their next steps on the work of previous inventors. You've probably heard the old saying about how it is pointless to reinvent the wheel. If all inventors and researchers constantly went back to square one and began anew in their idea development and research, we would lose a great deal of progress. Thus, both inventors and researchers make it a priority to know what has happened and is happening in their fields.

As you begin to tell the story of how your research area developed, make it clear that the second article you include in your paper built on the ideas and findings from the first article. The *Publication Manual of the American Psychological Association* (American Psychological Association [APA], 2020, p. 76) emphasizes that you should trace the progression of background research serving as historical antecedents to later work. This admonition should carry on through your entire paper. You should base each new article on the previous article you cited and make sure it builds on or adds to the information from that previous article. If you simply chose 8 or 10 articles about your topic at random and attempted to write a paper based on those articles, you would probably find it very difficult to compose a coherent paper. The problem with that strategy is that choosing articles at random makes it unlikely that they will be closely linked together, even if they *are* related to your overall topic.

As mentioned in the discussion of PsycINFO searching earlier in this chapter (and in Chapter 5), you have the option to limit your search results to only articles that are available in full-text versions at your library. As I pointed out, you could miss some good articles by using this approach. Another real possibility when choosing only the full-text-available articles is that those articles will not relate well to each other, making it almost impossible to write a paper that tells a coherent story about your topic. When I read a student paper that appears to be a collection of articles chosen randomly or based solely on full-text availability, I struggle to find any semblance of a story of the development or evolution of a research field. If *you* cannot find a link between two articles that you found in your search, it is highly unlikely that your instructor will see a link when you write about those two articles. A term paper composed in this manner is not likely to meet the requirement that an instructor has in mind and will probably result in a grade with which a student writer will not be happy.

Finding Related Articles. Developing a coherent paper is a skill with which many students struggle. From my subjective analysis of the hundreds (thousands?) of papers that I have read, the greatest difficulty that students have seems to be finding articles that are directly related to each other. Here, I suggest some pointers intended to help you find such articles.

Of course, one of the best ways to find related articles is through efficient PsycINFO searching. Nevertheless, depending on the number of hits your search turns up, not all of the articles may be as related to each other as you would hope. In the example cited earlier in the chapter, adding "preschool age" and "academic journals" to a search on "social facilitation" yielded 50 hits. More than likely, 50 articles is many more than you need for your paper—perhaps your assignment requires 8 or 10 articles (be sure to pay attention to the guidelines from your instructor). Thus, you want to find only those articles that most directly relate to each other.

Now it is time to examine the specific hits. As explained in Chapter 5, the title of each article is hyperlinked to the full record for that particular hit (see Figure 5.3). Reading the abstracts of your articles will provide a good indication of what the content of each article is and whether the articles are related. Also examine the "Subjects" field for main topics that you might not have considered as possible search terms. This step is particularly important if you are having difficulty finding relevant articles. In examining a few of the hits from the example search on social facilitation, I saw two additional terms that could be helpful: "peer pressure" and "conformity." Because I had no trouble finding relevant hits in this search, I chose not to search using these two terms. However, this pointer could be helpful as you search for relevant articles.

Another good indication that two articles are related is if the newer article cites the earlier article in its introduction and lists it as a reference. In the introduction of an article, the author does exactly what you are trying to do — paint a picture of the research that is vital to and led up to the current article's research. Thus, reading introductions to research articles is a great way to find articles that link together well. If the author of a 2019 article included a 2017 article in the introduction, it *must* be because some information in the 2017 article led to or contributed to the research in the 2019 article. Thus, one good way to find important, related articles is to work backward — that is, to use newer articles to work back in time to older articles. For this strategy to be successful, however, you must first find a recent article that is highly relevant to your topic. Conversely, if you have found an older article, it would be nice to have a way to work forward in time — that is, to find out who has cited that article since its publication. One method of working forward is to use a citation index (e.g., Social Sciences Citation Index, Science Citation Index) if your library provides access to them. A citation index allows you to input information about an article and find all the articles that have included the original article as a reference. The IN PRACTICE: Google Scholar box on the next page describes a more current alternative to using citation indexes. By using the strategies summarized in this paragraph and the IN PRACTICE box, you can find related articles by searching either backward in time *or* forward in time.

Another way to find related articles is to use PsycINFO in a slightly different manner. When I examined the hits I obtained in the social facilitation search, I saw something interesting: One author's name appeared several times in the first few articles (Peter C. Herman). This finding illustrates an important point about researchers in psychology (and other disciplines): They tend to engage in **programmatic research**, which involves a series of experiments on the same narrow topic. This approach enables them to become experts in their research areas and keep

IN PRACTICE

Google Scholar

A more recent alternative to using a citation index is to use Google Scholar (https://scholar.google.com/). When you open Google Scholar, you can type (or cut and paste) the title of an article into the search bar. Running a search on a title will pull up the article title, author(s), and abstract. Immediately under the abstract, you should see a link labeled "Cited by [number]," where [number] indicates how many articles published *after* the title you entered also included that article as a reference. Clicking on that link pulls up entries for all those subsequent articles. Some entries will probably show PDF links that enable you to get full-text versions of those articles. The entries without PDF links have clickable titles that will take you to full versions of the abstracts or a slightly more detailed summary, perhaps even including a list of references for the new article. You can search for these entries on PsycINFO to determine whether your library provides full-text access to any of them.

up with the latest trends and findings more easily. Imagine how difficult it would be to try to be an expert in more than one research area or topic. This specialization is akin to what happens in the field of medicine: Although you might visit your family doctor or a general practitioner first when you are ill, if the problem persists or is difficult to pinpoint, your doctor may refer you to a specialist for treatment — a doctor who specializes in a specific bodily system or organ. Thus, your doctor might refer you to a nephrologist for a kidney problem or an orthopedist for a bone issue, and your dentist might refer you to an endodontist or oral surgeon for a difficult dental problem.

This same type of specialization in research can help you identify related articles if you alter a PsycINFO search to include a specific author's name, known as an **author search**. Continuing with the previous example, I might search for "social facilitation" and "Herman" as an author. To conduct this search, I enter "social facilitation" in the first search box and select "DE Subjects [exact]" for its field, and then I type "Herman" in the second search box and select "AU Author" for its field. (Note: If you are entering a common last name such as Smith or Brown, you might want to specify first and last names [e.g., Randolph Smith] to avoid getting many hits for the wrong authors.) In this particular case, running the search yielded 10 hits, which is quite productive. The change to using an author search may not be large, but it could help you find more related articles in some cases.

What if I Have Too Many Related Articles? If you are writing about a topic that has a long history of research or is very popular, you may have trouble narrowing down your results to the number of articles that your instructor requires for your paper. Suppose that you have found 25 articles that seem highly related to your topic and to each other but your instructor requires only 10 articles for your paper. You could ask the instructor about including all 25 articles, but that option would probably result in an overly long paper and more work (time that you could devote to other classes). The *APA Publication Manual* (APA, 2020, p. 76) actually provides some guidance on this topic: It says that your literature review should be succinct, so a comprehensive historical picture of all research is not necessary. Thus, part of writing a good paper is sifting through relevant articles and choosing only a selection of those articles to include. You should avoid including articles that are only peripherally related to your research. Given these guidelines, it is clear that you do not need to include three or four articles that contain essentially the same information; instead, you should find what you believe is the best article with that information and include it in your paper. Obviously, the best article can be a subjective judgment—in some cases, it might be the first article because of historical significance or a later article because the relevant information seems clearer to you in that article. Generally speaking, I would argue that the simplest, most straightforward article containing the information you want is the best, because sometimes complex articles with many different types of information end up somewhat obscuring the information that you wish to include and spotlight.

How an Annotated Bibliography Can Help You

Chapter 5 explained how to compile an annotated bibliography. As I pointed out then, compiling an annotated bibliography can be helpful as you work on a term paper—now let me convince you of its utility. As you are searching PsycINFO for articles to include in your term paper, you will come across some that you believe will be vital to writing your paper. What should you do at that point? If you gradually build an informal annotated bibliography along the way, you can refer to it as you plan your paper. Typing up the APA-Style reference to an article and writing some notes about it (your annotation) will take a few minutes but will likely save you considerable time in the future. As you are searching, there is a degree of uncertainty about whether you will actually use any article in your paper, so it is probably wasteful to find and print every article at this point. On the one hand, you will likely change your mind about articles you found early in the search as you continue to search. On the other hand, it can be quite frustrating to try to find an article for a second time when you remember having seen it *somewhere* during the searching process! When you end your searching and have the requisite number of articles selected, having an informal annotated bibliography for the articles will be quite helpful as you begin to write your paper.

The annotations in your bibliography will help as you arrange the articles in order for your paper, as I describe later in this chapter. An annotated bibliography in a computer file makes it a simple matter to cut and paste the entries and sort them into the desired order of presentation. Even better, you will have references for all your articles ready to cut and paste into the paper's reference list. Thus, even without the assignment of creating an annotated bibliography as a precursor to your term paper, it is a useful strategy to compile one as you are searching PsycINFO.

Finding Your Articles

Once you have conducted your PsycINFO searches and decided which articles to include in your paper, you must obtain copies of those articles. There is simply not enough information or detail in the abstracts from PsycINFO to use them for writing your paper. Avoid the temptation to write about a study based on another author's description of that study (known as using a **secondary source**) because of potential inaccuracy. Find *all* the articles that you wish to include in your paper, so you can read them yourself. In this way, you will be using **primary sources**.

Ideally, at least some of the articles found through searching will be easy to obtain—all you will need to do is to click the "PDF Full Text" icon near the bottom of the record. When you click this link, an exact copy of the article as it appeared in the journal should open on your screen. Buttons on the right side of the screen allow you to print the article, email it to yourself (or someone else), or save the article in a folder (which you can later save or email). There is even a Cite button that can save the reference in several different formats, including APA Style. However, there is a potential problem with these formatted references that you should recognize: The reference formatting is *not* perfect for APA-Style references and might not yet be updated for the newest edition of the *Publication Manual* (APA, 2020). Thus, if you use the references as formatted with the Cite button, you will probably lose points on APA formatting in your paper. The fact that errors occur in the formatting is confusing and frustrating for students—but be aware that EBSCOhost is the provider for PsycINFO, so the reference formatting is not done by an entity of APA. The formatting by a third party makes the errors somewhat more understandable, though no less frustrating.

Another strategy for trying to find a full-text version of an article revolves around DOIs (digital object identifiers), which first appeared in 2000 (but now have been applied to older articles and books, too). Most recent journal article references end with a DOI (see Chapter 5 section "References for Journal Articles"), which is a string of characters that provides a permanent link to the article. Thus, when you read an article online, the DOIs for the article's references are clickable links. You can click on a link and go to either a full-text version of the reference or an abstract of the article with instructions about how to purchase a copy of the article. In most cases, you will probably *not* want to purchase these articles. The prices are typically quite high, and you might not even want to use an article when you read it in its entirety. Instead, read the subsequent paragraphs to find low-cost options for procuring articles that interest you.

Records without a full-text icon will be a little more challenging to get. The strategies that you can use to obtain such articles will depend to some extent on your library, so some possibilities that I mention here may not work. Back in the olden days (before the widespread use of computers and electronic records), libraries bought subscriptions to journals much as you might subscribe to a magazine. Each time a **journal issue** (one installment of a journal published multiple times yearly) was published, the library received a copy in the mail. At the end of the year, the library would have all of the issues from the year bound in a hard cover and filed on the library's shelves. Somewhere in your library, there are probably shelves and shelves of bound journals and an index to those journals. If you are fortunate, your library may have copies of journal issues that contain some of the articles you need.

When you look at a PsycINFO record, you will see the article's title, followed by the authors' names and the journal title. Immediately after the journal title, you will see the volume number of the journal (followed by the issue number in parentheses), followed by the date and page numbers. To find an article on the shelf, you will need the journal title, volume and issue numbers, and page numbers. Locate the journal on the shelf either by its title or its call number (which one you use will depend on how your library files bound journals). Once you have found the journal, you will probably see many bound copies, which will differ by year and volume (many journals publish one volume per year, so the volume and date may be redundant information). Within a volume, there will likely be several issues—journals often publish four, six, or 12 issues per year. The issue number may not be important to you because most journals use **continuous pagination** (each issue begins with a page number based on the previous issue) throughout the year. In such a case, you would simply find the correct volume number and leaf through it until you find the relevant page number of the article. However, a small number of journals **repaginate by issue** (begin each issue with page 1), in which case you *would* have to know the relevant issue number to find your article. If you find your article in the hard copy of the journal, it will be necessary to go "old school" and actually make a copy of the article on a copy machine or scan the article so that you will have an electronic copy.

If a particular PsycINFO record does not link to full text and your library does not have a hard copy of the journal you need, you are still not necessarily out of luck in terms of getting the article. If your college is located near other colleges, you could go online to other college libraries and check their journal holdings to find out if they have a hard copy of the needed journal. If so, a trip to that library could help you procure the articles you need. If you have a friend at another college, that friend could search PsycINFO for the articles you need to find out if the library at that school has full-text availability of any of the articles—if so, the friend can download the full-text version and email it to you.

By far, the best strategy for finding articles that you cannot find in your library is to use interlibrary loan (ILL). ILL is a method of transmitting articles electronically from a library that has an article to a patron (you) of a library that does not have that specific article. I addressed the use of ILL in Chapter 1 (see also that chapter's A CLOSER LOOK box), where I noted that each library has a slightly different way of implementing ILL. You should be able to find out how ILL works at your library by looking at the library's home page or speaking to a librarian in person. In the old days, ILL required making a hard copy of an article at one library and then mailing it to the library that requested it, with your library contacting you when the article arrived. Today, transmission of articles is electronic, so a copy will probably show up in your email. Thus, the ILL process is much faster now than it was in the past, but it still requires some time. For this reason, you should budget some extra time in your term paper timeline to allow for articles that you request by ILL to arrive. Obtaining books or dissertations by ILL is a different matter, as explained in the IN PRACTICE: Obtaining Books and Dissertations via Interlibrary Loan box.

IN PRACTICE

Obtaining Books and Dissertations via Interlibrary Loan

You can also order books by interlibrary loan (ILL), though this process usually takes more time than obtaining articles by ILL because the lending library has to actually mail the book to your library. Books are usually less desirable sources for term papers than are journal articles. Many professors require that you use original sources for your paper, and books are rarely original sources for research findings because they typically summarize research originally published in journal articles. Also, books are usually behind the times because their writing and publication times are both longer than those for journal articles; in fact, even newly published books are probably a year or two (or even more) behind on the latest research.

Obtaining a dissertation through ILL is almost impossible. Unlike books, which can be held by many libraries, a dissertation in hard copy is usually held only at the library where the doctoral student did the research. Libraries will typically not lend a dissertation because it is irreplaceable if lost. If you get a good hit on a dissertation, my advice is to conduct an author search to see if the author ended up publishing the dissertation work as a journal article. If that approach fails, you could try to locate the author and contact her or him directly.

Writing Your Paper

Once you have found your articles, it is time to move toward writing the paper. Before you actually begin to write, however, it would be wise to do some preliminary work.

What Do I Do With These Articles?

Once you have your articles in hand, you must figure out how to use them to tell the story about the development of the research area you are covering. The critical first step is to decide the order of the articles you will include in your paper. If you have done a good job with your PsycINFO searching and finding related articles, this step should be fairly simple. As I mentioned previously, one logical process would be to arrange your articles chronologically. If the articles truly are related or linked, then your earliest chronological article would logically lead to the next chronological article. What do I mean by "logically lead"? One possibility is that the authors of the second article directly based their research on the results from the first article. In such a case, they would have included the first article prominently in their introduction section and spotlighted that they were attempting to answer a question or address an issue raised by the first article. This type of coverage is the best possible signal that your articles are related to each other. This process would continue on to the third, fourth, fifth, and subsequent articles throughout your paper.

Think back to my earlier example of writing a history of the development of cell phones. There had to be a series of research discoveries that enabled the development of cell phones. Typically, that series of discoveries would have come in a specific order — that is, the second step in development could not take place until the first step had occurred. This type of progression of thought and research findings is exactly what you are attempting to show in your paper.

It is possible, of course, that your articles are not so clearly linked. In this case, you will need to work a little harder at putting the articles into the order that you will cover them in the paper. Arranging the articles chronologically is still a good starting point. Once you have arranged the articles, then look at the first two articles to determine if you can find a link between them. Even if the earlier article is not cited in the second, later article, can you find some common thread between them? How did the information in the second article advance the knowledge about the topic from the first article? How does the second article add to or build on the information from the first article? If you cannot determine any such link, then those two articles may not be a good fit for your paper.

It is *possible*, however, that chronological order is not the perfect arrangement. Suppose your third article (chronologically) relates directly to the first article, and the second article (chronologically) then links to the third article. This type of arrangement would still allow you to show how your line of research developed over time. Chronological order is not a perfect indicator because different journals may take different amounts of time to publish articles already accepted for publication. Thus, a later article might actually precede an earlier article in terms of how the research area has developed and evolved.

Regardless of the chronology involved, it is vital that you trace the thread of thought from one article to the next. Your instructor can easily detect if you have constructed your paper by simply throwing articles together with no regard for telling a story; this approach results in the perception of reading about study after study with no coherent theme development. It is your job to let your professor know how this research field developed over time, and a disjointed paper will not accomplish that objective. Imagine reading a novel in which the chapters have been randomly scrambled—it would be impossible to follow the plot development. A term paper with articles haphazardly thrown together will make it impossible for your instructor to follow the train of thought about how your research topic evolved and developed over time.

Using Your Articles to Write the Paper

When you arrive at the point of actually writing your paper, much of the difficult work is done. You have thoroughly searched the psychological literature about your research topic, you have narrowed that search to a handful of articles resulting in a narrow and well-defined topic, you have found copies of your articles, and you have arranged those articles in an order that will allow you to tell a clear coherent story about how your research topic developed over time. This kind of preparation for writing the paper is as important as actually writing it. Now that you are ready to write, the question of *what* to write comes up.

What Information Do I Include? As a general guideline, the previous edition of the *APA Publication Manual* (APA, 2010, p. 28) said to focus only on important details: "emphasize pertinent findings, relevant methodological issues, and major conclusions." This information is helpful because many students believe that they should include every detail of an article when they write about it in their paper. From experience, I can tell you that your instructor will probably not understand why you included a specific article if you cover every single detail of that article. Remember that your topic is narrow, so the information you use from the article should also be narrow. Include enough detail from an article so that it is clear how and why the article relates to your topic and adds new information about it. As an example, if every article that you include had college freshmen as subjects, then that detail is probably not important enough to include. If, however, your final study took information gleaned from research with college freshmen and applied that information to preschool children or senior adults, then that aspect of that final study is important enough to cover. Including irrelevant details from articles is much more likely to obscure your story about how the research area developed than it is to make that story clearer.

Ideally, your instructor will give you some guidelines about what details from the articles to include in your paper. For example, I once taught a course with a goal of helping students learn to read and evaluate research articles. Their term paper assignment was a critical evaluation of research articles in a narrow research area. I prepared a handout about writing such a paper and included information to help students know what to include from their research articles. I have adapted that handout for your use while working on your paper (see Table 6.1).

TABLE 6.1	**Assignment Checklist for Information to Include About Research Studies**	
Information to Include	**Required?**	**Have I Included the Information?**
Purpose of study		
Researchers' hypotheses/ predictions		
Type of research participants (include important demographic characteristics)		
Type of research method(s) used to test hypotheses/predictions		
Types of data collected		
Results obtained		
How results contributed to existing body of knowledge about topic		
Scientific evaluation of merits and limitations of study		
	Yes	
	Yes	

Note. You can use this checklist to ensure that you have covered the material your instructor requires about research studies in your term paper or literature review. For each category of information listed here, indicate whether your instructor requires that information (*Yes/No*). Note the two blank categories at the bottom of the table; you can use them to insert categories that I did not include but that your instructor requires. As you are writing about each study, check off the categories in the third column as you write about each category for that study. Using this table for each research study you cover in your paper will help you to avoid leaving out important information that your instructor wants you to include.

My goal was to leave nothing to the students' imaginations about the information I wanted to see from each article that they included in their paper. However, this assignment was somewhat different from a traditional term paper, so it is possible that your instructor would not want you to include all of these types of information about each article or might want you to include details that I did not list, which is why Table 6.1 is flexible for your needs. Given the variability in instructors and their requirements for term papers, it is best to ask your instructor directly about their preference. For example, I required students to include information about the research methodology used because my course dealt with research methods. Instructors who teach content-based courses in areas such as learning, developmental psychology, abnormal psychology, and the like are probably less likely to have you address methodology issues, but I would expect variability even for those types of courses. So, to be safe rather than sorry, I advise you to ask your instructor directly about what type of information to include about each article. As an instructor, I would be happy to provide a student with an answer so that the term papers I read are on target with what I expected!

How Do I Write About a Research Article? To some extent, the answer to this question depends on what information your instructor tells you to include about each article. Here, I'll focus on general pointers about how to write about research articles.

One of the best pointers I can give is to encourage you to consider the information in Chapter 2 about differences in APA-Style writing and humanities-based writing. In particular, the section in that chapter titled "Write for Clarity and Communication, Not Entertainment Value" provides valuable tips and some important writing guidelines for APA Style. A *concise* summary of those ideas would be that you should write as clearly and as briefly as you can in communicating your message.

All too often, students write about research studies in an indirect manner—something I attribute to writing papers for English classes. APA Style, in contrast, is as direct and brief as possible. For example, to introduce a study, students often use constructions such as "In a study by Smith and Jones in 1984 at the University of Nowhere, the researchers found …"; they may also introduce an article by using its title. If you begin a paragraph by writing "Smith and Jones (1984) found that …" or "Smith and Jones (1984) studied …", then you have placed the direct emphasis on the researchers and their findings or area of study rather than on peripheral details such as the date, title, or location. This direct style of writing often seems foreign to students, perhaps because it seems abrupt in contrast to the type of writing they have done in the past. Nevertheless, such an approach allows you to add the details from the article that your instructor has requested (remember to use Table 6.1 to assist as you write about each article).

Another problem that arises frequently in student writing is difficulty in telling a story about the development of research over time. Recall that you should focus on how and/or why each study leads to the next one (or follows the previous one): How does the next study *build on* or *add to* the information from the previous one? A key element in telling this story are the transitions between paragraphs. Transitions play an important role in helping to explain the order of your studies and their relation to one another. For example, imagine that I read this transition sentence in a paper: "Smith et al. (2016) conducted an experiment to confirm and extend Davis's (2010) research." Do you see how it is logical that the student covered Smith et al.'s study in the paper *after* Davis's study? It would not make sense if the student described the studies in the opposite order! This simple transition sentence helps the reader understand the ordering of the articles in the paper and sets the stage for how a later study built on and added to an earlier study. Be sure to pay attention to and work on your transitions (see the Chapter 7 A CLOSER LOOK box) from one article to the next.

As emphasized earlier, different instructors will want to see different information from the articles that you include in your paper. Here is a good example of what a student, Eric Morton (2016), wrote in a recent paper for me:

> Following Smith et al.'s (1994) finding that caffeine (3 mg/kg) increased alertness on an attention task, MacPherson et al. (1996) compared varying doses of caffeine on memory for reading passages. Groups received 0, 2, or 4 mg of caffeine per kg of body weight. Participants read six short stories at their own pace on a computer terminal. When participants finished reading, researchers instructed participants to recall what they had read. Participants who ingested caffeine took longer to read the stories, but recalled more idea units than the placebo group (MacPherson et al., 1996).

This paragraph covers the MacPherson et al. (1996) experiment well — it briefly summarizes both the methodology and the results of the study. It also places the MacPherson et al. study in context: You can see that the researchers compared differing doses of caffeine (0, 2, or 4 mg/kg) in contrast to the previous research cited (Smith et al., 1994), which had used only one dosage level. In addition, MacPherson et al. used a different type of task and dependent variable than Smith et al. did. If you have no information from your instructor about what information to include from articles you cite, this paragraph can serve as a good model. Once more, however, I urge you to ask about your instructor's preferences.

What Else Should I Include in a Term Paper? In addition to the articles that you cover in your term paper, be sure to include introductory and concluding paragraphs. In your introductory paragraph, set the stage for your topic and provide a foreshadowing of where your paper will go. In the introductory paragraph of a paper covering the example topic shown earlier in this chapter (social facilitation in preschool children), you might write about the general topic of social facilitation and about developmental changes from preschool to later ages. Information about these topics might come from scholarly sources such as textbooks, academic books, professional articles, or even from research articles. For example, you might refer to Zajonc's (1965) groundbreaking reinterpretation of confusing social facilitation results that showed both facilitating and hindering effects of the presence of others on performance. You might also note that the existing research on social facilitation has dealt, to a large degree, with adult subjects. You could then point out that testing young children in a social facilitation paradigm is a logical extension of laboratory work on social facilitation because the results will help establish whether social facilitation is a universal phenomenon regardless of age. In this case, you would have based your line of thought on scholarly work and provided a rationale for the application of that scholarly work to real life and a rationale for your term paper. The grounding in scholarly work is important—most professors will take a dim view of students using nonscholarly sources such as Wikipedia or internet sources with dubious credibility. Basing the premise of your paper in a combination of scholarly work and real-world application makes for a nice introduction to your paper.

Do not end the paper by simply stopping after you have written about your final article. Stopping in this manner will be too abrupt and not leave a good final impression. Just as your paper needs a good starting point, it also needs a good ending point. The *APA Publication Manual* (APA, 2020) does not address writing term papers because it is geared toward manuscripts submitted for publication. It does, however, briefly mention literature reviews, which are the closest type of published articles to term papers. Literature reviews have four functions (APA, 2020, p. 8):

- Describe and spell out the problem,
- review previous research,
- show trends and problems in the literature, and
- propose research needed to resolve the problem.

The first bullet seems to approximate your introductory paragraph, and the second bullet describes your coverage of the articles you include in your paper. Thus, we might look at the last two bullets as possible information to include in the concluding paragraph.

Showing trends and problems in the literature might be similar to writing a summary or overview of the research articles you covered. If you summarize the findings, it would certainly make sense to point out elements of agreement or disagreement or missing information in the literature. This approach may serve as an adequate conclusion to your paper. However, you may also wish to address the fourth bullet by suggesting avenues for future research. Making such suggestions would demonstrate to your instructor that you truly understand the area of research and would likely be an impressive addition to the paper. This type of closing would be particularly important as well as appropriate for the writing assignment covered in Chapter 7 — the research proposal.

APA-Style Considerations

Chapters 2 and 3 presented important considerations for writing in APA Style. These points are important as you write your paper because your instructor will likely grade the papers on adherence to APA Style as well as on content.

Citations

In Chapter 2, I first mentioned using citations in written assignments. Every time you use information from a source, you must give credit to that source—both in the paper at the point where you use the information by giving a citation and at the end of the paper in a list of references. You must cite *every* source used for information in your paper. A citation gives you the basic information a reader needs—name(s) and date—to find a reference to an article or book or some other type of source. For example, every time that I have used information from the *APA Publication Manual*, you have seen this citation: (APA, 2020). That citation tells you that there is a corresponding reference for that source. There are a few simple rules for formatting citations, depending on the number of authors and the previous citations you have made.

Sources With One Author

If you read an article written by Smith in 2014 and wanted to cite it in the text, you have two options. On the one hand, if you want to focus on the research rather than the researcher, you could use a parenthetical citation such as "Research (Smith, 2014) has shown that. . . ." On the other hand, if you want to name the researcher, you can use the name in the sentence: "Smith (2014) found that. . . ."

Sources With Two Authors

For sources written by two authors, you have the same options as for one-author sources. You could write "Results of caffeine use depend on the dosage (Smith & Jones, 2014)" or "Smith and Jones (2014) noted that caffeine's results depend on the dosage level." Note the use of the ampersand within parentheses, in contrast to the use of "and" when the authors' names appear in the text.

Sources With Three or More Authors

When a source has three or more authors, APA Style uses "**et al.**" (Latin for "and others") to keep citations brief. *All* citations substitute "et al." for the authors other than the first author; thus, the correct parenthetical citation for an article by Smith, Jones, Brown, White, and Black would be "(Smith et al., 2014)" and the correct text citation would be "Smith et al. (2014) found. . . ." Note that you never use "et al." with two-author sources. When you read articles published prior to the most recent *APA Manual* (2020), you will see citations with three to five authors listing all names on the first citation and using et al. only for second and subsequent citations.

Exception to the et al. Rule

Some potentially problematic situations force modifications to the guidelines just listed. Imagine having two articles to cite:

> Smith, Jones, Brown, White, and Black (2014)
> Smith, Brown, Jones, Black, and White (2014)

Using the "et al." guidelines, both citations would shorten to Smith et al. (2014), which would lead to a reader not knowing which of the two articles you were citing. The rule in this case is to list as many names as necessary to distinguish the two articles and then add "et al." Thus, the two citations would be Smith, Jones, et al. (2014) and Smith, Brown, et al. (2014). Table 6.2 on the next page summarizes all of these citation rules.

Duplicated Names

Chapter 5 explained how to format references if the authors' names and dates are identical. Recall that you arrange the references alphabetically by title and use a lowercase letter with the date. Just as you need to differentiate such articles in your list of references, you must do the same in citations. Thus, if you have both Smith and Jones (2015a) and Smith and Jones (2015b) in your reference list, you must cite them in the same manner—be sure to include the lowercase letter with the date in your citation, just as you do in your reference list.

TABLE 6.2	APA Citation Styles	
Number of Authors	**Type of Citation**	**Citation Format**
1	In text	Smith (2014)
	Parenthetical	(Smith 2014)
2	In text	Smith and Jones (2014) (never use et al.)
	Parenthetical	(Smith & Jones, 2014) (never use et al.)
3 or more	In text	Smith et al. (2014)
	Parenthetical	(Smith et al., 2014)
Exception to et al. Rule		
3 or more (e.g., articles by Smith, Jones, Brown, & White **and** Smith, Brown, Jones, & White, both published in 2014)	In text	Smith, Jones, et al. (2014) Smith, Brown, et al. (2014)
	Parenthetical	(Smith, Jones, et al., 2014) (Smith, Brown, et al., 2014)

Dealing With Multiple Citations

It is often the case that you will want to cite two (or more) studies at the same time, such as when multiple studies have the same or similar information. In this case, you should cite them in the same order that they appear in the reference list. Thus, if you wanted to cite Smith and Brown (2017) and Jones and White (2015) in the same sentence, you should use this type of wording and sentence construction: "These results are consistent with previous research (Jones & White, 2015; Smith & Brown, 2017)."

References

At the end of your paper, you will include a list of references — a list of all the sources that you actually used (and cited — be sure to cite *all* your references) in writing your paper. A reference list is different from a bibliography that you may have learned about in other disciplines; it does *not* contain any sources that you consulted but did not use in the paper. Different types of sources require different reference styles. Chapter 5 covered the APA reference style for journal articles, so we will examine only the reference styles for books in this chapter—journal articles and books are types of sources you would most commonly use in writing a term paper.

Books

One potential source of information for your term paper (*if* your instructor allows it) is books. The general format for book references also uses a specific order for the various elements of the source: author(s), date, book title, publisher name, and DOI (if the book has one) or URL for an online book. Just as with journal articles (actually, *all* references), the first line is left justified, with subsequent lines indented (remember to use a hanging indent, not tabs!). Here is an example of a correct reference for a book:

Crawford, L. A., & Novak, K. B. (2018). *Individual and society: Sociological social psychology* (2nd ed.). Routledge. https://doi.org/10.4324/9781315269313

Notice that you format authors' names and the date in the same manner as you do for journal articles. Type the title of the book in italics, capitalizing only the first word of the title, proper nouns, and the first word after a colon (use only one space after a colon). If the book is in a second or later edition, include that information in parentheses with no italics, as shown in the example. Finally, you must provide the publisher's name. For the publisher's name, "do not include designations of business structure (e.g., Inc., Ltd., LLC)" (APA, 2020, p. 296). If the author and the publisher happen to be the same (as in the case of the *APA Publication Manual*), omit the publisher's name because it is repetitious (see this chapter's reference list for an example). If the book has a DOI or URL, list it after the publisher; otherwise, end the reference after the publisher's name. When you see references to books in older journal articles, you will see a location listed before the publisher's name. This information was part of a book reference in the previous edition of the *Publication Manual* (APA, 2010).

Chapters in Edited Books

An edited book has chapters written by a variety of authors and is coordinated (edited) by one or more individuals. It is somewhat more probable that you would include edited books (compared to authored books) as references in your paper because chapters in edited volumes are more likely to include research findings. The reference style for a specific chapter in an edited book is something like a combination of a journal and book reference:

Cialdini, R. B., & Griskevicjus, V. (2010). Social influence. In R. F. Baumeister & E. J. Finkel (Eds.), *Advanced social psychology: The state of the science* (pp. 385–417). Oxford University Press.

In case this type of reference is unfamiliar to you, it refers to a chapter ("Social Influence") written by Cialdini and Griskevicjus, which appeared in a book (*Advanced Social Psychology: The State of the Science*) edited by Baumeister and Finkel that was published in 2010. The chapter authors' names appear first, followed by the publication date of the book and the title of the chapter (capitalized as you would a journal article title). Next, provide the book editors' names, followed (in parentheses) by "Ed." (if one editor) or "Eds." (for multiple editors), the title of the book (italicized and capitalized as you would a book title), and inclusive page numbers of the chapter (in parentheses and not italicized). Finally, provide the publisher's name and DOI or URL (if the book chapter has either;

provide the DOI or URL for the book if the book has one but each individual chapter does not).

Other Types of Sources

In the discussion here and in Chapter 5, I have included the major types of sources that you would be most likely to access and use in writing a term paper or literature review. However, the *APA Manual* (APA, 2020, pp. 316–352) provides 114 different reference examples, so you will need to consult the *Manual* if you use other types of sources and need to know how to reference them.

Compiling Your Reference List

Your term paper should end with a list of all your references — every source from which you took information should be listed here, and all sources listed should be cited somewhere in your paper. For more instructions on formatting your reference list, see Chapter 5. Remember to be compulsive with your reference list — avoiding errors here is paramount! I provide a helpful hint for compiling your reference list in the IN PRACTICE: Don't Forget a Reference! box on the next page.

Typing Instructions

Before you begin typing a manuscript, make sure that you have the correct settings for APA Style in Word (see the Chapter 2 IN PRACTICE box and the Chapter 5 section "Typing Instructions"). This is the first writing assignment covered in the book that will require APA Style throughout. You can refer to advice in the Chapter 2 section before the IN PRACTICE box about using a saved APA-Style file or using the APA-Style template (for APA, 2020) from Microsoft. The *APA Manual* (APA, 2020, pp. 50–67) contains pages from sample manuscripts to which you can refer if some element of formatting your paper in APA Style is not clear.

IN PRACTICE

Don't Forget a Reference!

It is not unusual for me to read a student paper that has a citation but no corresponding reference or a reference with no corresponding citation. To avoid forgetting a reference, when I begin writing a paper, I insert a manual page break (Control + Return on a PC; Command + Return on a Mac) and type the "Reference" header bolded and centered at the top of the new page. Every time I insert a citation in my writing, I go to the Reference page and enter the name(s) and date for the citation (in alphabetical order). At that point, I don't type the full reference because I don't want to interrupt my writing flow. At the end of my writing session or at the end of writing the paper, I have a prompt for every reference so that I don't forget to list a particular reference.

NOTE. To begin a new page in Word, do not press the enter key on your keyboard repeatedly until a new page shows up. The problem with that strategy is that any revision to the paper will make the information on that new page move up or down, depending on your edits.

Title Page

For a term paper or literature review, you would format a title page as outlined in Chapter 5 (see Figures 5.4 and 5.5). Remember that you need to find out from your professor whether to compile a professional or student title page and whether all of its components are required.

Page 2

As noted toward the end of in Chapter 5, you should see your all-CAPS running head at the top of Page 2. On the first line, retype your title (centered and bolded). Be certain that the titles on Pages 1 and 2 match perfectly. On the next line, begin the text of your paper, making sure to use an indent for each paragraph.

As a possible departure from the previous paragraph, your instructor might want you to include an abstract (see Chapter 4) on Page 2. This requirement would be somewhat unusual for a term paper or literature review, but it is certainly possible. If you need to include an abstract, see Chapter 8 for formatting instructions. An abstract (if required) stands alone on Page 2, even though there will be blank space under the abstract. Thus, in this case, you would begin the text of your paper on Page 3, as described in the previous paragraph.

Reference Page

After you complete the text of your paper, begin a new page for your list of references. On this new page, type "References" (centered and bolded) on the first line (type "Reference" if you have only one reference — but I would suggest that you *never* write a term paper with only one reference!). When you go to line 2, change to left justification and begin typing the first reference. Format the references as outlined in Chapter 5 (the section "References for Journal Articles") and in this chapter, being sure to use hanging indents for the second and subsequent lines of each reference. Also, be sure to alphabetize your references by the first author's last name. In the Chapter 5 section "Arranging the Annotated Bibliography," I provided pointers for tricky alphabetizing situations such as multiple articles by the same author.

Headings

APA format uses different types of headings to organize a manuscript (APA, 2020, pp. 47–49). This book uses APA-formatted headings throughout. You have probably noticed that most textbooks use headings throughout chapters to break the information you are learning into manageable chunks and provide an organizational scheme. You may wish to divide your paper into different sections based on content, main topic, or some other scheme. If so, headings will help point out these divisions to the reader. Table 2.3 of the *APA Manual* (p. 48) denotes the differing levels of headings, as shown in Figure 6.2 on the next page.

Figure 6.2 How to Format APA-Style Headers, With Examples from the Chapter

APA-Style Headers	Examples of APA-Style Headers from Chapter 6
Level 1 Heading	**What Is a Term Paper?**
Level 2 Heading	**Reducing the Stress of Writing a Term Paper**
Level 3 Heading	*Choosing a Topic for Your Term Paper*
Level 4 Heading.	**Further Narrowing Your Topic.**
Level 5 Heading.	*Consult Your Advanced Textbook.*

As Figure 6.2 suggests, headings are similar to outlining— something you probably learned early in your school career. Thus, a Level 2 heading denotes a subdivision of information under a Level 1 heading, and so on. The *APA Manual* (APA, 2020, p. 48) says to begin with a Level 1 heading and go down the list, depending on how many levels of headings you want in your paper.

Editing Your Paper and APA-Style Considerations

After you finish writing your paper, you should edit it thoroughly before you submit it to your instructor. Your editing should focus on grammar, APA Style, and content because all are critical to your writing success. Reading your paper in its entirety will likely spotlight some problems that you can correct before submission. Many students find it difficult to edit their papers, perhaps because they know what they are saying (or trying to say), so they see that information even if it is not clearly expressed. I have five suggestions that may help with this problem.

First, when writing the paper and later editing it, pay attention to the grammatical help that Word provides. You will probably see colored squiggly lines under some words and phrases as you type. Red lines indicate possible misspellings; blue (PC) or two blue (Mac) lines indicate possible grammar problems. If you right-click on a red squiggly line, you will see possible correct spellings (Word often marks names as misspellings; make sure you spell authors' names correctly and then ignore the red marks). Right-clicking on a blue squiggly line (PC) or two blue lines (Mac) will show you the grammatical issue (e.g., "Passive Voice [consider revising]"). If you do not see any squiggly lines, on a PC, click on File, Options, Proofing and make sure the first four boxes under "When correcting spelling and grammar in Word" are checked. On a Mac, click on Tools, Spelling and Grammar, Options, and make sure that "Check spelling as you type" and "Check grammar as you type" are checked.

My second editing suggestion is to read your paper aloud to yourself. When we read silently, we tend to go faster and gloss over problems that are there — hearing those problems when you read aloud may make them jump out at you.

Third, assuming your instructor has no objections, enlist a peer from your class, swap papers, and read and edit each other's work. Several studies (e.g., Cathey, 2007; Haaga, 1993; Kennette & Frank, 2013) have shown that students find this process, known as peer review, to be helpful and believe it helps improve their papers.

My fourth suggestion for editing your paper is to look at the "Proofread and Edit/Revise" section of Chapter 1. In that section, I contrasted proofreading with editing and revising a paper. Both approaches to working on your paper are important, but they involve different processes. Also, I provided pointers from writers to help you as you work on a draft of your paper to make it a better final product. Finally, the new *APA Manual* (2020, pp. 125–127) now contains a section titled "Strategies to Improve Your Writing" that provides helpful suggestions you can implement. Advice on revising a paper receives the most attention in this section of the *Manual*.

My final editing suggestion will allow you to benefit from my many years of experience trying to help students write better. Over many years of reading and editing student papers, I have developed a dual-purpose resource to help students improve their writing. I noticed that most students tend to make the same types of mistakes—and writing the same notes on paper after paper took me a great deal of time. To deal with these issues, I compiled a Common Writing Problems, Explanations, and Solutions list (see Appendix C, part A). Much of this list deals with APA-Style issues, but it also covers some grammatical problems. When I'm reading papers, I can simply make a brief mark on the paper (see the first column) and provide a more detailed comment about that problem in the list (explanation/ solution column). At the end of the list, I included other types of writing problems that didn't fit the column format as well (see Appendix C, part B). By using this list, I can make fewer marks on the paper but still provide students with detailed instruction about correcting these common mistakes. After using this list for a few semesters, I changed my approach: Rather than simply using it as a grading tool, I now give students the list *before* they write and submit their papers so that they can try to avoid these errors on their own. If you read this list and learn the various points listed, you will likely find that your APA-Style writing will improve. Use this list for all APA-Style writing assignments, not just term papers.

Concluding Thoughts

This chapter has dealt with what is perhaps the most common type of writing assignment for psychology courses—the term paper or literature review. You could encounter this type of assignment in any course at any level, from freshman to senior. This chapter provided insights and tips intended to make an often-dreaded assignment an easier task to tackle. There are two keys to making a term paper an easier assignment: You should pick a topic that interests you and then narrow that topic so that you can write a well-focused paper rather than attempting to explain too much in too little time or space.

Critical Thinking Writing Assignments

As you work on these writing assignments, keep in mind a friend who needs to pick your brain for your expertise on guidelines that apply equally to assigned writing assignments for term papers and literature reviews.

Assignment 1

Imagine you have a friend whose major is different than yours. He emails and asks your advice about how to get started on choosing a topic for his writing assignment. Write a paragraph of advice as a reply to him.

Assignment 2

Your friend contacts you again about her writing assignment. She has begun searching on her topic in PsycINFO but complains that she has found hundreds of relevant articles. Write an email to her with pointers on what to do about this problem.

Assignment 3

Attempting to be proactive, write your friend an email with advice about how to deal with citations and her reference list so that she will not be penalized by her instructor.

References

American Psychological Association. (2010). *Publication manual of the American Psychological Association* (6th ed.).

American Psychological Association. (2020). *Publication manual of the American Psychological Association* (7th ed.). https://doi.org/10.1037/0000165-000

Bem, D. J. (1995). Writing a review article for *Psychological Bulletin*. *Psychological Bulletin, 118*(2), 172–177. https://doi.org/10.1037/0033-2909.118.2.172

Cathey, C. (2007). Power of peer review: An online collaborative learning assignment in social psychology. *Teaching of Psychology, 34*(2), 97–99. https://doi.org/10.1177/009862830703400205

Chen, S. C. (1937). Social modification of the activity of ants in nest-building. *Physiological Zoology, 10*(4), 420–436. https://doi.org/10.1086/physzool.10.4.30151428

Haaga, D. A. F. (1993). Peer review of term papers in graduate psychology courses. *Teaching of Psychology, 20*(1), 28–32. https://doi.org/10.1207/s15328023top2001_5

Kennette, L. N., & Frank, N. M. (2013). The value of peer feedback opportunities for students in writing intensive classes. *Psychology Teaching Review, 19*(2), 106–111. https://files.eric.ed.gov/fulltext/EJ1149732.pdf

MacPherson, J., Sternhagen, S., Miller, T., Devitt, M., Petros, T. V., & Beckwith, B. (1996). Effect of caffeine, impulsivity, and gender on the components of text processing and recall. *Experimental and Clinical Psychopharmacology, 4*(4), 438–444. https://doi.org/10.1037/1064-1297.4.4.438

Morton, E. (2016). *The effects of caffeine on memory and recall* [Unpublished manuscript]. Department of Psychology, Moravian College.

Smith, A. P., Maben, A., & Brockman, P. (1994). Effects of evening meals and caffeine on cognitive performance, mood and cardiovascular functioning. *Appetite, 22*(1), 57–65. https://doi.org/10.1006/appe.1994.1005

Zajonc, R. B. (1965). Social facilitation. *Science, 149*(3681), 269–274. https://doi.org/10.1126/science.149.3681.269

Zajonc, R. B., Heingartner, A., & Herman, E. M. (1969). Social enhancement and impairment of performance in the cockroach. *Journal of Personality and Social Psychology, 13*(2), 83–92. https://doi.org/10.1037/h0028063

7

Writing a Psychology Research Proposal

Do You Know?

How do you pick and then narrow a research idea?

How can you find research studies that are relevant to your research idea?

How do you write differently in the beginning, middle, and end of an introduction for a research proposal?

What subsections should you put in a Method section for a research proposal?

What information do you include in each Method subsection?

A research proposal is a plan for conducting research. Putting the plan in writing facilitates getting constructive, specific feedback on its adequacy.

—Orcher, 2014, p. 91

If you are typical of many psychology majors, at some point your department will require you to conduct a psychological experiment. A task force from the 2008 National Conference on Undergraduate Education in Psychology (Dunn et al., 2010, p. 57) recommended that "students majoring in psychology should be well versed in scientific methodology, including descriptive and inferential statistics and research methods." Departments of psychology at colleges and universities across the United States tend to follow this recommendation. A 2014 survey (Norcross et al., 2016) showed that 98% of more than 300 responding baccalaureate psychology programs required a course in research methods. Perlman and McCann (2005) found that 79% of almost 200 undergraduate psychology programs surveyed required at least one course that involved a research opportunity. Research methods instructors typically have a course goal of teaching psychology students to think critically (Beins, 2008, p. 199; Saville et al., 2008, p. 149). Most, if not all, psychology faculty would agree with the statement issued by the Curriculum Task Force at a national conference on undergraduate psychology: "The fundamental goal of education in psychology, from which all the others follow, is to teach students to think as scientists about behavior" (Brewer et al., 1993, p. 169). When you conduct a research study, you must think about behavior from the viewpoint of a psychological scientist. Conducting a research study may give you the chance to generate new psychological knowledge—to ask a psychological question that no one has asked before.

If you are required to conduct an original experiment, you will likely have to develop a research proposal before conducting that experiment. The *Publication Manual of the American Psychological Association* (American Psychological Association [APA], 2020) does not address writing research proposals, but the sections that you will likely have to write for a proposal are some of the same sections that will appear in a research report. A research proposal typically consists of an introduction, a Method section, and a reference list (see Chapter 4). In the introduction, you present a survey of psychological literature relevant to your topic and develop your research question. In the Method section, you present the proposed methodology for conducting your experiment. The references document the sources that you consulted in developing your ideas and that you cited in your proposal. A research proposal allows your instructor and your school's **Institutional Review Board (IRB)**, a committee that scrutinizes research proposals to determine their ethicality, to evaluate your idea ahead of time to determine if it seems logical, doable, and ethical.

Levels of Student Research Projects

Students may potentially propose several different levels (or types) of research projects. These levels vary based on the degree of student originality in the research.

Replication Study

In a **replication study**, you simply copy a previous experiment as closely as possible in an attempt to verify the results of the previous study. If you have taken a psychology course with a lab component, you may be familiar with this approach. It is modeled on the chemistry lab approach: When you mix chemicals together in a chemistry lab, you replicate previous chemistry research. The chemistry lab instructor can predict with certainty what will happen when you mix two specific chemicals—they might change to a new color, foam, or produce some other predictable chemical reaction. After all, predictability is important because these instructors cannot take the chance of an explosion or another dangerous outcome!

Psychology instructors often use replication studies to demonstrate classic findings from the discipline—you might remember demonstrations of such findings if you have taken an introductory psychology course. For example, if you read a long list of words to a group of people and then ask them to remember the words, they are more likely to remember words from the beginning and the end of the list, demonstrating the classic serial position effect (Robinson & Brown, 1926; Rundus, 1971). Another classic replication example often used by instructors is the Stroop effect (Stroop, 1935), in which subjects naming colors of the letters of words are significantly slower if the words are printed in different colors from the word (e.g., blue letters spelling RED) than when the colors are consistent with the word (e.g., blue letters spelling BLUE).

Instructors replicate classic studies not only because they demonstrate classic findings to students but also because the outcomes of these classic studies are predictable. But it is precisely this predictability that makes a replication research study somewhat less interesting: Although replicating results does increase our confidence in them, it does not yield new information. Much of the scientific enterprise revolves around discovering new information. Thus, although replicating previous results might be an acceptable lab activity, it is not typically what psychology faculty desire when having students propose and conduct research studies. Instead, the requirement is typically for you to design a study designed to uncover new information. This requirement leads us to the other two types of student research projects.

If your assignment is to complete a replication study, you may not have to write a research proposal. The goal of a replication study is to teach you about the process of conducting research rather than about actually generating a research idea. The original researchers have already done the background work of a literature review, so there is little need to conduct a literature search and then propose a study.

Original Study

If you have the assignment to propose an **original study**, your task is to ask a totally new and original question and generate an idea for an experiment from that question. This description does *not* mean that you have to discover a new area of research; rather, you must generate a proposal for a new question within an area of research that already exists. In other words, after reviewing an area of research literature (see Chapter 6), you develop a totally new question based on that literature review. This type of assignment is difficult because it requires a high level of originality. Interestingly, it is extremely rare that researchers conduct a truly original study. This fact makes your task somewhat easier because you can probably conduct the type of study described in the next section.

Replication-With-Extension Study

A **replication-with-extension study** is like taking the next logical step in a line of research. You must survey the existing literature, find a gap in that literature, and figure out how to fill that gap. Thus, you base your experiment on previous research and add to that existing research. You are not asking a totally new question, but rather a question that is partially new. Typically, as the name implies, you would partially replicate previous research but extend it in some way. In Chapter 6, I described a hypothetical replication-with-extension study regarding social facilitation. The majority of research on social facilitation has involved college-age participants, so a student who wanted to examine social facilitation in preschool children would conduct a replication-with-extension study. Finding that social facilitation also occurs in preschoolers would both replicate *and* extend the findings about social facilitation. Another example of research that uses the replication-with-extension is **cross-cultural research**, or research conducted in different cultures to determine whether psychology's research findings generalize to those cultures. Thus, cross-cultural research seeks "to determine whether research results and psychological phenomena are universal (found in individuals from different cultures) or specific to the culture in which they were reported" (Smith & Davis, 2013, p. 144). In summary, one way to conduct a replication-with-extension study is to change some critical feature of a previous experiment—use a different context, research subjects, research materials, or some other aspect of that study.

Another good strategy for generating a replication-with-extension study is to focus on programmatic research—research in which a researcher asks a question, conducts an experiment in an attempt to answer that question, develops a new question based on the results of the experiment, conducts a new experiment to answer the new question, and so on (see Chapter 6 for additional information on this process). It is not unusual for researchers to write about existing questions left unanswered or new questions raised by their studies in their published journal article. In fact, the *APA Publication Manual* (APA, 2020, p. 90) specifically instructs authors that they might address such unresolved or new issues in their Discussion sections. The benefit for you when you are working on your research proposal is that you can read about these unanswered or new questions when you find articles for your literature review. If the article you are reading is old, chances are that researchers have already answered the questions raised—although you *can* conduct a PsycINFO search (see Chapters 5 and 6) to confirm that assumption. By contrast, if you are reading a recent article, answers to those questions may not yet have been published. The researchers may be working on those questions, but if no published answer is available, the questions are fair game for you to propose a replication-with-extension study. To see if you understand this concept, try the assignment laid out in the IN PRACTICE: Research Ideas in Discussion Sections box.

IN PRACTICE

Research Ideas in Discussion Sections

On the previous page, I dropped a hint about developing an idea for an experiment by reading the Discussion sections of previous studies: "It is not unusual for researchers to write about existing questions left unanswered or new questions raised by their studies in their published journal article." To make certain that you understand this concept, find five recent (less than one year old) journal articles. Look at their Discussion sections and try to generate an idea for a further research study from each of the five.

Given that virtually all research experiments build on previous experiments in some important way(s), it is easy to see why replication-with-extension experiments are quite common. They are more valuable than pure replication studies because they add new information to the psychological knowledge base. At the same time, they help strengthen our confidence in previous research findings because they, at least in part, replicate those findings.

Begin Your Research Proposal With a Literature Review

The title of Chapter 6 is "Writing a Term Paper/Literature Review." In that chapter, I more or less equated term papers and literature reviews. In the context of a research proposal or research report, the introductory section is almost always a literature review. A literature review is essentially the same as a term paper, with one critical difference. In writing a term paper, your primary goal is to survey the psychological literature on a particular topic, typically beginning with early research and ending with the most current research. In writing a literature review for a research proposal, however, your primary goal is to survey the psychological literature leading up to your research idea.

You cannot develop a research idea without a literature review because you would not know what questions have already been studied. Once you know what researchers have studied and what findings exist, you can develop a question that does not have an answer. It is still likely that your literature review will begin with older research and end with newer research studies. Nevertheless, if the most current research information about a topic of interest comes from a study published in 2010, then you might not write about studies published after that date. If more recent studies have not resolved the issues or questions raised in the 2010 study, then they are not actually relevant to your literature review for your research proposal.

Preparing a Literature Review

The primary steps in preparing a literature review for your research proposal are mostly the same as those outlined in Chapter 6. Let's quickly review those steps, highlighting any potential differences between them for the two different types of assignments.

Choosing Your Topic

As with the term paper, choosing your topic carefully is critically important for your success in writing a literature review for your research proposal. In fact, identifying a narrow topic for your research proposal may be even *more* critical than for your term paper. A term paper that is not as narrow as it should be does not necessarily prevent it from being a good term paper. However, a literature review that is not sufficiently narrow will not lead you to a researchable idea, which is something you must have for a good experiment. Let's review the considerations in choosing a term paper topic (see the "Choosing a Topic for Your Term Paper" section in Chapter 6 for more details).

Relevance to the Course Topic. Oftentimes, this consideration is not one you will need to address in planning a research proposal because you are most likely to write a research proposal for an Experimental Psychology or Research Methods course. These courses deal with learning techniques of research rather than with a specific topic area. In this case, your subject area is probably relatively wide open. In contrast, an instructor for a content-based course (e.g., Learning, Social Psychology, Personality) might assign a research proposal as one of the class requirements. In that case, you should be certain that your proposal is relevant to the course topic.

What Interests You? This consideration is also perhaps more important for a research proposal than for a term paper, depending on one factor. *If* your research proposal is an assignment that will lead to you actually conducting your proposed experiment, you will spend much more time with this subject matter than you would for simply writing a research proposal or term paper. Thus, you definitely want to choose a topic that will sustain your interest over the long run. It would not be unusual for you to spend two semesters on this project—one semester in which you develop your research proposal and a second semester in which you conduct your experiment. Perhaps your program or department will even provide you with additional research opportunities after the experimental or research course—an independent study or independent research course, for example. You might carry on with this project in that type of course, thus beginning your own line of programmatic research. You should begin by selecting as narrow a topic as you can. You might begin with a topic chosen from a previous textbook, a class lecture, or some everyday situation that interests you.

Practical Issue. Practicality is not a consideration covered in Chapter 6—because when you are writing a term paper or a literature review (not leading to a research proposal), any topic is fair game. You can write about esoteric topics that deal with narrow subject populations (e.g., people with schizophrenia, children with learning disabilities), highly specialized equipment (e.g., functional magnetic resonance imaging [fMRI] scanners, brain electrodes), or unusual abilities (e.g., animal language, synesthesia). In contrast, when you are writing a literature review for a research proposal that you will actually carry out, you *must* consider practical issues. Look at the examples just mentioned: Would you have access to a population of people with schizophrenia or children with learning disabilities? Could you use an fMRI scanner or implant brain electrodes? Do you have an ape to study whether animals can use language or know many people who have synesthesia? If you propose an experiment that you will actually conduct, it must be practical enough for an undergraduate research project. This practical consideration means that some topics that typically pique students' interest, such as abnormal psychology, child development, and therapy, are often not appropriate as research proposal topics simply because you will not be able to deal with such topics as an undergraduate.

A related practical issue is ethical considerations. APA (2002) has developed a code of ethics that applies to both human and animal research. If you have taken (or are taking) a research or experimental course, you can probably find information about ethical considerations in your text. A discussion of research ethics is beyond the scope of this book, but ethics remains a practical consideration for your topic. For example, it is unlikely that your instructor or your school's IRB would approve a research proposal involving shocking subjects or giving them drugs. Typically, an instructor requires research proposals to involve only **minimal risk** (see https://www.ecfr.gov) so that participants do not face any danger of physical or psychological harm. If you do not plan to actually conduct the proposed research, then your instructor may potentially relax this minimal risk requirement. In any event, as you consider your research topic for the proposal, take ethical considerations into account.

Narrowing Your Topic. Your impression of a narrow topic may actually be fairly broad when you examine the research literature. At this point, PsycINFO searching will be highly important to your success. Both Chapters 5 and 6 covered searching PsycINFO, so I will not rehash that information here. Note, however, that using multiple search boxes is likely to be the most successful strategy for narrowing your research proposal topic. Although you may find the limiting options on the left side of the PsycINFO screen under "Refine Results" helpful when searching for only journal articles ("Academic Journals") written in English (shown under the "Language" option), you will almost certainly need to use two or even three search boxes to run a search narrow enough to develop a research proposal.

Let me provide an example of the importance of narrowing your search. I once had a student from Russia, Maria Khersonskaya, in my Experimental Psychology class. Because of her background, she was interested in studying cross-cultural differences. However, searching PsycINFO for that term (even using the DE option) yielded many thousands of hits. After taking a Social Psychology class, Khersonskaya became interested in the topic of how people perceive other people in terms of physical attractiveness. A PsycINFO search on physical attractiveness (using DE) located many fewer hits, but still more than a thousand. Combining both terms ("cross-cultural differences" and "physical attractiveness") using the DE search option yielded only 92 hits for me in a recent search; Khersonskaya was in my class in the late 1990s, so she would have found many fewer hits using both terms back then. She proposed and conducted a study on cross-cultural differences in perception of physical attractiveness and even ended up publishing her research (Khersonskaya & Smith, 1998). Although I wrote "cross-cultural differences" in the previous sentence, see the IN PRACTICE: The PsycINFO Thesaurus Rules box on the next page for an important search pointer about hyphenated terms.

IN PRACTICE

The PsycINFO Thesaurus Rules

Running a search on "cross cultural differences" uncovered an important hint for searching PsycINFO. The correct form for this term, according to APA Style, is "cross-cultural differences" because APA specifies hyphenating an adjectival phrase that precedes the noun it modifies (APA, 2020, p. 163)—"cross-cultural" is a phrase used to modify "differences." Interestingly, when you use PsycINFO's online Thesaurus, you find "Cross Cultural Differences" listed as a DE term. When I searched for "cross cultural differences in DE," I got more than 48,000 hits. However, when I searched for "cross-cultural differences in DE," I got *zero* results. The implication is clear—you must search a DE term *exactly* as it appears in the Thesaurus to get the results you seek.

Your goal in PsycINFO searching with multiple DE terms (plus specifying journal articles and English from "Refine Results") should be approximately 100 hits—perhaps even fewer, although I must admit that figure is somewhat arbitrary. The important point is that your search is narrow enough that all the hits are highly related and that the hits are not too numerous for you to look through. A narrow search is even more important for a research proposal than for a term paper because in the former situation you have to develop a narrow idea for an actual experiment. When you think you have narrowed your search as much as possible, take another look, trying to come up with other possibilities. You might even enlist a classmate or your instructor to help uncover other possibilities—they won't have the preconceived mental set that you have.

Let's return to my earlier example of finding 92 hits on "cross cultural differences" and "physical attractiveness" as DE terms. If you think about that search in a literal sense, some of the hits *might* deal with the question of whether individuals from various cultures actually are more or less physically attractive than people from other cultures. That question was *not* what interested my student—her topic (and the title of her article) dealt with *perception* of physical attractiveness, not *actual* attractiveness. Therefore, I used the PsycINFO Thesaurus to look up "perception." I found both "perception" and "social perception" as DE terms. However, when I narrowed my search by adding either term as a third search term (combined with "cross cultural differences" and "physical attractiveness" as DE terms), I found only one hit by adding "perception" and eight hits using "social perception" (only six of which were journal articles). Scrolling through the six hits showed the titles to be on target because they dealt with perception of physical attractiveness. That number is quite low, however. To determine if adding "perception" in any way might help narrow my search, I entered it in the third search box as a free-text term (by typing "perception" but not using the pull-down menu). In this search, I found 31 journal article hits—again, a quick scroll through the records showed that many were clearly on target. As this example suggests, sometimes a free-text search can be helpful and productive—but note that I used only one of the three search terms as a free-text term; I used DE terms for the other two.

From Choosing a Topic to Writing Your Research Proposal

After tentatively completing your PsycINFO searching, it is time to turn your attention to actually writing the proposal. I used the word "tentatively" in the previous sentence because you may find gaps that you need to fill and that require a return to PsycINFO.

Writing Your Introduction

Let's assume that you have 100 or fewer PsycINFO records on a narrow topic, such as my example of 31 hits on "physical attractiveness (DE) + cross cultural differences (DE) + perception." Just as with a term paper, you must now decide which articles to choose for the literature review of your research proposal.

The goal is to describe to your reader how this area of research has evolved over time, again similar to what you would write in a term paper. However, the important difference with this literature review is that it *must* lead directly into your research idea. In other words, all the articles should focus on research ideas and findings that lead to *your* idea for an original experiment. Some articles found in your PsycINFO search may relate to the topic, yet may not be relevant to your literature review because their research is not directly relevant to your research idea. For example, my PsycINFO search that led to 31 hits included a study by Gitter et al. (1983) about cross-cultural differences in perceptions of female physical characteristics. Khersonskaya was interested in *facial* physical attractiveness: Thus, this study was related to the general topic, but was far less relevant to her literature review. Similarly, articles dealing with body weight, leg length, and waist-to-hip ratio were not particularly relevant to facial attractiveness. Conversely, she might have chosen to include studies with variables such as hair color, skin tone, and facial symmetry in her literature review because those factors *are* related to facial attractiveness.

In Chapter 6, I pointed out how compiling an informal annotated bibliography could help you write your term paper or literature review. The same idea holds true for working on a research proposal. As you find articles that you believe will be helpful in writing your proposal, build an annotated bibliography (even a rough one) from those articles. By formatting the references in APA Style and making a summary annotation, you will have information about a number of articles in a brief format so that you can deal with them more easily. This arrangement will help you get an idea of how the articles could fit together (and in what order) to develop the background for your research idea.

Another important consideration for your literature review is how specific or general you should be when writing your introduction. I like to use the analogy of a funnel as a shape for the introduction (Smith & Davis, 2013, pp. 342–343). A funnel

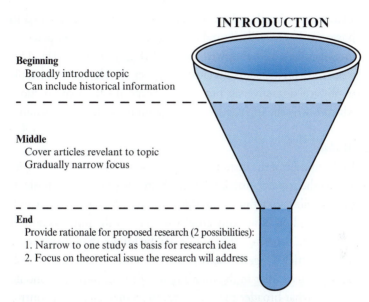

INTRODUCTION

Beginning
Broadly introduce topic
Can include historical information

Middle
Cover articles revelant to topic
Gradually narrow focus

End
Provide rationale for proposed research (2 possibilities):
1. Narrow to one study as basis for research idea
2. Focus on theoretical issue the research will address

Figure 7.1 The shape of a funnel serves as an analogy for the introduction section to a research proposal—broad at the beginning and narrowing toward the end.

(see Figure 7.1) starts out very wide at the top, gradually narrows, and ends in a very narrow opening. Likewise, your introduction should begin with a broad overview of the research topic, narrow as you cover relevant research, and finally hone in on one specific study or theoretical issue on which you are basing your proposed experiment. The research idea should be the next logical research step derived from the final study covered in your introduction.

Beginning

In the first paragraph or two of your introduction, you typically introduce the topic in a broad sense. If you wish to cite some of the historical pioneering research in this area, that information belongs here. If you need to define or describe overarching terms or concepts, this paragraph would be a good location. In her article (Khersonskaya & Smith, 1998), Khersonskaya cited Feinman and Gill's (1978) idea that having physical attractiveness standards ensures that desirable traits would endure through genetic selection. She also covered the notion of the physical attractiveness stereotype, whereby physically attractive people are assumed to possess other socially desirable traits such as social competence, intelligence, and being well adjusted (Eagly et al., 1991). This research that Khersonskaya cited was generally relevant to the topic of physical attractiveness but not to her specific research question, which is why she included it at the beginning of the introduction.

Middle

In the middle of the introduction, you should begin to cover (write about) the research articles that are more relevant to your topic. It is impossible to define the middle in terms of length—the length will depend on how many articles you cite in the introduction. If you cover 20 articles, the middle will be longer than if you cover only 10 articles. Again, though, think in terms of the funnel analogy. Articles earlier in the middle part of the introduction should be somewhat broader than the ones that come later in the introduction. Khersonskaya's first sentence of her second paragraph should give you a good sense of how the transition from broad to more specific proceeds: "Evidence of the importance of physical attractiveness in human interaction exists in many cultures" (Khersonskaya & Smith, 1998, p. 39). The narrowing here occurs through Khersonskaya's inclusion of both of her main topics—physical attractiveness *and* cultural comparison. At the same time, the sentence is still somewhat general because it doesn't yet address cross-cultural comparisons or facial attractiveness.

As you continue to write the middle section of your literature review, keep narrowing the focus of the research articles. As noted in Chapter 6, be sure to carefully link your articles together logically—that is, each new article that you write about should build on the results of the previous study. These logical links (transitions) will help you document the development of knowledge in the field over time about your research topic. For more information about writing effective transitions, see the A CLOSER LOOK . . . at Transitions box. Can you see the logical link and the narrowing in the following two sentences (Khersonskaya & Smith, 1998, p. 39)?

> White adults responded positively to neonate features when judging both men . . . and women. . . . Further research showed that adult faces with neonate features received higher attractiveness ratings from participants of 13 nationalities. . . .

(I omitted citations from the sentences so that you can better concentrate on the wording.) The logical link is that both sentences cite research about studying reactions to adult faces with neonatal features (e.g., large eyes, smooth skin, small nose). There are two good examples of narrowing: The first sentence refers to "White adults," whereas the second sentence mentions "participants of 13 nationalities." Thus, the subject pool in the second sentence is much broader and more typical of cross-cultural research. Also, the dependent variable mentioned vaguely in the first sentence is "responded positively to," whereas it is "attractiveness ratings" in the second sentence. Thus, the second outcome variable is more specific and more in line with Khersonskaya's interest.

A CLOSER LOOK
at Transitions

In Chapter 6, I emphasized the importance of transition sentences to telling the story of how your research area developed over time. It is critical for a reader to be able to follow your train of thought as you transition from one study to the next and from one paragraph to the next. Your paragraphs *must* flow smoothly so that they tell a story rather than appearing to be descriptions of research studies randomly pieced together one paragraph at a time. To help emphasize the importance of transitions in your writing, I have compiled some advice from experts.

Continued • • •

"As a rule, begin each paragraph either with a sentence that suggests the topic or with a sentence that helps the transition. If a paragraph forms part of a larger composition, its relation to what precedes, or its function as part of the whole, may need to be expressed" (Strunk & White, 2000, p. 16).

"When editing your writing, use additional transitional devices to make it less choppy" (APA, 2020, p. 112).

The *APA Manual* suggests using transitional words to help your flow of thought, such as a pronoun referring to a noun in the previous sentence (also helps to reduce repetition); but make sure that the reference is clear (APA, 2020, p. 120). You can also use transitional words to show links (APA, 2020, p. 112) such as time (e.g., "then," "next"), cause–effect (e.g., "therefore," "as a result"), addition (e.g., "in addition," "furthermore"), or contrast (e.g., "but," "however").

Sternberg (2003) noted that even clearly written sentences that are missing transitions can result in disjointed and choppy writing. You may be writing sentence A and already be thinking about sentence B. By the time you finish writing sentence A, your thinking has skipped forward to sentence C, so you write sentence C without actually writing sentence B. Although your thought process likely is clear to you, it may not be clear to the reader.

"Missing transitions can be inserted if you reread your paper, checking carefully whether each sentence follows logically from the sentence immediately preceding it" (Sternberg, 2003, p. 75).

Notice how each of these ideas captures the importance of intentionality in your writing. To write clearly with transitions linking your ideas together, you must intentionally focus on writing good transitions. To take Sternberg's advice, you must intentionally complete your writing early enough so that you have the time to carefully reread it to look for problem areas. These ideas dovetail nicely with the advice provided in Chapter 1 of this book.

You should continue this pattern of narrowing your literature review throughout the middle section of the introduction. As people read the introduction, they should get a better and better idea of your specific research topic and direction. This continual narrowing throughout the introduction is the key feature that distinguishes this type of literature review from the term paper/literature review covered in Chapter 6, which primarily concerned tracing the development from older research to the most current research.

End

At the end of your introduction, typically in the last paragraph, you will introduce the specific rationale for the proposed experiment. As noted earlier, at this point you narrow the discussion to one specific study or theoretical issue on which you base your proposed experiment. Perhaps the simpler of these approaches is to base your proposed experiment on one specific study. Typically, this process would entail reading a relatively recent journal article, realizing that an unanswered question remains, and proposing an experiment to answer that question.

For example, Elizabeth Posey, another student from one of my research classes, became interested in the self-serving bias after taking a Social Psychology class. As she read more about that topic, she found two important gaps in the research literature: Whitley and Frieze (1985) showed that children displayed self-serving bias in artificial experimental tasks but noted that researchers tended to avoid using academic tasks in their studies because students might not use lack of effort as an excuse for failure, thereby making it difficult to find evidence of self-serving bias. Posey wished to test this idea, so she used an academic task in her experiment. Based on the Whitley and Frieze study, she narrowed her focus to one specific question: "I sought to determine whether an academic task made a difference in whether children exhibited the self-serving bias" (Posey & Smith, 2003, p. 154).

Rather than focusing on one specific study, Khersonskaya addressed a theoretical issue at the end of her literature review (Khersonskaya & Smith, 1998). This approach is often somewhat more complex than deriving your research idea from one research study. In her introduction, Khersonskaya focused on two threads of research. One thread showed that people from different cultures had similar ideals of physical attractiveness (Cunningham, 1986; Cunningham et al., 1990; Cunningham et al., 1995; Langlois et al., 1991; Perret et al., 1994). However, another line of research (Cunningham, 1986; Cunningham et al., 1995; Thakerar & Iwawaki, 1979) showed that there were cultural differences regarding images of physical attractiveness. These sentences spotlight an important search strategy described in the IN PRACTICE: Author Searching box.

IN PRACTICE

Author Searching

The sentences describing the two threads of research Khersonskaya (Khersonskaya & Smith, 1998) focused on highlight an important literature-searching tip first mentioned in the previous chapter—searching for a specific author. Researchers often engage in programmatic research, studying a narrow topic more and more deeply. When you look at my two sentences about the lines of research above this box, you will see the name Cunningham cited as an author in three different studies. When Khersonskaya found the first study by Cunningham, she was able to conduct a search by using his name and found the other two highly related studies.

Based on these studies, Khersonskaya faced dueling lines of research that would lead to different predicted outcomes. She predicted that she would find differences between cultures when they rated attractiveness of members of one culture (Americans), hypothesizing that same-culture attractiveness ratings would be higher than different-culture ratings. She specifically predicted that ratings of American faces would be

higher by American participants than by European participants. The difference in theoretical predictions was why Khersonskaya proposed the experiment that she conducted. The
rationale for her experiment is clear-cut, as is the question that
she asked. Achieving these two objectives—clear rationale *and*
question—should be your goal for the end of the introduction.

Writing Your Method Section

As covered in Chapter 4, a Method section typically contains
information about the subjects who participated in the experiment, the equipment or materials used in the experiment, and the
procedures that the experimenter used and the subjects experienced during the experiment. Your proposed Method section will
contain the same information except that you are presenting your
future plans for each of these aspects of the methodology. Each
of these aspects of information has its own subsection within
the Method section (see the next three chapter sections, starting
below). When you lay out your plans in this way, your instructor
and the IRB are able to scrutinize and comment on your ideas.

Participants/Subjects

When you read older journal articles dealing with humans, you
will see this subsection labeled "Subjects"; APA Style changed
to "Participants" in a previous edition of the *APA Publication
Manual* (APA, 1994). In the sixth edition of the *APA Manual*
(APA, 2020, p. 141), use of either term is deemed permissible—
although "participants" seems a little more dignified to me than
"subjects" does. If you plan to use animals in your research, "subjects" is the preferred term. To show respect for your subjects,
avoid the word "use" when describing their participation (e.g., do
not write "I plan to use 40 subjects in my experiment."). Thus,
although you may read different labels for this subsection, its purpose remains the same in different articles.

In this subsection, you will provide important details about
the subject population you intend to work with in your experiment. As the *APA Manual* (APA, 2020, pp. 82–83) specifies, you

must describe your sample well. Given that you are writing a proposal, you will be unable to provide many of the details about the
participants that you will eventually include in the final report—
information such as average age, sex breakdown, exact number,
and so on. However, you are presenting a plan, so detail how
many participants you *plan* to include in your experiment. Also
note how you plan to recruit or find participants: Will they come
from a subject pool of psychology students or be volunteers? Will
participants have any inducement for participating such as extra
credit or partial class credit? If you plan to have any inclusion or
exclusion criteria (i.e., any characteristics that participants must
have to participate [e.g., 20/20 vision] or any characteristics that
would exclude people from participating [e.g., cannot be younger
than age 21]), you should list them in the proposal.

Apparatus/Materials/Testing Instruments/Measures

This subsection also has different names as possibilities. In
this subsection, you will describe what you plan to use in your
experiment to manipulate each independent variable (IV) and
measure each dependent variable (DV). Select the term that
is most appropriate for what you plan to use. The most clear-
cut term is "apparatus"—if you use any equipment, that term
is appropriate. You might plan to use equipment for either
presenting your IV or for measuring your DV. The remaining
terms are more flexible. "Materials" would seem to apply well
to stimuli (typically IVs) such as slides, pictures, videos, and the
like. "Testing instruments" and "measures" would seem to fit
primarily DVs, particularly paper-and-pencil tests (e.g., personality tests) or forms. "Testing instruments" seems to fit standardized tests; "measures" is probably better for tests that you plan to
devise or that you find in the research literature. If you plan to
use more than one of the categories listed, you can combine the
names. Thus, you might use the title "Materials and Apparatus"
or any other combination for this subsection. Table 7.1 briefly
summarizes the naming considerations when you are working
on your Method section.

TABLE 7.1	Naming the Second Subsection of the Method Section
Possible Name of Subsection	**Content of Subsection**
Apparatus	Equipment of any type
Materials	IV stimuli (e.g., words, pictures, videos)
Testing Instruments	Standardized psychological tests or assessments
Measures	Self-devised tests (or found on the web)

Note. The content used can refer to IV manipulations or DV measurements. If you use more than one type of content, use a name that reflects both (e.g., "Apparatus and Materials").

Just as in your Introduction, you should provide a citation and reference for any information that you use from previous researchers. Thus, if you use the same test or measure as previous researchers, be sure to give them credit for that idea.

It would not be unusual for your instructor or the IRB to require you to submit actual copies of any materials you plan to use. Thus, it is critical to pay attention to materials that previous researchers have used when you are reading the articles from your literature search: You should learn much more by reading previous research than simply what the researchers discovered.

Procedure

The Procedure subsection is where you describe your plan for actually conducting the experiment. Here, you will provide a step-by-step account of what you plan to do from the moment your participants arrive until they leave. Include important details of what you plan to do, but avoid unnecessary details. For example, if you plan to seat participants in every other seat so that they cannot see the work of other participants, you should include that detail. In contrast, it is probably not important to specify that participants will participate in a 30-seat (versus 50-seat) classroom or that they will use #2 pencils to complete the forms unless those details are part of your experimental manipulations. It is often difficult to plan exactly what you want to do, so be sure to write this section as a draft and then revisit it repeatedly over several days' time so that the plan makes sense, is logically designed, and is actually feasible. For example, planning to have participants complete 14 different measures in a 30-minute period is probably not a realistic plan. As always, if your planned procedures rely on ideas from other researchers, you should give them credit with a citation and reference.

This section is also where you should address your plans to deal with some prominent ethical concerns for researchers. Standard 8 of APA's ethical principles (APA, 2002, pp. 1069–1071) involves research and publication. Four principles are particularly important to you.

- *Principle 8.01* (p. 1069) mandates that you receive institutional approval for conducting your experiment. As mentioned previously, you will need to submit a proposal to your school's IRB.
- *Principle 3.10* (p. 1065) and *Principle 8.02* (p. 1069) spell out the requirement of **informed consent**, which says that you should obtain written agreement from your participants that they are willing to participate *after* you have described the research and any factors (e.g., risks, benefits, confidentiality) that might affect their willingness to participate and have given them the opportunity to ask questions. Be sure to read Principle 8.02, as it provides you with eight detailed descriptions of the type of information participants should receive from you.
- *Principle 8.07* (p. 1070) addresses the use of deception in research. Deceiving participants during an experiment is not something you should plan lightly. If you think that you need to mislead participants, you must provide adequate justification for doing so.
- *Principle 8.08* (p. 1070) says that you should plan to debrief your participants after they have completed the experiment. In other words, you should tell them everything you can about the experiment, what they did, why they did it, and what you are trying to find. Part of the rationale for requiring introductory students to participate in research is

for them to learn about the research process—if you don't debrief them fully, they won't understand what took place and why. If you did use any deception, you should tell the participants and justify why you used it.

If you used any **confederates** (people who appeared to be participants but were not), you should inform the participants and perhaps even reunite the participants with the confederates. The debriefing session is important to make certain that your participants leave feeling good about what they did and respecting the discipline of psychology. For more ideas and details about planning your debriefing session, consult Aronson and Carlsmith (1968, pp. 29–36, 70–73).

One last caution about debriefing: As you work on your proposal, be sure to take the debriefing session into account in your time schedule. If your experimental process will take a full 30 minutes, then proposing to give participants only 30 minutes of credit for participating will be inadequate because you have not included time for debriefing.

Design/Statistical Analysis

It is possible that your instructor will require you to add another subsection to your Method section beyond the three standard subsections described so far. In some cases, you may need to demonstrate that you understand what type of experimental design and what type of statistical analysis your proposed experiment will need. Such a requirement would be based on the fact that you have learned such information in a current or previous course devoted to statistics and/or research methodology. The type of information necessary to address such issues is beyond the scope of this text, but you should be able to glean the appropriate information from statistics or research methods textbooks.

References

Remember to end your proposal with a list of references formatted in APA Style. You can find pointers on APA-Style references for journal articles in Chapter 5 and for books and book chapters in Chapter 6. One of the most important steps is to confirm that your citations and references are an exact match—that is, the names and dates should be identical. If your instructor finds different spellings of a name or different dates for citations and references, it makes your work look sloppy. Every citation should have a corresponding reference, and every reference should have a corresponding citation. Finding citations with missing references or references with missing citations also makes your work look careless. Also, beware of typing a reference entry exactly the way it appears in a published article—that article may have been published before the current edition of the *APA Manual* (2020) and thus now be formatted incorrectly. See the IN PRACTICE: Avoiding Citation/Reference Mismatches box for hints to help you avoid errors.

IN PRACTICE

Avoiding Citation/Reference Mismatches

In Chapter 6 I provided a pointer that can help you avoid mismatched citations and references: Every time you insert a citation in your paper, put the corresponding name(s) and date into a draft reference list. There is no need to interrupt the flow of your writing and insert the complete reference at this point, but the listing of names and dates will prompt you to complete each reference later, either at the end of your writing session for the day or after you complete your proposal.

Another practice that will help you avoid mismatched citations and references is to use the "Find" function in Word after you complete your proposal. As you proofread your proposal and come to a citation, click on "Find" and type the author's name into the search window. You should get at least two hits for each search—one for the citation and one for the reference. If you find only one hit from the citation, then either you omitted that author from your reference list or you misspelled the author's name in one location. Likewise, if you find only one hit from your reference list, either you misspelled the name somewhere or you did not cite that author in your proposal.

APA-Style Considerations

The previous chapters covered quite a few APA-Style considerations. However, as with any specific type of writing assignment, there are critical differences in APA Style for a research proposal versus an annotated bibliography.

Completing Your Proposal

Your instructor might have different requirements, but a research proposal usually entails an introduction, Method section, and list of references. You will probably add a title page, formatted as shown in Chapter 5 (see Figure 5.4 or 5.5, depending on your instructor's preference). You should format the introduction as explained in Chapter 6 and the reference list as discussed in Chapters 5 and 6. For APA formatting throughout the entire proposal, refer to the advice from Chapter 2 about using a saved APA-Style file or using the APA-Style template that Microsoft has created (*if* it has been updated to the seventh edition of the *APA Manual*).

Formatting the Method Section

After you complete your introduction, the Method section follows immediately on the next line—no new page, so it could begin at the top, middle, or bottom portion of the page. The word "Method" is a Level 1 heading (APA, 2020, pp. 47–49; see Figure 6.2 for information on headings), centered, boldfaced, and capitalized (first letter only). Your first subsection (Participants or Subjects) on the subsequent line is a Level 2 heading (APA, 2020, pp. 48–49), flush left, boldfaced, and capitalized (first letter only). To add the information about your participants, go to the next line, indent, and type in your regular font. You will format the other subsection headings identically to the first, although capitalize only words of four letters or more (APA, 2020, p. 167). Thus, if you used a subsection that included both apparatus and materials, the correct format would be shown as **Apparatus and Materials** flush against the left margin of the page.

Headings

Recall that APA format uses different types of headings to organize a manuscript (APA, 2020, pp. 47–49). Figure 6.2 presents the five levels of headings used in APA papers.

Writing Considerations

The first writing consideration I mention here is not an APA-Style guideline because the *APA Manual* (APA, 2020) does not cover research proposals. Because a research proposal is a plan for an experiment that you will conduct in the future, you should use future tense for verbs in your proposal's Method section (unless your instructor says otherwise). A research report uses past tense verbs because the researcher conducted the experiment in the past (such as the research you cover in your introduction). Thus, as you write your proposed methodology, remember that you will likely use the word "will" a great deal—it is the typical way of expressing simple future tense.

The remaining writing considerations are components of APA Style and are reminders from earlier in the book. Chapter 3 addressed the APA guideline of trying to avoid passive voice (APA, 2020, pp. 118, 142). The *APA Manual* does not totally forbid using passive voice if your focus is on an object rather than the actor: For example, writing "The computers were placed on the table" would focus attention on the location of the computers, not who placed them there, which is the appropriate focus for the Method section (APA, 2020, p. 118).

Based on my experience, when attempting to write in future tense, many students lapse into using passive voice along with future tense. By being alert to passive voice, however, you can avoid this type of problem. For example, in your discussion of the proposed methodology, you might write, "A math test will be completed by participants to delay the recall test," which would be passive voice ("will be completed"). The "math test" is not actually the subject of that sentence (it is not doing anything) but rather the object. One way to avoid the passivity here is to write, "Participants will complete a math test to delay the recall test." In this case, the participants *are* doing something and thus serve as the subject of the sentence. Another way to avoid passive voice is to use yourself as the subject of the sentence: "I will administer a math test to participants to delay the recall test." Although many psychology instructors believe that APA Style precludes using first person, it does not. The *APA Manual* (APA, 2020, pp. 119–120) even includes two example sentences using first-person subjects to avoid passive voice. Furthermore, the *APA Manual* (p. 120) cautions against using third person to refer to yourself as the experimenter (e.g., "The experimenter will administer a math test . . . ." when you are the experimenter) and provides a first-person example as a substitute.

The second reminder for APA Style (see Chapter 2) is to use scientific style in your writing. I have often read proposed Method sections that students wrote in a conversational or informal style. Writing scientifically is important for all writing in psychology; it is especially critical in your proposed Method section, where you are attempting to clearly and concisely communicate your plan for your experiment, including operational definitions of the IV and DV. If you are not familiar with operational definitions, refer to Chapter 3 (see the "Nouns" section). You *must* define your variables in terms of the operations you used to bring them about. As noted in Chapter 3, rather than referring to hungry rats, you could operationally define "hungry" as the number of hours of food deprivation that the rats have experienced. Rather than labeling your proposed participants as "children" or "adults," you should provide a specific age range, minimum age (for the adults), or some similar precise definition. See the *APA Manual* (2020, p. 135) for the appropriate terms to use for different age groups. Although there is no guarantee that you will be able (eventually) to get the exact participants you propose, you should still be precise about your proposed methodology. Be sure to avoid vague writing everywhere, but especially in this section: Be "certain that every word means exactly what you intend" (APA, 2020, p. 113).

Editing Your Paper/APA-Style Considerations

As emphasized in Chapter 6, you should thoroughly edit your proposal before turning it in to your instructor. Carefully scrutinize the writing in terms of both grammar and APA Style as you edit. I provided several tips in the previous chapter to assist you during this process. First, pay attention to Word's grammatical help feature. Second, read your paper aloud so that you can more easily detect grammar problems and odd-sounding phrases and sentences. Third, work with a peer to edit each other's papers. Fourth, look back at Chapter 1 for proofing, editing, and revising suggestions. Fifth, look at my table with Common Writing Problems, Explanations, and Solutions in Appendix C.

Concluding Thoughts

This chapter has dealt with a common type of writing assignment for psychology majors: a research proposal. If you are among the majority of psychology majors nationwide who have a program requirement of conducting an original experiment, this type of proposal may well be a precursor to conducting and reporting on that research project. By contrast, you might take an upper level psychology course that requires you to develop a research proposal without any expectation that you conduct the proposed experiment. In either case, the points in this chapter should be relevant. Next on this book's agenda is guidance on writing your final research report after having completed your experiment.

Critical Thinking Writing Assignments

Write a paragraph in answer to each of the following questions aimed at a student who has the assignment to write a term paper or develop an experimental idea but who has no idea where to begin.

Assignment 1
What is a research proposal? How can compiling an annotated bibliography help you develop a research proposal?

Assignment 2
Why is it critical to prepare a literature review as part of your research proposal?

Assignment 3
Why is the shape of a funnel a good analogy for a literature review (introduction) of a research proposal?

Assignment 4
What is the purpose of a Method section in a research proposal?

References

American Psychological Association. (1994). *Publication manual of the American Psychological Association* (4th ed.).

American Psychological Association. (2002). Ethical principles of psychologists and code of conduct. *American Psychologist, 57*(12), 1060–1073. https://doi.org/10.1037//0003-066x.57.12.1060

American Psychological Association. (2020). *Publication manual of the American Psychological Association* (7th ed.). https://doi.org/10.1037/0000165-000

Aronson, E., & Carlsmith, J. M. (1968). Experimentation in social psychology. In G. Lindzey & E. Aronson (Eds.), *The handbook of social psychology* (2nd ed., Vol. 2, pp. 1–79). Addison-Wesley.

Beins, B. C. (2008). Why we believe: Fostering critical thought and scientific literacy in research methods. In D. S. Dunn, J. S. Halonen, & R. A. Smith (Eds.), *Teaching critical thinking in psychology: A handbook of best practices* (pp. 199–210). Wiley-Blackwell. https://doi.org/10.1002/9781444305173.ch17

Brewer, C. L., Hopkins, J. R., Kimble, G. A., Matlin, M. W., McCann, L. I., McNeil, O. V., Nodine, B. F., Quinn, V. N., & Saundra. (1993). Curriculum. In T. V. McGovern (Ed.), *Handbook for enhancing undergraduate education in psychology* (pp. 161–182). American Psychological Association. https://doi.org/10.1037/10126-000

Cunningham, M. R. (1986). Measuring the physical in physical attractiveness: Quasi-experiments on the sociobiology of female facial beauty. *Journal of Personality and Social Psychology, 50*(5), 925–935. https://doi.org/10.1037/0022-3514.50.5.925

Cunningham, M. R., Barbee, A. P., & Pike, C. L. (1990). What do women want? Facialmetric assessment of multiple motives in the perception of male facial physical attractiveness. *Journal of Personality and Social Psychology, 59*(1), 61–72. https://doi.org/10.1037/0022-3514.59.1.61

Cunningham, M. R., Roberts, A. R., Barbee, A. P., Druen, P. B., & Wu, C.-W. (1995). "Their ideas of beauty are, on the whole, the same as ours": Consistency and variability in the cross-cultural perception of female physical attractiveness. *Journal of Personality and Social Psychology, 68*(2), 261–279. https://doi.org/10.1037/0022-3514.68.2.261

Dunn, D. S., Brewer, C. L., Cautin, R. L., Gurung, R. A. R., Keith, K. D., McGregor, L. N., Nida, S. A., Puccio, P., & Voigt, M. J. (2010). The undergraduate psychology curriculum: Call for a core. In D. F. Halpern (Ed.), *Undergraduate education in psychology: A blueprint for the future of the discipline* (pp. 47–61). American Psychological Association. https://doi.org/10.1037/12063-003

Eagly, A. H., Ashmore, R. D., Makhijani, M. G., & Longo, L. C. (1991). What is beautiful is good, but …: A meta-analytic review of research on the physical attractiveness stereotype. *Psychological Bulletin, 110*(1), 109–128. https://doi.org/10.1037//0033-2909.110.1.109

Feinman, S., & Gill, G. W. (1978). Sex differences in physical attractiveness preferences. *Journal of Social Psychology, 105*(1), 43–52. https://doi.org/10.1080/00224545.1978.9924089

Gitter, A. G., Lomranz, J., Saxe, L., & Bar-Tal, Y. (1983). Perceptions of female physique characteristics by American and Israeli students. *Journal of Social Psychology, 121*(1), 7–13. https://doi.org/10.1080/00224545.1983.9924460

Khersonskaya, M. Y., & Smith, R. A. (1998). Cross-cultural differences in perception of physical attractiveness. *Psi Chi Journal of Undergraduate Research, 3*(1), 39–42. https://doi.org/10.24839/1089-4136.jn3.1.39

Langlois, J. H., Ritter, J. M., Roggman, L. A., & Vaughn, L. S. (1991). Facial diversity and infant preferences for attractive faces. *Developmental Psychology, 27*(1), 79–84. https://doi.org/10.1037//0012-1649.27.1.79

Norcross, J. C., Hailstorks, R., Aiken, L. S., Pfund, R. A., Stamm, K. E., & Christidis, P. (2016). Undergraduate study in psychology: Curriculum and assessment. *American Psychologist, 71*(2), 89–101. https://doi.org/10.1037/a0040095

Orcher, L. T. (2014). *Conducting research: Social and behavioral science methods* (2nd ed.). Pyrczak. https://doi.org/10.4324/9781315266626

Perlman, B., & McCann, L. I. (2005). Undergraduate research experiences in psychology: A national study of courses and curricula. *Teaching of Psychology, 32*(1), 5–14. https://doi.org/10.1207/s15328023top3201_2

Perrett, D. I., May, K. A., & Yoshikawa, S. (1994). Facial shape and judgements of female attractiveness. *Nature, 368*(6468), 239–242. https://doi.org/10.1038/368239a0

Posey, E., & Smith, R. A. (2003). The self-serving bias in children. *Psi Chi Journal of Undergraduate Research, 8*(4), 153–156. https://doi.org/10.24839/1089-4136.jn8.4.153

Robinson, E. S., & Brown, M. A. (1926). Effect of serial position upon memorization. *American Journal of Psychology, 37*(4), 538–552. https://doi.org/10.2307/1414914

Rundus, D. (1971). Analysis of rehearsal processes in free recall. *Journal of Experimental Psychology, 89*(1), 63–77. https://doi.org/10.1037/h0031185

Saville, B. K., Zinn, T. E., Lawrence, N. K., Barron, K. E., & Andre, J. (2008). Teaching critical thinking in statistics and research methods.

In D. S. Dunn, J. S. Halonen, & R. A. Smith (Eds.), *Teaching critical thinking in psychology: A handbook of best practices* (pp. 149–160). Wiley-Blackwell. https://doi.org/10.1002/9781444305173.ch13

Smith, R. A., & Davis, S. F. (2013). *The psychologist as detective: An introduction to conducting research in psychology* (6th ed.). Pearson.

Sternberg, R. J. (2003). *The psychologist's companion: A guide to scientific writing for students and researchers* (4th ed.). Cambridge University Press. https://doi.org/10.1017/CBO9780511819261

Stroop, J. R. (1935). Studies of interference in serial verbal reactions. *Journal of Experimental Psychology, 18*(6), 643–663. https://doi.org/10.1037/h0054651

Strunk, W., Jr., & White, E. B. (2000). *The elements of style* (4th ed.). Pearson Education.

Thakerar, J. N., & Iwawaki, S. (1979). Cross-cultural comparisons in interpersonal attraction of females toward males. *Journal of Social Psychology, 108*(1), 121–122. https://doi.org/10.1080/00224545.1979.9711969

Whitley, B. E., Jr., & Frieze, I. H. (1985). Children's causal attributions for success and failure in achievement settings: A meta-analysis. *Journal of Educational Psychology, 77*(5), 608–616. https://doi.org/10.1037/0022-0663.77.5.608

8

Writing a Psychology Research Report

Do You Know?

Can you list the elements and sections that belong in a research report?

What material from your research proposal do you need to revise for your research report?

What information should you include in your abstract?

How do you write your statistical results in your Results section?

How can you create a table to display your findings?

How can you create an APA-Style graph using Excel?

How do you provide the bottom line for your research report?

"Once you have analyzed your data and thought about your results, you are ready to report them."

—Sternberg, 2003, p. 47–53

As a psychology major, you will probably conduct a psychological experiment at some point in your career (see Chapter 7). The goal of this chapter is to help you with the final step in the research process—writing a report about your research.

Why Do You Need to Write a Research Report?

Since the 1890s, psychologists have focused on writing relatively brief accounts of their research because of the influence of Joseph Jastrow (Blumenthal, 1991). Jastrow wrote a series of brief reports about research studies conducted at the University of Wisconsin laboratory that contrasted with the longer essays published in psychology journals up to that time. "These short articles first stated a simple problem, described a research method, then findings and data analysis, then a conclusion, all in a few pages" (Blumenthal, 1991, p. 82). Thus, there is a long tradition of psychologists writing experimental reports about their research. As you may be able to tell from the description of Jastrow's articles, he set the standard for what we know today as APA Style.

An important part of the scientific enterprise is sharing results with other scientists. The only way for scientists to build a body of knowledge about a topic is to publish their findings so that other scientists can read those findings and add to them. If you think back to the process of writing an introduction for your research proposal, you can see how important the publication process is. If other psychologists had not published their findings, you would have had nothing on which to build your research idea. Likewise, our knowledge about psychology would not advance much because people would be doing research willy-nilly, without any regard for what other researchers before them had found. Even if your career goal is to become a practicing psychologist such as a clinician or counselor, you should appreciate the importance of research knowledge. Without research results to back up practice, psychologist practitioners might use dangerous or useless techniques with their clients. Just as you would not want a physician to use untested treatments on you, you should not want to use untested techniques with your (future) clients. Even if you do not conduct any research projects in the future, the ability to write an experimental report will help you read and interpret journal articles that could be important to your practice.

It is these traditions, then, that led up to the assignment to write a research report about your experiment. Your instructor is helping indoctrinate you into the ways of research psychologists. If you do plan to go to graduate school for further training, having conducted an experiment and written a research report will be helpful for your graduate school entrance chances. In Chapter 4, I related the experience of Eugenio Peluso (now PhD) who conducted undergraduate research to help get into a clinical psychology graduate program. Appendix A spotlights his published article (Peluso, 2000).

What Goes in Your Research Report?

Earlier chapters in this book covered the elements of journal articles, so we will not rehash all of that information here. The following list identifies the elements that belong in your experimental report and the chapters in which information about these elements appears:

Title page (Chapters 4, 5, and 6)

Abstract (Chapters 4, 5, and 6)

Introduction (Chapters 4, 6, and 7)

Method (Chapters 4 and 7)

Results (Chapter 4)

Discussion (Chapters 4 and 7)

References (Chapters 4, 5, 6, and 7)

Footnotes/Appendices/Supplemental Materials (Chapter 4)

The chapters on specific writing assignments (Chapter 5: annotated bibliography; Chapter 6: term paper or literature review; Chapter 7: research proposal) provide information about how to create a title page, introduction, Method section, and reference list. This chapter focuses on the tasks remaining for you—writing an abstract, a Results section, and a Discussion section. Those sections, combined with all the others listed previously, will end up forming your research report. To help make this chapter more concrete, you can refer to Appendix C, where you will find Peluso's manuscript that led to his article. Although Peluso wrote his manuscript using an older edition of the *APA Manual*, I marked his article in Appendix A with edits (see Appendix B) necessary to reflect the current edition of the *Publication Manual of the American Psychological Association* (APA, 2020). Appendix C contains a Word version of Peluso's manuscript updated to the current version of APA Style (APA, 2020) based on the edits in Appendix B.

The Good News

There is good news about writing your research report *if* you previously wrote a research proposal as outlined in Chapter 7. That proposal likely consisted of a title page, introduction, Method section, and references. Therefore, you will have already written nearly half of the final paper for your experimental report. The major new work you have left will be writing the abstract, Results, and Discussion sections. You may or may not need to compile appendices or footnotes. Perhaps your introduction and references will need some touch-up work, and you will definitely need to rework the Method section. So keep plugging away: The end is in sight!

Revising the Material You Have Already Written

The information in this section assumes that you wrote a research proposal before you conducted your experiment. If you did not have to submit a proposal, then you will need to read the information about these sections covered in the previous chapters.

Title Page

Given the material on your title page (title, author, affiliation; see Figures 5.4 and 5.5), it is unlikely that you would need to edit any of that information at this point. However, be certain to check with your instructor about which type of title page (professional or student) you should use. Because you have now completed your experiment, double-check your title (and, therefore, your running head, if required) to make sure it still fits the entire research project and report. Sometimes unexpected findings can turn what was originally a good title into something of a misfit at this point. Although it is unlikely to be relevant to your experimental report, remember that you can provide information about a change in your current institution in the Author Note (if one is required)—for example, if you submitted a paper you wrote at your undergraduate institution for publication after you went to graduate school.

Introduction

It may be tempting to leave your introduction (literature review) untouched from your research proposal (see Chapter 7). However, as a conscientious student, you should revisit it in a couple of ways.

Update Your Literature Review

First, you should check PsycINFO to determine whether you need to update your review of the literature. Have researchers published any important studies about your topic in the time since you originally wrote the proposal? The likelihood of new studies depends on the timeline of your proposal and your actual experiment. Two departments in which I taught offered research courses that spanned an entire year, with the proposal written in the first semester and the experiment conducted in the second semester. With several months' time intervening between the two activities, it is certainly possible that new and important studies have come out. By comparison, if you are in a class in which you develop a proposal *and* conduct your study in a single semester, the likelihood of new studies being published is much lower, though still possible.

Update Your Experiment Rationale

In the last paragraph of the introduction you wrote for your proposal, you most likely laid out the rationale or hypotheses for your planned experiment. You should recheck this paragraph (and more, if necessary) to make sure your rationale makes sense given the results you found and the conclusions you will draw. Also, check your verb tense: Now that you have conducted your experiment, you should use past tense. For example, "I hypothesize that . . . " (in your proposal) would become "I hypothesized that . . . " (in the final paper).

Method

You will definitely need to update at least one thing in your Method section—the verb tense. In your proposal, you should have used future tense because you wrote about the plan for your experiment (see Chapter 7). Now that you have conducted the experiment, you should change the verbs to past tense because you are writing about things you have already done.

Another element of your Method section may also need updating. It is often the case that the methodology you originally proposed and the methodology you actually ended up using will not be the same. It is difficult to anticipate exactly how your proposed methodology will work out until you actually attempt to implement it. So, if you had to modify the methodology that you proposed, you need to update your Method section to reflect what you actually did while conducting the experiment. Presumably, these changes will be minor, but you do need to incorporate them in your final report.

References

The updating you need to do for your references (see Chapters 5 and 6 for information about how to format references) will depend on any updating you have done for your introduction/ literature review. If you added new articles (citations) to the introduction, make sure to add the corresponding references to this section. None of the information related to your original references will have changed.

Writing New Material for Your Report

As mentioned earlier, the new material you will write is an abstract, the Results section, and the Discussion section. Let's look at what is required for each of these elements.

Abstract

Chapter 4 explained that an abstract is similar to a summary of your entire research project. The *APA Publication Manual of the American Psychological Association* (American Psychological Association [APA], 2020, p. 38) says that abstracts typically contain no more than 250 words, but does not set a specific length. Thus, you should ask your instructor about the specific word limit for your abstract.

The *Publication Manual* (APA, 2020, p. 74) identifies five items that should go in an abstract for an empirical study: the problem, information about participants, study methodology, findings, and conclusions and implications/applications (see Chapter 4 for further details). However, the *Manual* (p. 74) also notes that you should "include only the four or five most important concepts, findings, or implications." Additionally, the *Manual* (2020, p. 73) recommends the use of active voice in the abstract. Clearly, writing a good abstract is a challenge!

Many published abstracts likely do not cover all the bulleted points listed in the *APA Manual* (APA, 2020). But don't rely on others' deficiencies as an excuse for writing an incomplete abstract! There really is no need to attempt to write your abstract until you have finished writing the rest of your paper. When you are ready to write your abstract, go back and read the abstracts of articles that you cited and referenced in your paper. Rereading those abstracts will help you get comfortable with the style that other experimenters have used for this important element of an experimental paper.

As an example, look at the abstract for the sample published journal article (Peluso, 2000) included in Appendix A, which consists of 122 words. Can you find information about the problem, participants, methodology, findings, and conclusions/

implications in that abstract? As mentioned earlier, you may not find information pertaining to all of the *APA Manual*'s (APA, 2020, p. 74) critical points in all abstracts. For help in locating the important information in the abstract, see A CLOSER LOOK . . . at Peluso's Abstract With Comments.

A CLOSER LOOK
at Peluso's Abstract With Comments

Abstract and comments

Skilled Motor Performance as a Function of Types of Mental Imagery

[1]*This study examined the effects of mental imagery on skilled motor performance.* [2]*Participants, 48 volunteers from introductory psychology classes, were assigned to either of two treatment groups or to a control group.* [3]*Skilled motor performance was assessed by the number of errors and the speed with which participants performed pick-up jacks and mirror tracing tasks. Between trials, participants engaged in either relevant imagery (i.e., the tasks), irrelevant imagery (i.e., scenic environments), or no imagery. Analysis of variance was used to test for differences between groups.* [4]*Following five imagery sessions, participants in the relevant imagery group committed significantly fewer errors than those in the other groups.* [5]*Directions for further research include an assessment of imagery for tasks emphasizing speed versus fine motor coordination.*

> (1) In the sentence numbered 1, Peluso (2000) addressed the problem. It may not be very clear to you what the problem is, but the topic (effect of imagery on motor performance) is clear. On the other hand, to a reader who knows the mental imagery research literature, the problem might be clear. Part of the idea behind you reading journal articles in your research area is to understand that area and develop some expertise about it.
>
> (2) The sentence numbered 2 provides information about the participants.
>
> (3) The two sentences after number 3 give information about the study's methodology.
>
> (4) The sentence numbered 4 lays out the results of the experiment.
>
> (5) The sentence numbered 5 provides a direction for future research rather than a conclusion or implication.

A simple strategy for writing your abstract is to write a sentence (or two, at most) for each of the five bulleted points in the *APA Manual* (APA, 2020, p. 74). See the IN PRACTICE: Abstract Verb Tense box for an important pointer. Let's look at each facet of the abstract in order.

IN PRACTICE

Abstract Verb Tense

Choosing the verb tense for an abstract might seem confusing. Fortunately, the *APA Manual* (APA, 2020, p. 74) directly addresses this question: Use past tense for the majority of your abstract describing what you did; use present tense only for conclusions and implications/applications.

Problem

Begin by writing a sentence that captures the essence of your problem and/or question. Writing this sentence may be challenging for you because you now know so much about your topic—condensing that information to a single sentence forces you to synthesize a great deal. Remember that readers of an article are typically informed readers—they are already familiar with the topic, so your sentence does not have to spell out all the background and previous findings about your topic. Craft this sentence until a peer from your class can read it and understand the problem.

Participants

Writing the sentence that identifies the participants in your study should be fairly simple. The *APA Manual* (APA, 2020, p. 74) says to specify only "pertinent" features of the participants. The key word in that phrase is "pertinent." If your participants came from the college's subject pool, then describing them as "college-aged" or "college students" is probably relevant. If the participants came from a population other than college students, that point is relevant. The fact that your study involved a mix of male and female participants is not relevant, but using a single-sex sample would be. Likewise, the fact that you studied a mixed-race group or all-Caucasian sample is probably not important, but the use of a sample taken from a single ethnic or racial group would likely be relevant. The sample size could be useful information for the reader, but don't make that number a focal point; simply weave it into a sentence (e.g., "a sample of 28 introductory psychology students").

Methodology
You may find this sentence to be challenging to write, particularly if your experiment's methodology was complex. As noted in the *APA Manual* (APA, 2020, p. 38), your space (words) is limited—so cover only interesting or crucial aspects of your method. Thus, you should not attempt to communicate every single element of your Method section in one sentence. Instead, include just the critical details so that readers will have an idea what your research participants did in the study.

Findings
The *APA Manual* (APA, 2020, p. 74) instructs authors to include only the basic results in the abstract. As with the methodology, writing one sentence about your results can be challenging if you conducted a complex experiment. In this case, once again, you must focus on the highlights: What is the primary finding (or two) from your experiment? Actual statistics are not necessary for this sentence (with the exception of significance level or effect sizes); instead, concentrate on writing the results as if you were summarizing them to a friend or relative.

Conclusions and Implications/Applications
In this sentence, you should concentrate on communicating the take-away message from your experiment: What is the meaning or implication(s) of what you found in your experiment? If

your experiment was complex, there might be several important messages, but pick and choose so that you can condense this information to a single sentence. My preference is to emphasize a conclusion rather than an implication/application (although your instructor may have a different preference); therefore, my advice is to focus on your most important conclusion in this sentence. That conclusion is likely to be the one most directly related to what you wrote at the end of your introduction, where you described your specific problem or question or hypothesis. Remember to use present tense for this sentence in contrast to past tense for the previous sentences.

Pulling It Together

After you complete writing the five sentences, then you must put them together and see if they flow together. An abstract is not necessarily supposed to flow as well as, say, your introduction, but you should smooth over any rough or jarring transitions. If you are in a class with other students, offer to exchange (and read) abstracts with a classmate. It is often easier for someone other than you to spot flaws in your writing. Be sure to get the word count for your abstract to make certain that it falls within your instructor's guidelines. (Word shows the word count at the bottom of the screen when you select a passage.)

Results

Unfortunately, no clearly delineated set of guidelines exists for writing about your results, unlike the case for writing your abstract. The description of the Results section in the *APA Manual* (APA, 2020, pp. 86–89) is much more general than the corresponding description of the abstract. For example, the statement "summarize the collected data and the results of any analyses performed on those data relevant to the discourse that is to follow" (APA, 2020, p. 86) does not provide any specific guidelines or step-by-step instructions.

Generally speaking, you could provide four types of statistical information in your Results section, although all of them may not be appropriate in every case. In the following subsections, we'll look at these four types of information and what you might write about each type. As you read the following paragraphs, you will find descriptions of basic statistical concepts that are essential to writing a research report. You have encountered (or will encounter) these concepts in an introductory statistics course; in this book, the Glossary includes these terms along with their definitions.

The *APA Manual* (APA, 2020) gives relatively clear guidance about reporting statistics with decimal fractions. Generally, for most numbers, you should use two decimal places (APA, 2020, p. 180). The exception to this generality is when you report your ***p* value** (**probability value** or **probability of chance**): The *APA Manual* specifies that you should report exact probability values to two or three decimal places. See the IN PRACTICE: Statistical Analysis Packages Are Stupid box for a caution about reporting your *p* values.

IN PRACTICE

Statistical Analysis Packages Are Stupid

Some statistical analysis packages will list a *p* value of .000 for your statistical probability. If you see this number, you should remember your statistics training (if you have taken such a course) and recognize that the **probability of chance** can *never* equal zero—there is always some probability, no matter how small, that the effect could be due to chance. If you see a value of .000 on a printout, you should report $p < .001$.

Descriptive Statistics

As you may remember from previous courses, **descriptive statistics** are numbers that *describe* sets of data. The two most commonly encountered types of descriptive statistics are measures of central tendency and variability.

Central Tendency. Measures of **central tendency** tell us about the "average" score of a set of scores. The most commonly used measure of central tendency is the **mean**, the arithmetic average of a set of scores, symbolized as $\bar{X}$ (or μ for a population). See the IN PRACTICE: How Do I Create $\bar{X}$? box for a pointer that will probably cause you to breathe a sigh of relief.

IN PRACTICE

How Do I Create $\bar{X}$?

If you have ever tried to create the symbol $\bar{X}$ in Word, you know it can be a bit of a pain in the neck. You'll be glad to know that APA Style (APA, 2020, p. 184) allows you to use **M** in your paper if you are reporting means in statistical results, whether parenthetically or in tables. If you use this term in text, simply type the word "mean" (APA, 2020, p. 187).

The other two measures of central tendency are the **median** (middle score) and the **mode** (most frequent score); the mean is used most frequently. The mean gives us some idea about the typical (average) score in a group or groups. You will usually report group means related to your statistical comparison in your Results section. If you have three or fewer means, you can include them in the text (APA, 2020, p. 181)—for example, "the mean score for boys was 12.4; the mean score for girls was 12.5"—or place them within parentheses—for example, "(boys' $M = 12.4$; girls' $M = 12.5$)." If you have many means to present, you should consider displaying them in a table or a figure (covered later in this chapter).

The mean is not an appropriate measure of central tendency if you have **skewed data**—that is, when the majority of scores fall at the high or low end of the distribution rather than in the middle. Extreme scores (the cause of skewed data) pull the mean higher or lower, depending on the magnitude of the extreme scores, so they give an inaccurate estimate of the average score. In such a case, you might report group medians (*Mdn*) rather than means.

Variability. Measures of central tendency give you only half the story about a set of scores. It is also important to know about the spread of scores in a distribution, known as **variability**. For example, if you find out that you scored 5 points above the class mean on an exam, you would probably be happy. But *how* high that score actually is depends on the variability of the class's scores. If the scores are quite variable, your score may be just above the mean. However, if the data have relatively little variability, your score could be in the 90th (or higher) percentile!

The most commonly used measure of variability of a sample of scores is the **standard deviation**, symbolized as *s* (σ for a population). Authors typically include standard deviations along with means, which provides the reader with more context about the means and any differences between those means. See the IN PRACTICE: Standard Deviation Symbol box for information about presenting standard deviations in your report.

IN PRACTICE

Standard Deviation Symbol

Just as with the mean, APA Style (APA, 2020, p. 185) allows you to use an alternative symbol for the standard deviation in your paper: *SD*. It would be rare that you would mention standard deviations in text, but if you do, spell it out as "standard deviation."

Standard deviations are usually presented in the text in conjunction with means. For example, you might write, "The mean score for boys was 12.4 (*SD* = 1.24); the mean score for girls was 12.5 (SD = 1.32)." If you use a table to display multiple means for your data, you would probably also include standard deviations in that table (see Table 4.1 for an example).

Correlation. We use the **Pearson product–moment correlation**, symbolized as r, to assess the degree of relation (linear) between any two numeric variables, such as height and weight or age and income. Other correlation statistics exist for measuring relations that are nonlinear, involve more than two variables, or have one dichotomous variable (Spatz, 2019), but we'll focus on the Pearson correlation here because it is the most commonly used. Not all statistics texts agree on calling correlation a descriptive statistic, but it does describe a relationship between variables.

As with the mean, you can report correlation coefficients in two ways: in a table if you have many correlations to report or in text if you have a small number of correlations. You would write about an in-text correlation finding in this manner:

> The correlation between height and weight of the students was significant, $r(24)$ = .68, p < .001.

Notice that the statistical symbols (r, p) are italicized (as you will also see for subsequent symbols) and that spaces separate each component of the description, just like words in a sentence. Also, remember that the **degrees of freedom** (the number within parentheses) is equal to the number of pairs of scores minus two.

Inferential Statistics

Although psychologists conduct experiments on samples of subjects, they are not interested in only those subjects; that is, they would like to apply the results from a sample to a larger population. Thus, we use **inferential statistics** to test our sample data for significance and then to make informed decisions (draw inferences) about a population beyond our sample. Fortunately, the *APA Manual* (APA, 2020) gives explicit advice about the information you should include when writing about your inferential statistics results:

> For inferential statistical tests (e.g., *t*, *F*, and chi-square tests), include the obtained magnitude or value of the test statistic, the degrees of freedom, the probability of obtaining a value as extreme or more extreme than the one obtained (exact *p* value), and the size and direction of the effect. (APA, 2020, p. 88)

You can use many different inferential tests to analyze the data for your experimental report. For the purposes of this discussion, let's focus on the three tests listed in the previous quote. If you use a statistical test other than one of these three, consult the *APA Manual* (APA, 2020) for information about presenting those specific results.

***t* Test.** A *t* test compares two sample means from a single independent variable (IV) to determine whether they differ on some score—a dependent variable (DV). Imagine that you compared two groups of rats in maze performance, with one group of seven rats receiving a dose of amphetamine before running the maze and a control group of six rats receiving no amphetamine. To cover the statistical results (data from Spatz, 2019), you might write a sentence something like this:

> Rats dosed with amphetamine ($M = 39.71$, $SD = 8.54$) ran the maze in fewer seconds than did rats without amphetamine ($M = 57.33$, $SD = 12.63$), $t(11) = 2.99$, $p = .012$.

Notice that this sentence contains all the elements outlined by the *APA Manual* (APA, 2020, p. 88). The value of the *t* test was 2.99, and there were 11 degrees of freedom (7 rats + 6 rats − 2 groups). The exact probability of obtaining a *t* of 2.99 or more was .012 (see an important note in the IN PRACTICE: *p* Values box). The sentence indicating that the amphetamine-dosed rats ran the maze faster (took less time) than the rats without amphetamine shows the direction of the effect.

IN PRACTICE

p Values

You can provide an exact probability statement (such as $p = .012$) only if you analyzed your data with a statistical analysis package such as SPSS, because computer packages provide exact probabilities. If you calculated your statistics by hand, you must gauge the probability from a table (probably as you would in a statistics class). You will see this difference play out in journal articles: Older articles are more likely to have probability statements such as $p < .05$, whereas new articles will have exact probabilities such as $p = .012$.

F Test. The **F test** is perhaps better known as **analysis of variance (ANOVA)**. Sir Ronald Fisher, a British statistician, developed ANOVA in the 1920s; Snedecor named the test F in Fisher's honor in the 1930s (Kirk, 1968, p. 39). The two basic types of ANOVA are covered next.

One-way ANOVA. A **one-way ANOVA** extends the *t* test by comparing three or more sample means (from a single IV) to determine whether those means differ. Imagine that you compared the effects of three different doses of amphetamine on the maze performance of rats, with one group receiving 5 mg of amphetamine, a second group receiving 10 mg, and a third group receiving 15 mg (each group had four rats). The following sentences provide one way you might present the statistical results (data from Spatz, 2019):

A one-way ANOVA showed that the number of maze errors rats made differed by dosage, $F(2, 9) = 11.26$, $p = .0035$. Tukey post hoc tests showed that rats receiving 5 mg of amphetamine made fewer errors ($M = 2.25$) than rats receiving 10 mg of amphetamine ($M = 7.25$; $p = .005$) and rats receiving 15 mg of amphetamine ($M = 6.75$; $p = .009$). Rats receiving 10 mg or 15 mg of amphetamine did not differ in maze errors ($p = .90$).

This sentence contains all elements outlined by the *APA Manual* (APA, 2020, p. 88) for statistical findings. The value of the F test was 11.26, and there were 2 (3 groups − 1) and 9 (12 rats − 3 groups) degrees of freedom. The exact probability of obtaining an F of 11.26 or more was .0035 (which you could report as $< .01$ or $< .004$ to follow APA's guideline regarding decimal places). The sentence indicating that the low-amphetamine-dosed (5 mg) rats made fewer errors in the maze than either group of rats that received higher amphetamine doses (10 mg, 15 mg) shows the direction of the effect. Because there were three levels of the IV (5 mg, 10 mg, 15 mg), there were three possible comparisons of means (5 versus 10, 5 versus 15, 10 versus 15) for the **Tukey post hoc test**—one type of post hoc test, which is needed when the F test shows significance because there are three (or more) means to compare. With more levels of the IV, there would be more mean comparisons to make, and the description of the results would need to be longer (see the IN PRACTICE: How Long Should My Results Section Be? box for the rationale). For example, with four levels of an IV (A–D), you could potentially make six comparisons: A versus B, A versus C, A versus D, B versus C, B versus D, and C versus D.

· ·

IN PRACTICE

How Long Should My Results Section Be?

You may have noticed that the account of results for the one-way ANOVA was three sentences compared to one sentence for the *t* test and was more than twice as long. It is simpler to decode the results from a *t* test than the results from ANOVA: A significant finding from a *t* test tells you that the two means are different, so you can simply examine those means to determine which group outperformed the other. Significance in a one-way ANOVA, however, tells you that there is a significant difference somewhere among the three (or more) means. To determine exactly where the significance lies, you must compute a **post hoc test**, such as the Tukey test mentioned in the previous findings.

Factorial ANOVA. A **factorial ANOVA** compares group means from two or more independent variables IVs to determine whether significant differences exist between/among the means for the different IVs. Unlike the difference between *t* tests and one-way ANOVAs, the number of levels of each IV is irrelevant: As long as you have two (or more) IVs, a factorial ANOVA is necessary. The simplest possible factorial ANOVA is a **2 × 2 factorial design**, which means there are two IVs (because there are two digits), each of which has two levels (because each digit is a 2). Although there are two IVs, you get more than twice as much information with this factorial ANOVA as you would from two separate *t* tests or one-way ANOVAs: In addition to the result from each IV, you get information about the simultaneous effect of the two variables. As you can imagine, because a factorial ANOVA provides more statistical information, your recounting of the results will be longer when you perform such an analysis. Be sure to include *all* results—don't ignore some findings because they aren't significant or aren't of interest to you (APA, 2020, p. 86).

Imagine that you conducted an experiment in which you gave rats either a high or low dose of amphetamines *and* tested their performance in simple and complex mazes. One IV is amphetamine dose (2 levels = 5 mg or 10 mg), and a second IV is type of maze (2 levels = simple or complex). The solitary effect of each IV is a **main effect**; the joint/simultaneous effect of the IVs is an **interaction**. The DV is maze performance, which you measured as the percentage of correct decisions that the rats made in the mazes. Here is a way that you might cover the findings from this experiment in your write-up (data from Spatz, 2019):

> A two-way ANOVA testing the percent of correct decisions showed that the main effects of dosage (M_5 = 34.0%, M_{10} = 38.5%), $F(1, 16)$ = 0.36, p = .56, and maze complexity (M_{Simple} = 41.0%, $M_{Complex}$ = 31.5%), $F(1, 16)$ = 1.60, p = .22, were not significant. However, the interaction between dosage and maze complexity was significant, $F(1, 16)$ = 13.41, p = .002. The group means (M_{5C} = 43; M_{10C} = 20; M_{5S} = 25; M_{10S} = 57) showed that rats performed better in a simple maze with the higher dose of amphetamine but better in the complex maze with the lower dose of amphetamine.

As before, this explanation covers all aspects of the findings as specified by the *APA Manual* (APA, 2020, p. 88). For the main effect of amphetamine dosage, the value of the F test was 0.36, the degrees of freedom were 1 (2 groups [levels of amphetamine] − 1) and 16 (20 rats − 4 treatment combinations [2 × 2]), and the exact probability of that F ratio was .56. For the main effect of maze complexity, the value of the F test was 1.60, the degrees of freedom were 1 (2 groups [levels of maze complexity] − 1) and 16 (20 rats − 4 treatment combinations [2 × 2]), and the exact probability of that F ratio was .22. For the interaction between amphetamine dosage and maze complexity, the value of the F test was 13.41, the degrees of freedom were 1 (2 groups − 1) and 16 (20 rats − 4 treatment combinations [2 × 2]), and the exact probability of that F ratio was .002. Of the three effects (main effects of amphetamine dose and maze complexity plus interaction of those two variables), only the interaction was significant—the direction of that effect is indicated by the sentence explaining that rats showed better performance on the simple maze with a high dose of amphetamines, whereas they performed better in the complex maze with a low dose of amphetamines. The IN PRACTICE: Factorial ANOVA Results box shows you an important point to remember when reporting results from factorial designs.

IN PRACTICE

Factorial ANOVA Results

When you conduct a factorial ANOVA, you should always check the significance of the interaction first. If the interaction is significant, then that effect supersedes the main effects. A significant interaction tells you that the effects of one IV depend on the level of the second IV, so interpreting a main effect alone is oversimplifying and would be misleading. Thus, you should focus on reporting the results from the interaction rather than the main effects. If the interaction effect is *not* significant, then you should interpret and report the two (or more) main effects just as you would in a one-way ANOVA.

As noted earlier, a 2×2 factorial design is the simplest possible version of a factorial design. There are two ways that you might make your factorial design more complex, both of which would slightly alter what you would need to cover when explaining your results.

The first design variation involves using more than two groups for one or both of your IVs. Thus, continuing with the previous example, you might have three dosage levels of the amphetamine (high, medium, and low). In this case, you would have a **3×2 factorial design**. As suggested by the explanation of factorial designs provided earlier, 3×2 means the design has two IVs (because there are two digits), but in this case, one IV (amphetamine) would have three levels and the other IV (maze complexity) would have the same two levels. If the interaction of the two IVs was *not* significant and the amphetamine effect *was* significant, you would need to add the results from post hoc tests to your report (such as the Tukey post hoc test, mentioned earlier in the one-way

ANOVA section) to explain which level of amphetamine led to the best maze performance.

The second design variation that would require adding more information about your results would involve using more than two IVs, which creates more possible interaction terms in addition to more main effects. For example, in addition to amphetamine dose and maze complexity, you might include age (young versus old rats) as a third IV. If you used only two levels of amphetamine, you would have a $2 \times 2 \times 2$ **factorial design** (three digits signifying three IVs, each with two levels). If you have three IVs (A, B, C), you would end up with three two-way interactions (AB, AC, BC) and one three-way interaction (ABC). Adding a fourth IV would create a multitude of possible interactions (two-way: AB, AC, AD, BC, BD, CD; three-way: ABC, ABD, BCD; four-way: ABCD). Your report of the results would need to cover *all* of the main effects and interactions, so your Results section could get quite long and involve much more writing. See the IN PRACTICE: Be Cautious When Adding Independent Variables (IVs) box for a cautionary note.

IN PRACTICE

Be Cautious When Adding Independent Variables (IVs)

Although they may provide interesting results, interactions involving more than two variables are typically more complex to interpret and write about than two-variable interactions. Thus, in planning your experiment, you may want to avoid designs with several IVs.

χ^2 **Test.** A **chi-square** (χ^2) **test** compares frequency counts or percentages/proportions, whereas t tests and ANOVAs compare means from sets of scores. Rather than measuring a subject's score on a DV, you would simply sort subjects into categories, such as men/women, Democrat/Republican/Independent, or high school/college.

Statisticians use chi-square tests for two different purposes (Spatz, 2019). First, they may serve as a **test of independence**—a test that measures whether two variables are independent of each other, such as sex and political party. On the one hand, if variables are independent, then we cannot use one to predict the other. On the other hand, if variables are related or contingent, then knowing one helps predict the other.

As an example, data show that sex and political party are likely related: A survey by the Pew Research Center (2016, p. 17) revealed that men identified or leaned Republican by a 51% to 41% margin, whereas women identified or leaned Democrat by a 54% to 36% margin. Imagine you surveyed 100 men and 100 women about their political identification and, for those people who provided a response, you found percentages that exactly matched the Pew data (men: 51 Republicans, 41 Democrats; women: 36 Republicans, 54 Democrats). You would use a chi-square test to determine whether sex and political party are independent of each other.

Interestingly, the current *APA Manual* (APA, 2020) does not provide a specific example of writing about chi-square results in text (see APA, 2020, p. 214, for tabular chi-square results), but a previous *APA Manual* (APA, 2001, p. 139) did. The following sentence shows how you might write your results:

> Results showed that sex and political preference were not independent, $\chi^2(1, N = 182) = 4.34$, $p = .037$. Men were more likely to identify as Republicans (51% to 41%), whereas women were more likely to identify as Democrats (54% to 36%).

These sentences contain all the information specified in the *APA Manual* (APA, 2020, p. 88). The chi-square value was 4.34, there was 1 degree of freedom (true for all 2×2 chi squares), the exact probability of the chi-square test was .037, and the second sentence indicates the direction of the result.

The second use of the chi-square test is as a **goodness of fit test** that compares actual frequencies to the predicted outcomes from a hypothesis or theory. For example, suppose you are interested in the frequency of different colors of plain (milk chocolate) M&M's. You know from eating M&M's that the colors include blue, brown, green, orange, red, and yellow. You hypothesize that these six colors are equally represented in the population of M&M's. To test this hypothesis, you would have to undergo the "hardship" of buying a large quantity of M&M's and then count them by color. The real-life data would likely tell you that your hypothesis is incorrect—the population of plain M&M's has traditionally shown large differences by color (Smith, 2008).

The good news for reporting the results of your chi-square test is that the format is the same, regardless of which type of chi-square test you used. Suppose you bought a bag of M&M's and found 18 blue, 6 brown, 9 green, 11 orange, 5 red, and 8 yellow M&M's in the bag (the observed frequencies for your χ^2 test; data adapted from Spatz, 2019). Given that your bag had 57 M&M's spread across six colors, the expected number per color *if* the colors are evenly distributed would be 9.5 (57/6; the expected frequency for your χ^2 test). Given these data, here is an example of how you might write about your findings:

> The hypothesis that the six colors of milk chocolate M&M's are equally distributed was not supported, $\chi^2(5, N = 57) = 11.53$, $p = .042$. Frequencies of the six colors ranged from 5 (red) to 18 (blue).

These sentences contain the *APA Manual*'s (APA, 2020, p. 88) specified information. The chi-square value was 11.53, there were 5 degrees of freedom (number of categories minus 1), the exact probability of the chi-square test was .042, and the second sentence indicates, to some degree, the direction of the result.

Effect Size. Estimates of **effect size** allow you to gauge the strength of an inferential statistical effect. Researchers use several different effect size measures; the discussion here focuses on two such measures and considers how to include them in the write-up of your statistical results. Effect size measures are technically descriptive statistics; however, researchers use these measures to assess inferential findings.

d. Researchers use *d* to assess the effect size of a difference between two means (Spatz, 2019). Calculating *d* is not difficult: You simply subtract the two means and divide by the standard deviation (Lakens, 2013), which means that *d* is a measure of standard deviation units. Cohen (1988) categorized a *d* of .20 as a small effect, .50 as a medium effect, and .80 as a large effect. Because *d* is appropriate with two means, we can incorporate it into the *t*-test results we covered earlier in the chapter:

> Rats dosed with amphetamine ($M = 39.71$, $SD = 8.54$) ran the maze in fewer seconds than did rats without amphetamine ($M = 57.33$, $SD = 12.63$), $t(11) = 2.99$, $p = .012$. The effect size was large, $d = 1.63$.

This effect size result shows that the two means are 1.63 standard deviations apart. As you can see, reporting *d* is simple and straightforward. An even briefer version of the results is also possible, in which you would simply follow the probability statement with the effect size (e.g., $p = .012$, $d = 1.63$). This second presentation would assume that the reader is familiar enough with *d* so as not to need any context for it. As a beginning writer, it is probably a good idea for you to present more information rather than less, so I would advise using the slightly longer version shown above.

η^2 (Eta Squared). Researchers use **eta squared (η^2)** to measure the amount of the total variance that can be attributed to the effect of a particular variable (Becker, 1999). This effect size measure is an extension of r^2 (Lakens, 2013), which statistics instructors teach as a measure of effect size for correlation. You can calculate η^2 for each effect (main effects and interaction) in ANOVA (Wuensch, 2015), so it is the preferred effect size measure for ANOVA (Becker, 1999; Lakens, 2013; Wuensch, 2015). Given the earlier factorial

ANOVA results from this chapter, here is how you could write the information about the effect sizes:

> A two-way ANOVA testing the percent of correct decisions showed that the main effects of dosage ($M_5 = 34.0\%$, $M_{10} = 38.5\%$), $F(1, 16) = 0.36$, $p = .56$, $\eta^2 = .01$, and maze complexity ($M_{Simple} = 41.0\%$, $M_{Complex} = 31.5\%$), $F(1, 16) = 1.60$, $p = .22$, $\eta^2 = .05$, were not significant. However, the interaction between dosage and maze complexity was significant, $F(1, 16) = 13.41$, $p = .002$, $\eta^2 = .43$. The group means ($M_{5C} = 43$; $M_{10C} = 20$; $M_{5S} = 25$; $M_{10S} = 57$) showed that the rats performed better in the simple maze with the higher dose of amphetamine but better in the complex maze with the lower dose of amphetamine.

This report shows that the amphetamine dosage accounted for only 1% and maze complexity for only 5% of the variability in maze performance. However, their interaction accounted for 43% of the variability in maze performance, which is a strong effect (Cohen, 1988). Reporting effect sizes for a **nonsignificant effect** ($p > .05$) remains a topic of debate among statisticians, but reporting them allows readers to have full information about the various effect sizes.

Ancillary Presentation

Authors often provide ancillary information to supplement their statistical results. Such information serves to help the reader better understand and interpret the statistical findings. The most common types of ancillary information are tables and figures. Tables and figures are so important and so widely used that the *APA Manual* (APA, 2020) devotes an entire chapter to them (Chapter 7, pp. 195–250).

Tables. Although the *APA Manual* (APA, 2020, p. 195) notes that tables can be used to display numbers or text (such as stimuli) in columns and rows, most tables in Results sections display numerical data. Tables are typically easier than figures to compose for your report because you can simply type them as you type your report (although they do belong on a separate page, as noted subsequently). When thinking about the appropriateness of a table, an important consideration is whether to include numbers in the text or in a table. The *APA Manual* (APA, 2020, p. 181) gives a general rule: It advises authors to try to use a sentence when they have three or fewer numbers, to try to use a table when they have four to 20 numbers, and to try to use a figure for more than 20 numbers. The first part of this rule explains why I did not list the six different colors of M&M's and their frequencies in the sentence describing the second set of chi-square results presented earlier. If I wanted to present the full frequency data, I would construct a table because there were six colors of M&M's, which fits within the four to 20 numbers guideline.

There are usually multiple ways to format data into a table, so you must make choices about the best way to organize your data. For example, in presenting the M&M's data, should I list the colors alphabetically, in increasing order, or in decreasing order? That is a decision you would have to make, based on which presentation you believe would be most informative for the reader. For one possible presentation of the M&M's data in a manuscript, see Figure 8.1 on the next page. Also, my description of the findings would change slightly from the earlier presentation in the chapter because I am including a table; one possible way to describe the results appears below:

> The hypothesis that the six colors of milk chocolate M&M's are equally distributed was not supported, $\chi^2(5, N = 57) = 11.53$, $p = .042$. Frequencies of the six colors appear in Table 1.

The most important factor about formatting a table is to display the information so that it maximally helps the reader to understand the data (APA, 2020, p. 181). Also, you should not duplicate information in both the text and a table (see the IN PRACTICE: Tables Provide Supplemental Information box on the next page).

Figure 8.1 Manuscript page with table for M&M's data

M&M's FREQUENCIES   10

Table 1

Frequency of M&M's Colors in a Bag

Color	Frequency	Percentage
Blue	18	31.5
Brown	5	8.8
Green	9	15.8
Orange	11	19.3
Red	6	10.5
Yellow	8	14.0

Note. Data are from a 1.69-ounce bag.

IN PRACTICE

Tables Provide Supplemental Information

Several important APA-Style considerations arise when you consider whether to use a table. Most importantly, the table should supplement—not duplicate—information in the text (APA, 2010, p. 130; see also APA, 2020, p. 196). In other words, do not include the same information in your paper and in a table. In my description of chi-square results that referred to a table, I deleted the information that I included when I did not refer to a table ("Frequencies of the six colors ranged from 5 to 18.").

In text, you refer to your table(s) by using an Arabic number (e.g., Table 1), just as I did at the end of the previous paragraph (APA, 2020, p. 197). When typing your manuscript (APA, 2020, p. 198), you typically type each table on a separate page and include the table(s) after your list of references (and footnotes page, if you have any)—although the *Manual* (APA, 2020, p. 198) mentions embedding tables within a manuscript, depending on journal or instructor preference. At the top of the page, type "**Table n**" where "n" represents the figure number. One double-spaced line below, type a figure title (in italics)—a brief explanatory title for the figure (APA, 2020, p. 201). The table itself appears under the title line. If you have an explanatory note (or notes), type it (or them) under the figure, preceded by the word "*Note.*" (or "*Notes.*"). The three possible types of notes (general, specific, probability) are explained in the *APA Manual* (2020, pp. 203–204). Notice that Figure 8.1 uses a general note. The *APA Manual* (APA, 2020, pp. 210–224) provides 24 examples of tables for you to consult as you plan how to format your table. For an overview of all the possible components of a figure, see Table 7.1 in the *Manual* (APA, 2020, p. 200). The sample papers included in the *APA Manual* include examples of tables on page 60.

Figures. According to the *APA Manual* (APA, 2020, p. 195), figures might include graphs, charts, drawings, photographs, or illustrations—basically, any nontextual depiction. My experience with both writing and reading journal articles tells me that graphs probably account for at least 90% of all figures, so I will address only graphs in this section (consult the *APA Manual* [APA, 2020] for information about other types of figures if you need to include something other than a graph).

The *APA Manual*'s (APA, 2020, p. 233) description of graphs says that they "typically display the relationship between two quantitative indices or between a continuous quantitative variable (usually displayed on the *y*-axis) and groups of participants or subjects (usually displayed on the *x*-axis)." The first example given (two quantitative indices) would most likely refer to an IV and DV (*t* test or one-way ANOVA) or two IVs and a DV (factorial ANOVA). The second example (of a continuous variable and groups of subjects) would most likely refer to a correlational result (note the mention of *x*- and *y*-axes). I will primarily refer to the first type of example, but the APA-Style guidelines would apply to any type of figure you might include in a paper or research report.

For an example, let's take another look at the data from the "Factorial ANOVA" section of the chapter. In that example, a researcher tested rats' correct maze decisions as a function of both amphetamine dose (5 mg/10 mg) and maze difficulty (simple/complex). Recall that the main effects of amphetamine dose and maze difficulty were not significant, but the interaction of the two variables was significant. This was the final sentence of those results:

> As the group means show, rats performed better in the simple maze with the higher dose of amphetamine but better in the complex maze with the lower dose of amphetamine.

To fully understand this sentence, the reader must examine the means based on the two IVs and try to visualize the pattern of those means. This task is a difficult one, which makes it clearly advantageous to add a figure. Although you could use a table to display the means, the reader would still need to imagine the pattern.

As is often the case when presenting data, you have choices about how to design your graph for your figure. Because you will be graphing an interaction, you will have three variables (two IVs and one DV) to represent on a two-axis graph. You should graph your DV on the y-axis (vertical axis) and one of your IVs on the x-axis (horizontal axis), which means you have to represent your second IV with different elements within the graph. Thus, given the example, you could represent either maze complexity or amphetamine dose as the IV on the x-axis and the other IV as different lines on the graph. Typically, one representation of the graph will seem to make more sense to you or be easier to explain than the other. By using Excel, it becomes relatively easy to draw both graphs and then determine which one works better for you. It is a fairly simple process to draw a graph using Excel that you can turn into an acceptable figure.

If you follow the step-by-step directions in Table 8.1, you'll be drawing good graphs in no time flat.

TABLE 8.1 **Beginning a Graph in Excel**
1. Begin by creating an Excel table with your IV labels and means, as shown in Figure 8.2a on the next page.
2. Making sure your cursor is positioned within the table, click on the Insert tab. (If your cursor is not in the table, you will end up with a graph with no data or lines.)
3. In the Insert options, you will see the Charts option. Select the option that shows lines. Click the pull-down arrow and select the option showing "Line with Markers" (PC) or "Marked Line" (Mac). You should now see a rough graph of your interaction with amphetamine dose on the x-axis and maze complexity represented with two lines, one for the simple maze and one for the complex maze (see Figure 8.2b in a few pages).
4. On top of the worksheet, you should see "Switch Row/Column" (PC) or "Switch Plots" (Mac) as an option. If you click this option, the graph will reverse so that the maze complexity appears on the x-axis and the amphetamine dose is represented with two lines. By toggling back and forth between the options, you can view both rough graphs and determine which seems easier or more logical to explain. In this example, I favor the graph that shows amphetamine dose on the x-axis because explaining this graph seems relatively straightforward. At this point, your screen should show both the data table and the rough graph (see Figure 8.2b).
5. Now you can begin to format the graph so that it is acceptable in APA Style (see APA, 2020, pp. 60, 234–250 for examples). You will do most of the formatting by clicking on the box with the large + sign to the right of the graph (PC) or selecting "Chart Layout" (Mac). The exact steps you take next vary considerably, depending on what version of Excel you are using and whether you are working on a PC or Mac. Rather than trying to cover an almost infinite number of possibilities, I'll list the general steps you should take from this point on. If you get stuck, I recommend performing a web search on a particular operation you are trying to accomplish.
6. Some of these elements may already appear in your rough graph, but here's a list of points to check:
• Make sure to check *Axes* so that you see the values (or options) labeled for each axis.
• Unclick *Chart Title* because you will not have a title centered over the graph.

(continued)

TABLE 8.1 (continued)

- Leave *Data Labels* and *Data Table* unchecked—you do not want to display the data values on the graph.

- *Error Bars* allows you to show variability around your data points (see examples in the *APA Manual* [APA, 2020, pp. 234–235]). Although error bars are helpful for showing variability, they sometimes make a graph difficult to interpret if the bars overlap.

- Uncheck *Gridlines* so that you do not have horizontal gridlines showing on the graph.

- Uncheck *Trendline* and *Up/Down Bars*.

- Be sure the font in the rough graph (see Figure 8.2b) is sans serif (e.g., Arial, Calibri, Lucida Sans Unicode) for better legibility (APA, 2020, p. 227).

7. Checking *Axis Titles* allows you to label each axis with its variable name. Make sure to check the *Legend* box so that the lines for your graph will have labels. Word gives you the option of moving the legend to various locations for the graph. According to the *APA Manual* (2020, p. 229), figure legends should appear within or below the figure to avoid empty space around the legend. Placement within the figure may make the figure difficult to interpret or look too busy; use your aesthetic sense to choose the best location if your instructor has no preference. All of these elements should be in a sans serif font, as mentioned in Step 6.

8. The default settings in Excel will make your lines appear in different colors, which is not appropriate in APA Style, because journal articles appear in black and white. Thus, you need to reformat the lines so that they appear in black. When you format the lines to black, you will also need to reformat one of the lines to be discernibly different from the others (e.g., a dashed line or different endpoints), which should also reformat that line in the legend box. At this point, you should have a figure that is ready to use in your paper (see Figure 8.2c in a few pages). Note that any page in your paper that contains a figure would also have a running head (if required) and page number.

Figure 8.2a Setup for Excel table of means with independent variable labels

	5 mg	**10 mg**
Simple Maze	25	57
Complex Maze	43	20

Figure 8.2b Excel table with rough graph of interaction

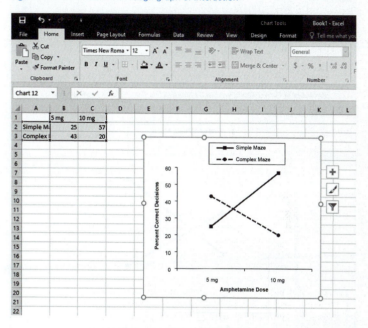

When you have a completed figure in Excel, you can copy and paste it onto a page in your experimental report in Word. Just as with tables, you should refer to figures with Arabic numbers (e.g., Figure 1). The *APA Manual* (APA, 2020, p. 43) indicates that figures follow tables in your manuscript, with each figure appearing on a separate page (APA, 2020, pp. 225–229). Format your pages with figures in the same manner as explained earlier for pages with tables (of course, type "**Figure n**" in this case). For an overview of all the possible components of a figure, see Figure 7.1 in the *Manual* (APA, 2020, p. 226). A final version of the figure that I have been describing, ready for inclusion in the manuscript, appears in Figure 8.2c of this chapter. Notice that Figure 8.2c uses a probability note. Because of this graphed interaction, the description of the results should change

Figure 8.2c Manuscript page for figure

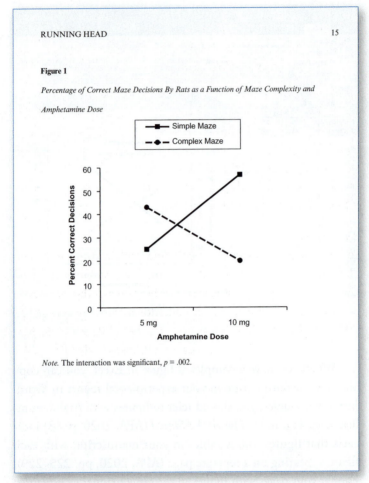

15

Figure 1

Percentage of Correct Maze Decisions By Rats as a Function of Maze Complexity and

Amphetamine Dose

Note. The interaction was significant, $p = .002$.

accordingly. Here is one possible way to write about these results from earlier in the chapter:

A two-way ANOVA testing the percent of correct decisions showed that the main effects of dosage ($M_5 = 34.0\%$, $M_{10} = 38.5\%$), $F(1, 16) = 0.36$, $p = .56$, $\eta^2 = .01$, and maze complexity ($M_{Simple} = 41.0\%$, $M_{Complex} = 31.5\%$), $F(1, 16) = 1.60$, $p = .22$, $\eta^2 = .05$, were not significant. However, the interaction between dosage and maze complexity was significant, $F(1, 16) = 13.41$, $p = .002$, $\eta^2 = .43$. As Figure 1 shows, rats performed better in the simple maze with the higher dose of amphetamine but better in the complex maze with the lower dose of amphetamine.

This discussion of how to write the results of your experiment has taken quite a few pages, primarily because we covered several different types of statistical tests and explored both tables and figures. Oddly enough, although this section of the chapter is quite long, your actual Results section might end up being the shortest section of your paper, unless you have complex or numerous statistical analyses to cover.

Discussion

In your Discussion section, you should explain your results and your conclusions based on those results (see the Chapter 4 section on "Discussion"). If your results bear on any theory or have practical implications, you should address those points (APA, 2020, pp. 89–90). In other words, you should draw the bottom line for your study in this section. The guidance about the Discussion section found in the seventh edition of the *APA Manual* (APA, 2020) is less succinct than the guidance offered in the fourth edition of the *APA Manual* (APA, 1994, p. 19). That earlier version provided three points to address in your Discussion:

- the contribution(s) of your study,
- how your research answered the original question, and
- the conclusions and theoretical significance of your study.

You should address the first bullet point in the first paragraph or two of your Discussion section. Specifically, you should focus on what your study adds to the research literature. Experimenters often begin their discussion by briefly summarizing their important statistical results, which allows you to point out the new information you found in your study. The *APA Manual* (APA, 2020, p. 89) advises that you address the support (or nonsupport) found for your research hypotheses early in your discussion, which should help you address how your study helped (or did not help) resolve the original problem (second bullet point). However, be careful not to restate what you have already written. If your data or conclusions have any limitations, be sure to mention them here. If you attempt to gloss over shortcomings of your research, readers may become suspicious or skeptical about your entire paper. At the same time, don't sell yourself and your research short: You made the best attempt you could to manipulate and measure your variables in a careful, methodical fashion.

Perhaps the most important point to address in your discussion is the third bullet point: What are your overall conclusions, and what are the implications of your results for theory in your research area? This type of information truly indicates the importance of your study and your results. Remember that the goal of research is to build a body of knowledge about various topics. Thus, it is important for you to address how your research has added to that body of knowledge. I liken this process to bricklaying: The bricks at the bottom form a foundation for bricks to be added on top of them, and then those new bricks become the foundation for still more bricks to be added. The previous foundation for your research study was the research you described in the introduction of the paper. You should point out the new foundation that your study provides for future researchers to build on.

Finally, you may address areas or ideas for future research in your discussion. The *APA Manual* (APA, 2020, p. 90) mentions that you could raise new or unanswered questions stemming from your research. In Chapter 4, I noted that this type of information might help you develop an idea for your research study. When you include your perceptions of future directions for research in your discussion, that information might provide ideas for future researchers *or* for you to pursue. Indeed, unresolved issues often lead a researcher to a new research idea or proposal to address those issues. As noted in Chapter 6, many researchers engage in programmatic research—they conduct continuing research studies in the same topic area by building on their previous studies.

Again, as I pointed out in Chapter 4, it is difficult to provide a blueprint of exactly what your Discussion section should include, because that section tends to vary more widely in style and content than any other section of a research report. For example, the Discussion section is the only area of your research report in which you can engage in some degree of speculation without having firm data on which to base your ideas. Your evaluation of the importance of your results will be, to some degree, based on your opinion rather than on cold, scientific facts. However, having opened the door to some speculation or opinion, I must point out that unfounded or biased opinions and ideas have no place in your discussion. You must remember that you are writing a scientific research report.

APA-Style Considerations

Throughout this book and in your copy of the *APA Manual* (APA, 2020), you will encounter many considerations that you must address and many rules that you must learn to correctly format an experimental report in APA Style. I would never undertake writing in APA Style without my trusty copy of the *APA Manual* by my side, and I have been writing in APA Style for more than 40 years! I urge you also to keep your *APA Manual* nearby as you write.

Students have often told me that it is difficult (impossible?) to know *all* the rules and specifications that go along with APA Style. This comment is one with which I can sympathize and identify—it has taken me years to learn APA Style, and it's not unusual for me to still learn new aspects or have to ask questions about APA Style. Also, just as I thought I was learning all the elements of APA Style in the sixth edition of the *Publication Manual* (APA, 2010), APA published the seventh edition of the *Manual* (APA, 2020)! This list of resources can help you better understand and apply APA Style:

- Refer to the advice from Chapter 2 about using a saved APA-Style file or using the APA-Style template that

Microsoft has created. Before using the Microsoft APA-Style template, however, be sure it has been updated to the most recent version of APA Style (APA, 2020).

- Examine the APA-Style editing marks in Appendix B; then check Appendix C to see how I resolved the needed edits.
- Use the Common Writing Problems, Explanations, and Solutions table found in Appendix D.
- Be sure your writing is consistent with APA-Style values (see that section in Chapter 2).
- Review the Grammar Counts section in Chapter 3.
- Pay attention to the Seven Guidelines for Revising in Table 1.1.
- Follow the guidelines on formatting journal article references in Chapter 5 and book references in Chapter 6.
- Use the APA Citation Styles guidelines from Chapter 6 (see Table 6.2).
- Be sure to format your headers correctly as shown in Chapter 6 (see Figure 6.2).
- Use the IN PRACTICE box in Chapter 2 to guide you in formatting your paper (e.g., font, margins, running head, hyphenation).
- There are many more APA-Style considerations to review: the sections for Nuts and Bolts of APA Style (see Chapter 2) and APA-Style Considerations (see Chapter 5 and Chapter 6).
- When you have a question about APA Style and cannot find an answer in the *APA Manual* (APA, 2020), consult the APA Style Blog (http://blog.apastyle.org/). This site posts frequent blogs dealing with APA-Style questions. Better yet, all posts are archived and searchable, so that you can often find help for difficult questions here.
- Remember to access the Purdue OWL site (owl.purdue.edu) for other APA formatting questions.
- If all else fails, conduct a web search for whatever aspect of APA Style you need help with.

Editing Your Report

Although APA Style is sometimes tough to master, grammar and writing well are certainly challenging, too! Although I have made this point previously in this book, I *must* remind you once again: After you compile your experimental report, read through and thoroughly edit it before you submit it. If you began your work with a research proposal that you wrote at some point in the past, your writing of this report has likely taken place over a span of several months. For this reason alone, you should take a close look at your writing to ensure that it is consistent in voice, tone, and quality throughout its entirety. Also, you may have learned new information about APA Style since you wrote your proposal, so you should double-check your report for APA Style correctness. You may be surprised at some problems you detect—and relieved that you can correct them before submitting your paper.

Concluding Thoughts

This chapter has focused on helping you write the final report for your experimental study. Although conducting the study itself is quite important, no research can have any impact until the researcher compiles and reports the results. Knowing how to compile this report is important and makes it possible for your study and results to receive their proper due.

Critical Thinking Writing Assignments

Write paragraph-length answers to the following questions aimed at students who will have an assignment to complete a report of their experimental projects in the upcoming semester.

Assignment 1
Why is it important to edit and/or update the material that you wrote for your research proposal when you are putting that material in your experimental report?

Assignment 2
Why is it critical to you *and* to other researchers to write a good abstract for your research report?

Assignment 3
Why do authors often include ancillary information such as tables or graphs in their Results sections?

Assignment 4
What are three important things to accomplish in your Discussion section? Explain each one fully.

Assignment 5
To make certain that you understand how to graph your results in Excel, use the data (from Spatz, 2019) provided below to draw a graph. Be sure that you can format the graph so that it is in APA format.

Consider the following circumstances: Imagine that you measured attitudes toward playing two types of games (cards, computers) as a function of the age of people surveyed (young, old). Mean attitude scores appear here (higher scores indicate more favorable attitudes). After you have graphed the interaction, explain it in words, as in a Results section.

		Factor A (Age)	
		Young	**Old**
Factor B	**Cards**	51	75
(Game Type)	**Computer**	78	47

References

American Psychological Association. (1994). *Publication manual of the American Psychological Association* (4th ed.).

American Psychological Association. (2001). *Publication manual of the American Psychological Association* (5th ed.).

American Psychological Association. (2010). *Publication manual of the American Psychological Association* (6th ed.).

American Psychological Association. (2020). *Publication manual of the American Psychological Association* (7th ed.). https://doi.org/10.1037/0000165-000

Becker, L. A. (1999). *Measures of effect size (Strength of association).* University of Colorado, Colorado Springs. https://www.uccs.edu/lbecker/glm_effectsize.html

Blumenthal, A. L. (1991). The intrepid Joseph Jastrow. In G. A. Kimble, M. Wertheimer, & C. L. White (Eds.), *Portraits of pioneers in psychology* (pp. 74–87). American Psychological Association. https://doi.org/10.4324/9781315799568

Cohen, J. (1988). *Statistical power analysis for the behavioral sciences* (2nd ed.). Erlbaum. https://doi.org/10.4324/9780203771587

Kirk, R. E. (1968). *Experimental design: Procedures for the behavioral sciences.* Brooks/Cole.

Lakens, D. (2013). Calculating and reporting effect sizes to facilitate cumulative science: A practical primer for *t*-tests and ANOVAs. *Frontiers in Psychology, 4.* https://doi.org/10.3389/fpsyg.2013.00863

Peluso, E. A. (2000). Skilled motor performance as a function of type of mental imagery. *Journal of Psychological Inquiry, 5,* 11–14.

Pew Research Center. (2016, September 13). *The parties on the eve of the 2016 election: Two coalitions, moving further apart.* http://assets.pewresearch.org/wp-content/uploads/sites/5/2016/09/09-13-2016-Party-ID-release-final.pdf

Smith, R. A. (2008). A tasty sample(r): Teaching about sampling using M&M's. In L. T. Benjamin Jr. (Ed.), *Favorite activities for the teaching of psychology* (pp. 8–10). American Psychological Association.

Spatz, C. (2019). *Basic statistics: Tales of distributions* (12th ed.). Outcrop.

Sternberg, R. J. (2003). *The psychologist's companion: A guide to scientific writing for students and researchers* (4th ed.). Cambridge University Press. https://doi.org/10.1017/CBO9780511819261

Wuensch, K. L. (2015). *Standardized effect size estimation: Why and how?* East Carolina University. http://core.ecu.edu/psyc/wuenschk/StatHelp/Effect%20Size%20Estimation.pdf

9

So I've Written a Psychology Paper — What's Next?

Do You Know?

What does a research presentation entail?

Where can you present your research?

How do you make a research poster for presentation?

Which journals publish undergraduate psychology research papers?

How do you submit a paper you have written for publication?

How should you revise a paper on which you have received editorial comments and suggestions?

"Scientific progress can be achieved only if researchers share their findings with one another and with the general public."

—Weiten, 2014, p. 34

Congratulations on making it to the last chapter in the book! Ideally, this progress means that you have completed writing a psychology paper . . . or that you are finding out what possibilities exist after you have written a paper. Much of this chapter is aimed at students who have conducted an experiment and completed a written report of their results, but it also describes options possible for students who have written a term paper or literature review.

Most universities evaluate their faculty not just on their teaching, but also on their research accomplishments. Psychologists are typically expected to publish their writing as part of their professional accomplishments. This expectation — informally described as "publish or perish" — is especially important to psychologists employed at colleges and universities and research-based organizations. Publishing research can help a psychologist obtain and maintain a job, earn promotion through the academic ranks, and gain tenure. Why does this pressure to publish exist? Universities and research organizations pride themselves on contributing to the body of scientific knowledge, and publication is the way that scientific knowledge typically advances. Indeed, most lists of the steps in a scientific investigation include some version of publication as the final step. For example, Weiten (2014, p. 34) listed "report the findings" as his last step of five. Smith and Davis (2013, pp. 4, 7–10) named "sharing your results: presentation and publication" as step 10 of 11. The *Publication Manual of the American Psychological Association* (American Psychological Association [APA], 2020) not only provides APA-Style information for authors, but also presents new ways of disseminating information such as online publication.

If you have plans to go on in psychology, the information in this chapter is particularly important. Many writers have emphasized that making a research presentation or publishing a journal article is particularly helpful for getting into graduate school (Helms & Rogers, 2015; Landrum & Davis, 2007; Morgan & Korschgen, 2006; Smith, 1985). Making a research presentation is often an intermediate step for psychologists along the road to publication. Thus, completing the final step in the research and writing process is a way to move toward becoming a full-fledged psychologist.

You can now see that your work is not necessarily done after you finish writing your paper for class. In this chapter, we will explore the options that are open to you when you have completed your paper.

Presenting Your Research

Many psychologists attend professional conferences to present their research findings before they submit a paper to a journal for potential publication. In this way, they receive feedback about their research from colleagues, which can provide valuable insights for consideration before they finish writing their manuscript and submitting it for publication. In addition, they can include the presentation on their **vita** (sometimes called a **curriculum vitae**, which is much like an academic version of a resume), which contributes to their professional reputation. For more information about how to proceed with your vita, see the IN PRACTICE: Vita Pointers box.

IN PRACTICE

Vita Pointers

If you plan to pursue a career in psychology, you should start building your vita at this point. A quick web search on "building your vita as an undergraduate" revealed many hits—of the first 10 hits I found, four were specific to psychology departments. Also, several university career centers provided more generic information about building a vita for all majors. Your faculty members would also probably be willing to give you advice about your vita. If you have a psychology club or **Psi Chi**—the national honor society for psychology (www.psichi.org)—chapter at your school, you might suggest this topic as an idea for an informational meeting.

As many as three to four levels of conferences may be available at which you could make a presentation. The most typical presentation at such a conference comprises a research presentation based on an experiment that you designed, conducted, analyzed, and interpreted. At some levels, it *might* be possible to make a presentation based on a term paper or literature review that you wrote for a class, but these opportunities are less frequent.

Local Conferences

You may be required to make an in-class presentation of your paper in the course that required you to write a paper. Although such a presentation provides good experience, you should not include it on your vita. Instead, you should look for presentation opportunities that are not mandatory—that is, voluntary presentations for which you must submit a proposal for consideration. Many colleges and universities now hold annual or semiannual research conferences for their students; this meeting might be titled Scholars' Day or something similar. For example, Moravian College (where I currently teach) sponsors a Student Scholarship and Creative Arts Day. These types of meetings typically spotlight the research and other creative accomplishments of students. Depending on your college's format, presenting term papers in addition to research papers might be allowed. Check with your psychology faculty to determine whether your college or university sponsors such a meeting. If it does, consider submitting a proposal.

Regional Student Research Conferences

In the 1980s, undergraduate psychology research conferences became commonplace, with 16 such conferences listed in a 1985 issue of the *APA Monitor* (Carsrud & Palladino, 1985). Faculty organizers of these conferences developed them to give undergraduates the chance to present the results of their research studies in a low-stress environment at a low cost. As models, these conferences use professional meetings typically geared toward faculty presenters (described in the next section). The experience of presenting at such a conference gives students an incentive to engage in research, helps them learn how to communicate their work to other interested students, offers an opportunity to create an entry for their vita, and helps them learn skills that can be valuable in job searches or graduate school admission (Carsrud et al., 1984). For students who have not yet conducted a research study, some of these conferences are open to presentations of term papers or literature reviews (check their listings or send the conference organizer an email if you are uncertain about this possibility).

Attending such an undergraduate conference will allow you to experience an atmosphere similar to one at a professional conference because it will take place away from your campus (unless your school hosts the conference). You will gain the experience of making a presentation and receiving feedback from peers and, perhaps, faculty whom you do not know. If you attend with a group of psychology majors from your school, you will enjoy the camaraderie that results from a trip with students who have similar interests. For all these reasons, I heartily recommend that you look for an undergraduate research conference at which to present your research (or other writing project).

A large number of undergraduate psychology research conferences exist, as well as similar conferences that are open to students from all disciplines. On the next page, Table 9.1 lists some of the conferences designed primarily for undergraduate psychology students. Although some listings of such conferences are provided on websites (see a list at https://www.cur.org), I could not find one as comprehensive as Table 9.1, and even this table is probably not all-inclusive — undergraduate conferences pop up almost every year. A web search on a conference name should turn up a link to the conference. (The web addresses change frequently because the conferences often rotate locations, and each host school may develop its own website for the conference.) If Table 9.1 does not list a conference that is convenient to you, ask your psychology faculty whether one meets nearby or conduct your own online search for other possibilities. Also remember to search for conferences that are open to students from all majors, not just psychology. To present your research at such a conference, you will likely have to submit an abstract of your work (probably online) ahead of time and wait to hear whether your presentation has been accepted for inclusion on the program. Because of this need to apply to present, you must plan ahead—check online to determine the application deadline. Most of these student meetings are quite supportive, so the acceptance rate is likely to be high.

TABLE 9.1 Undergraduate Psychology Research Conferences
Conference Name
Arkansas Symposium for Psychology Students (ASPS)
Association for Psychological and Educational Research in Kansas (PERK)
Carolinas Psychology Conference
Conference for Undergraduate Research in Psychology (Indiana)
Georgia Undergraduate Research in Psychology Conference
Great Plains Students' Psychology Convention (Kansas/Nebraska/Missouri)
Hudson Valley Undergraduate Psychology Conference (New York)
ILLOWA Conference (Iowa/Illinois/Missouri; claims to be the longest-running undergraduate psychology conference in America—47 years in 2020)
Laurel Highlands Undergraduate Psychology Conference (Pennsylvania)
Lehigh Valley Association of Independent Colleges Undergraduate Psychology Conference (Eastern Pennsylvania)
Making Waves: An Undergraduate Psychology Research Conference (Western United States/Canada)
Michigan Undergraduate Psychology Research Conference
Mid-America Undergraduate Psychology Research Conference (Indiana/Illinois)
Mid-Atlantic Undergraduate Psychology Conference (MAUPC; Maryland)
Minnesota Undergraduate Psychology Conference

TABLE 9.1 **(continued)**
Ohio Undergraduate Psychology Research Conference
Red River Psychology Conference (Minnesota/North Dakota)
Reid Undergraduate Psychology Conference (Virginia)
Science Atlantic Undergraduate Psychology Conference (Nova Scotia)
Tri-State Undergraduate Psychology Research Conference (Iowa/Illinois/Wisconsin)
UCLA Psychology Undergraduate Research Conference
Virginia State University Black Psychology Student Research Conference
Western Pennsylvania Undergraduate Psychology Conference
Western Psychology Conference for Undergraduate Research (California)

Note. For information about any of these conferences, search for the conference name on the web. My apologies to any conference organizers whose conference I omitted from this list. Please contact me with your information so that I can update the list.

You might be able to apply to receive funds to offset the cost of attending a student research conference. Your psychology club or Psi Chi chapter, your department, or your college may have funds set aside for these kinds of trips. Often, student organizations may hold fundraisers to generate money to support trips to student conferences. However, the cost of a regional student conference is typically low enough that you should consider going at your own expense even if funding is not available.

Regional and National Professional Conferences

Seven regional psychological associations affiliated with the American Psychological Association exist to support psychological research (see Table 9.2 on the next page). These regional associations serve faculty and students in two ways — both for attending and for making presentations. Most of them are student friendly and may even have sessions specifically geared for students to attend and/or present their research. At many of these meetings, Psi Chi sponsors student-oriented sessions.

TABLE 9.2 Regional and National Psychology Association Conventions

Association Name	Website	Upcoming Meetings
Eastern Psychological Association (EPA)	https://www .easternpsychological.org	March 12–14, 2020 Boston, MA March 4–6, 2021 Philadelphia, PA March 3–5, 2022 New York, NY March 2–4, 2023 Boston, MA
Midwestern Psychological Association (MPA)	https://midwesternpsych .org/	April 23–25, 2020 Chicago, IL (permanent site) April 22–24, 2021 April 21–23. 2022
New England Psychological Association (NEPA)	http://www .newenglandpsychological .org/	October 23–24, 2020 Worcester State University
Rocky Mountain Psychological Association (RMPA)	http://www .rockymountainpsych.com/	April 16–18, 2020 Denver, CO April 7–11, 2021 Albuquerque, NM
Southeastern Psychological Association (SEPA)	http://www.sepaonline .com/	April 1–4, 2020 New Orleans, LA March 17–20, 2021 Orlando, FL
Southwestern Psychological Association (SWPA)	http://www.swpsych.org/	April 3–5, 2020 Frisco, TX April 9–11, 2021 San Antonio, TX
Western Psychological Association (WPA)	http://westernpsych.org/	April 30– May 3, 2020 San Francisco, CA

TABLE 9.2 (continued)		
Association Name	**Website**	**Upcoming Meetings**
American Psychological Association (APA)	https://convention.apa.org	August 6–9, 2020 Washington, DC August 12–15, 2021 San Diego, CA August 4–7, 2022 Minneapolis, MN
Association for Psychological Science (APS)	https://www .psychologicalscience.org	May 21–24, 2020 Chicago, IL May 27–30 Washington, DC May 26–29 Chicago, IL

Regional conferences typically hold meetings in the spring of each year (check association websites for future dates); most have revolving locations. As with the student meetings, you must submit an abstract of your proposed presentation and await notification about acceptance. Getting accepted to present at these meetings tends to be somewhat more competitive than for student meetings, but your odds of acceptance are still pretty good. The lead time for submitting abstracts to these meetings tends to be considerably longer than for the student meetings, so you must plan several months in advance. The ratio of faculty to student presenters can vary widely among these conferences, but they are clearly not geared only to students (unlike the student research conferences).

Two major national psychology organizations also host annual meetings (known as conventions) that feature presentations by faculty and students (see the last two entries of Table 9.2). At these meetings, you will find a much higher percentage of faculty and graduate student presenters, but there are still sessions designed for undergraduate presenters. The APA's annual convention typically takes place in August; the

Association for Psychological Science (APS) usually holds its annual meeting in May. Planning ahead is even more essential if you hope to present at these conventions, as their submission deadlines are many months in advance.

Both regional and national meetings take place in larger cities and are much more expensive to attend than are regional student meetings. As mentioned previously, your college may potentially be able to provide the funding needed to attend one of these meetings. If you present your research at such a conference, the probability of being funded is likely higher than if you are simply attending a meeting to observe. If you are a member of Psi Chi (www.psichi.org), that organization makes available options for funding, with specific funding offered for attending regional meetings. Psi Chi also provides awards for presenting research at either the APA or APS conventions. Finally, Psi Chi provides funding for travel not covered by other travel grants (check their website about all funding opportunities for travel).

What Does a Presentation Entail?

Often, these psychology meetings (at all three levels) will offer multiple options regarding presentation style. You typically have to choose your presentation style when you submit an abstract for consideration. The two most common options are to make an oral presentation or a poster presentation.

Oral Presentation

The traditional style of presentation is to stand in front of an audience and give an oral summary of your research. This format closely resembles a classroom presentation — standing at a podium or teaching station and talking about your research. The time allotted for oral presentations is typically limited; you might have 10–15 minutes to give your presentation. As you might guess, use of PowerPoint (or newer presentation software such as Prezi) is ubiquitous in talks.

When presenting your research findings, your talk would follow a rough outline of your final research report. You would briefly introduce the topic, surveying *some* of the relevant background research; you would then talk about your methodology, findings, and conclusions. If you are presenting research from a term paper, you would briefly introduce your topic, survey the relevant research, and cover any conclusions that you drew from the research.

Regardless of whether you present your research project or your term paper, I strongly urge you to prepare notes at which you can glance during the presentation, rather than simply read the paper verbatim. Imagine how boring you would find it if someone read a paper to you — and a bored audience is *not* what you want to experience. I also strongly urge you to practice your presentation in front of an audience — and a friendly, helpful audience is best. Whenever I take students to a conference to present their research, we all meet a day or two before leaving, and the students practice their presentations. In this way, they get the support of their classmates plus feedback from both their peers and me.

Poster Presentation

A newer presentation style that has emerged since I first began attending research conferences is the poster presentation. In a poster presentation, you create a poster describing your study, display the poster at a designated location at a designated time, stand by it for some time period (usually 60–90 minutes), and converse with interested conference attendees as they walk through the area set aside for poster presentations.

Poster presentations have some advantages over oral presentations: They are somewhat less formal, which seems to reduce the anxiety of presenting. You are able to talk to people who are interested in your specific research rather than a roomful of people who may be interested in a talk other than yours. At the same time, you must be prepared to think on your feet: Some people may want you to summarize the entire project (as in an oral presentation), but others may just want to ask specific questions about aspects of your project.

Preparing a Poster. When making a poster for presentation, your goal is to create a summary of the research that is visually appealing—you want to attract people to your poster so that you can converse with them about your project. The photograph on this page shows my student Eric Morton presenting a poster at Moravian's Student Scholarship and Creative Arts Day. When posters first began to be featured at conferences, they tended to consist of individual pages of text or graphs printed in a large font. Today, the ability to use large-format printers has transformed poster making. Now, a poster is likely to take the form of one large piece of paper covered with a blend of text and graphics (see Figure 9.1). Your college likely has such a printer available, along

Randy Smith

My student Eric Morton presented his research ("The Effects of Caffeine on Memory and Recall") at the Moravian College 12th annual Student Scholarship and Creative Endeavors Day, April 19, 2017.

Figure 9.1 Close-up view of Eric Morton's research poster

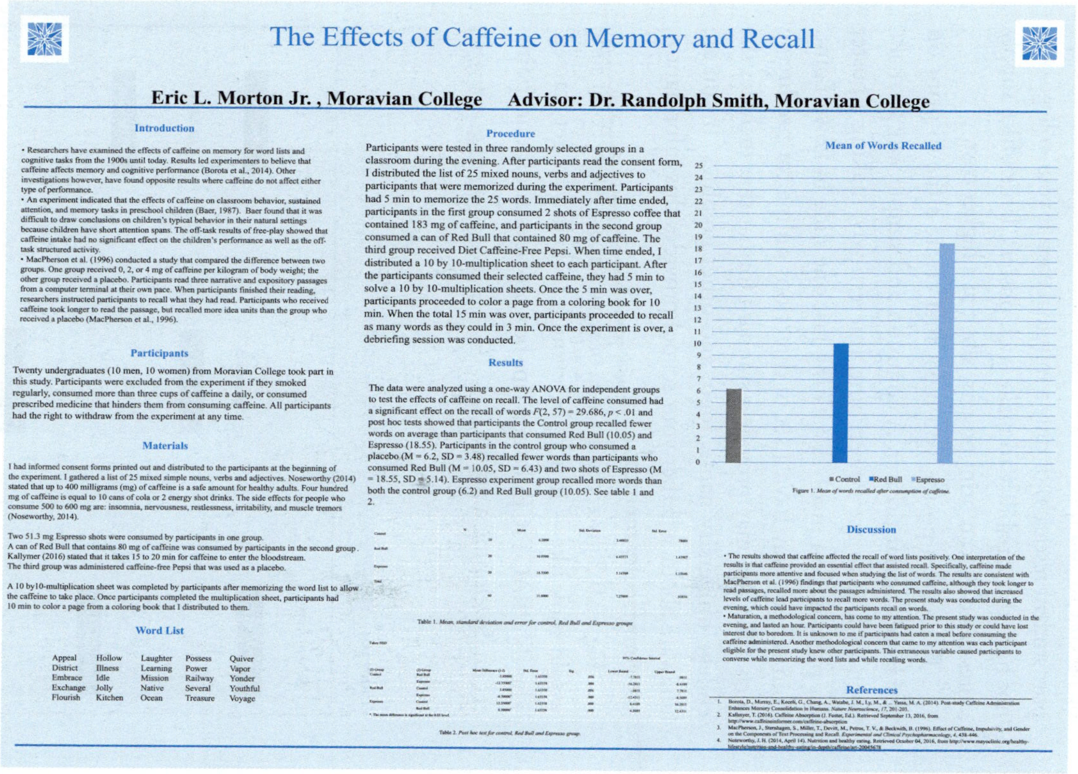

Used with permission of Eric Morton

with the resources needed to make your poster. Ideally, there will be no cost to you (provided by the college or department to support student research) or only a minimal cost. If your college does not have the capability to make such posters, large office supply stores typically can print posters, albeit at a higher cost.

To create a poster, you must first create a file to print on the large-format printer. A common and simple way to make such a file is to use PowerPoint. Interestingly, making a poster for presentation involves creating just one slide in PowerPoint. Your school may have a set of directions online for producing such a file and may provide a standard format that includes the college/university name, logo, and other graphics. If you are unaware about whether your school provides this information, ask your faculty mentor.

Figure 9.2 gives you an idea of what such a PowerPoint slide would look like—it may be enough to help you get started. The IN PRACTICE: Poster Tips box provides additional pointers on developing a poster.

Figure 9.2 Sample PowerPoint poster template

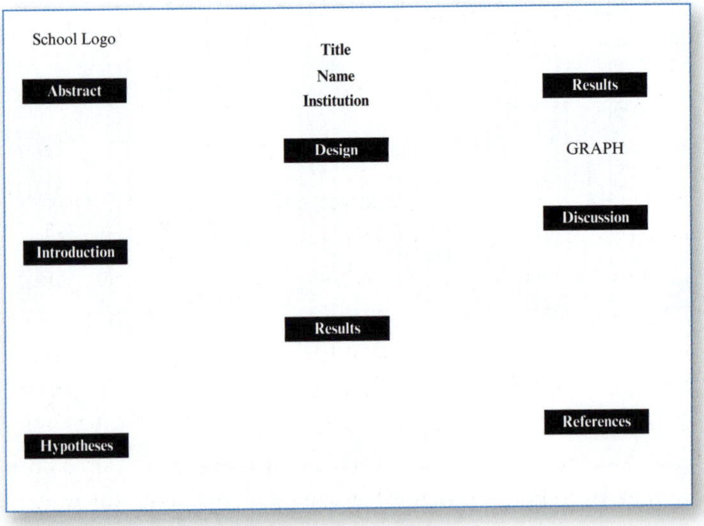

IN PRACTICE

Poster Tips

If your school does not provide information about producing a poster, you are still not on your own. I performed a web search on "make poster using PowerPoint" and got more than 4 million hits! When I narrowed the search to the specific version of PowerPoint I use, I still got almost 1.8 million hits. Many of the first hits were guides from colleges and universities, some of which referenced resources specific to their campus (details you would need to ignore), but the steps were still there to help you create a poster.

One of my hits was a YouTube video; when I clicked on it, I found many other YouTube videos that would help you create a poster. If you search the web for "poster presentation" and choose "Images," you will see a wide variety of research presentations via poster. By perusing these images, you can get ideas about how you might design your own poster.

One final tip/warning: If you run a web search for "poster templates PowerPoint," you will find many predesigned templates with which you can work. My warning revolves around the issue of whether the template is actually free or is linked to a company that will force you to have the company print your poster. Look very carefully if you find an online template! There is no need to pay for information and assistance that you can access at no cost.

Publishing Your Research

As I noted earlier in the chapter, publishing an article as an undergraduate can be helpful for your future, particularly if you plan on attending graduate school. Thus, I encourage you to pursue the publication process like other students whose published articles you have read about in this book (Khersonskaya & Smith, 1998; Peluso, 2000; Posey & Smith, 2003). The process of publishing your research involves several steps (Smith, 1998). The competition to get an article published can be stiff, so it is important to know exactly what you are doing along the way.

Selecting a Journal for Submission

This step is one of the most important in the entire publication process because submitting a manuscript to the wrong journal is almost certainly a kiss of death, at least for that journal. "All journals have a particular mission. Some journals publish articles only in narrow specialty areas; some publish only certain types of articles. It is your responsibility to submit your manuscript to the proper journal" (Smith, 1998, p. 51). Thus, you must do your homework before you even submit a manuscript for consideration (APA, 2020, pp. 373–376) — you must find a journal where your manuscript will have a fighting chance of being accepted. You have two types of journals from which to choose when submitting your manuscript.

Undergraduate Journals

There are many journals that publish student research. In a recent search, I found that the Council of Undergraduate Research (CUR) listed more than 240 journals that publish work by undergraduates (see a list at https://www.cur.org). Some of these journals publish work only by students from the college or university that sponsors the journal, but most are open to work by students from other schools. Some of the journals are open only to specific disciplines, but many are interdisciplinary in nature. From the CUR website, I compiled a list of 10 psychology-specific journals (see Table 9.3; search online to find each journal's current website). Of course, this number could change in the future, but at least the list provides you with a starting point. Many of these journals publish not only empirical research articles, but also literature reviews, term papers, and other specialty formats (consult the journal's website for additional details about the types of articles it publishes). In addition to these 10 journals, consult the CUR listing for other journals that might publish psychology articles because they are interdisciplinary journals — either totally (e.g., *American Journal of Undergraduate Research*) or partially (e.g., *Journal of Integrated Social Sciences*).

TABLE 9.3 Undergraduate Psychology Journals	
Journal Name	**Types of Articles Published (*in addition to* empirical research studies)**
Journal of European Psychology Students	Literature reviews, registered reports (in-progress reports)
Journal of Psychological Inquiry	Literature reviews, historical articles, special features
The Journal of Psychology and Behavioral Sciences	No specific guidelines; all topic areas in psychology
Journal of Undergraduate Ethnic Minority Psychology	Quantitative/qualitative empirical research, short reports
Modern Psychological Studies	Theoretical papers, literature reviews, book reviews
Psi Chi Journal of Psychological Research	Replication reports (also accepts articles by faculty authors)
Undergraduate Journal of Psychology	Literature reviews, hot topics
Undergraduate Journal of Psychology at Berkeley	Term papers, literature reviews
Undergraduate Research Journal of Psychology at UCLA	Literature reviews
Yale Review of Undergraduate Research in Psychology	Theoretical/literature reviews, short reports

Note. My apologies to any publishers or editors whose undergraduate journals I omitted from this list. Please contact me with your information so that I can update the list.

The good thing about submitting your manuscript to an undergraduate journal is that such journals tend to be less specialized than professional journals. (Here the term "professional journals" simply distinguishes undergraduate-oriented journals from the journals to which academic and research psychologists typically send submissions; it does *not* indicate that undergraduate journals are not professional in nature.) If you submit a manuscript to an undergraduate psychology journal, you do not need to worry that the journal might not publish articles in your area of psychology. If you submit a manuscript to an interdisciplinary undergraduate psychology journal, all you have to worry about is whether it publishes psychology articles. For example, it would not be wise to submit a manuscript to the *Armstrong Undergraduate Journal of History* unless your paper dealt with a history of psychology topic—even so, it would probably be wiser to submit that paper to an undergraduate psychology journal. Many of the journals in the CUR list include the words "undergraduate research" in their titles, so they may be appropriate outlets for your submission. Even so, you should check their websites to confirm that psychology manuscripts are appropriate for journals that appear to be interdisciplinary.

One other possible advantage of submitting your manuscript to an undergraduate journal is that the competition for publication might not be as strong as it would be for a professional journal, although it is difficult to know for sure. Journals differ widely in their acceptance (or rejection) rates—that is, the percentage of manuscripts that they accept (or reject). When I edited *Teaching of Psychology*, the **rejection rate** hovered between 75% and 80% of submissions, so I ended up accepting only one of every four or five manuscripts. When I edited the *Psi Chi Journal of Undergraduate Research*, the **acceptance rate** was much higher—perhaps as high as 50% of submissions. Undergraduate journals exist to support students in their research efforts, whereas professional journals exist to publish only the best research that they can. Thus, your odds of having a manuscript accepted for publication are likely higher if you submit your work to an undergraduate journal.

Professional Journals

Professional psychology journals vastly outnumber undergraduate psychology journals. The list of journals published by APA alone numbers more than 90. There are many additional publishers that publish psychology journals, which far outnumber the ones published by APA. Thus, it would be nearly impossible to create a list of all psychology journals similar to the list of undergraduate psychology journals in Table 9.3.

Unlike undergraduate journals, professional journals tend to be much more specialized by subject matter. If you submit a manuscript to one of these journals, it is *critical* that you select an appropriate journal based on the nature of your work. The first clue to the subject matter of a particular journal is its title — most journals have fairly specific titles that provide a clue to the subject matter that they publish. After you find one or more appropriately titled journals, you can peruse the contents of an issue or two to find out if your manuscript seems appropriate for each of these journals. Finally, when you have narrowed the list of possibilities, you should read the information that each journal provides to prospective authors. The "Instructions for Contributors," or something similar, is typical for this information; you can read it either in a hard copy of the journal (if your college's library carries the journal) or online by finding the journal's website. This information should give you additional insight into the types of articles the journal publishes, as well as any stipulations about types of manuscripts (e.g., word limits) appropriate for the journal. For example, you probably need to find out if the journal you are considering publishes one-experiment papers. Many journals seem to favor articles that include more than one experiment, so if you submit a single-experiment manuscript, it might have a low probability of being published in those journals. For more information on multiple-experiment articles, consult the *APA Publication Manual* (APA, 2020, pp. 4–5).

Your faculty mentor/research advisor will likely be an invaluable source of advice about selecting an appropriate journal for submitting your manuscript. Faculty members often have a good sense about the submission and publication process, particularly in their areas of expertise. If the faculty member directing your research project does not conduct research in your project's area, you could consult another faculty member who does conduct research in that specific area for advice about an appropriate journal.

Another valuable source of advice could be the APA's annual publication (typically in the July–August issue of *American Psychologist*) titled "Summary Report of Journal Operations." This report lists all APA and APA-division journals and provides information about the number of manuscripts received and published, as well as the rejection rate for each journal. In a recent report (APA, 2019), the rejection rates for the various APA journals ranged from 35% to 90% (average: 72%), which shows considerable variation among journals. If you have multiple journal options for submitting a manuscript, choosing the one with the lowest rejection rate may be a wise move.

Authorship

Determining authorship of a manuscript is an important enough issue that the *APA Publication Manual* covers it: Authorship entails not only the actual writing of a paper but also includes "those who have made substantial scientific contributions to a study" (APA, 2020, p. 24). Thus, you should likely include your research supervisor/mentor as an author on your manuscript. Given that the research was primarily your idea and your faculty mentor helped guide you throughout the process, you should list your name as the first author and your faculty mentor's name as the second author. If other students or faculty were involved in the process, "the name of the principal contributor appears first, with subsequent names appearing in order of decreasing contribution" (APA, 2020, p. 25).

Submitting Your Manuscript

In olden days, authors submitted multiple copies of their manuscripts via snail mail. Today, electronic submission is the rule, typically using one of two methods. One submission method is sending your manuscript and any other required documents via email attachments. This approach is fairly common for the undergraduate journals listed in Table 9.3. The alternative submission method is through a web portal established solely to receive manuscripts submitted to the journal. This approach typically requires you to register with the portal and set up an account. With an account, you can upload your manuscript and any other required documents to the portal (APA, 2020, pp. 381–382).

You should look for "Submission Instructions" (or some similar heading) either in the hard copy of a journal issue or on the journal's website. These instructions will provide all the information you need to submit your manuscript. Make sure that you read these instructions carefully: If you do not follow the instructions to the letter, you risk making a bad impression on the journal editor(s) or, even worse, not including required information or forms with your manuscript. In turn, your manuscript may be rejected and you will then have to resubmit it properly. Also, do not submit a manuscript in the same manner as novelists. It is fine to shop your novel around to different publishers; it is not OK to do the same with your research manuscript (see p. 2, https://www.apa.org/pubs/authors/new-author-guide.pdf). Submit your work to only one journal at a time!

One of the most important criteria listed for submitting a manuscript is that you format the manuscript in APA Style. This and previous chapters might have convinced you that I am obsessed with APA Style — and you wouldn't necessarily be wrong about that belief! In particular, I am obsessed with APA Style because editors and reviewers are also often obsessed with APA Style. Not following the required style gives people who read your paper (faculty, editors, reviewers) a ready reason to form a negative impression of your paper. In addition to using your *APA Manual* (APA, 2020) religiously, don't forget to use the Common Writing Problems, Explanations, and Solutions resource provided in Appendix D and the list of resources about writing and APA Style included in Chapter 8 to help you troubleshoot issues with APA formatting. Finally, refer to the "Checklist for Manuscript Submission" included in the previous edition of the *APA Manual* (APA, 2010, pp. 241–243), being sure to ignore outdated APA-Style guidelines (e.g., 12-word limit for title), and the list for the proper order of manuscript pages (see Table 9.4 on the next page).

TABLE 9.4	Page Order for Submitted Manuscripts in APA Style

Title page

Abstract (begin on p. 2)

Text of paper — begin with Introduction, showing the paper's title (p. 3)

Introduction, Method, Results, and Discussion sections (only Introduction begins on new page)

References (begin on a new page)

Footnote(s) (begin on a new page)

Table(s) (each on a new page)

Figure(s) (each on a new page)

Appendices (each appendix on a new page)

(APA, 2020, p. 43)

Before you submit your manuscript, it is a good idea to review Chapter 4 of the *APA Manual* (APA, 2020, pp. 111–127): Writing Style and Grammar. Also, Sections 2.25 (Paper Length) and 4.4 (Importance of Conciseness and Clarity) offer particularly important advice regarding the length of your manuscript. Journals have a limited amount of space — they can publish only the number of pages per year that their contract specifies. If authors submit overly long manuscripts, editors and reviewers often advise them to shorten their papers. By publishing shorter articles, editors can accommodate more authors and more articles. As the *APA Manual* (APA, 2020, p. 113) states, "Say only what needs to be said in your writing." If you are economical with your words and write a readable manuscript, your chance of being published increases. For one additional consideration you may have to take into account when you submit your manuscript, see the IN PRACTICE: Anonymous Submission box.

IN PRACTICE

Anonymous Submission

One possible option when submitting your manuscript is to choose masked or blind review (APA, 2020, pp. 378–379). If you select this option, you would need to remove all identifying information from your manuscript before submitting it. Masked review means that the people who review your manuscript would not know who authored it. Some research (Peters & Ceci, 1982) has indicated that reviewers may give harsher reviews to manuscripts submitted by authors from less prestigious institutions. Such bias might potentially extend to student authors, so submitting a masked manuscript may not be a bad idea, especially if it makes you feel less nervous about the process.

To be fair, not all authors believe that masked review is the answer to the potential for bias. "To date, there is little evidence that masked review is effective in redressing bias, even if we conclude that such bias exists" (Newcombe & Bouton, 2009, p. 64).

After You Submit Your Manuscript

Although exact procedures may vary from journal to journal, the review process is reasonably similar across the board. You can expect the editor to give your manuscript a quick look to confirm that it is appropriate for the journal and that you have followed the submission guidelines correctly. Assuming the manuscript clears this hurdle, the editor will send your paper to psychologists (in my experience, usually three) who are knowledgeable about your research area. They will read your manuscript and make recommendations to the editor about whether it is worthy of being published. The editor will consider the reviewers' comments, make a decision about the fate of your manuscript regarding publication, and communicate that decision to you.

It is important that you remain patient during the review process. According to the *APA Manual* (APA, 2020, p. 379), review times can vary, but the process usually takes two to three months. If you have not heard from the editor after three months, you are justified in contacting the editor to find out about the progress of the reviews.

Unfortunately, the review process usually takes longer than authors hope it will. This process depends on multiple people—the editor and the reviewers. All are typically faculty members, so they have to juggle their class, department, college, and family responsibilities along with reviewing manuscripts. The good news is that editors of the undergraduate journals (see Table 9.3) typically strive to have a faster review process than the other journals. Even so, the process will take time. Make a note of when you submitted your manuscript as a way to accurately track how long it has been out for review—the time will probably seem longer to you than it actually has been. Resist your urge to pester the editor about your manuscript until the three-month period (or whatever timeline the editor might have indicated) has passed.

Receiving Editorial Feedback

At some point after you submit the manuscript, you will receive feedback from the editor, probably via email if you submitted your paper electronically. The editor's letter to you will likely include one of three possible decisions.

Accepted

If you are fortunate enough to receive this verdict, you have cause to celebrate! Your manuscript is on the way to being published. The editor may request some minor changes to the manuscript, but it *will* be published at some point in the future. This decision is a rare one for an initial submission of a manuscript, however—so don't be surprised or disappointed if this is not the news you get. Although these data are old, Eichorn and VandenBos

(1985) reported that the acceptance rate for initial submissions was less than 2%. Clearly, even if this figure is somewhat outdated, acceptance on a first submission is highly unusual.

Rejected

If you receive a rejection letter, this decision typically means that you should not attempt to resubmit a revised version of the manuscript to the same journal. This decision could come for one of several reasons: (a) Your manuscript does not fit the journal's coverage area; (b) the manuscript has flaws, and the editor does not believe it can be salvaged; or (c) the editor believes the manuscript makes a minimal contribution to the field (APA, 2020, pp. 380–381). This decision is the most disappointing one, of course, but the editor and/or reviewers may still provide you with feedback that could help you strengthen the manuscript if you would like to revise it and submit it to a different journal. Although I noted earlier not to submit a manuscript to multiple journals at the same time, it *is* permissible to revise a rejected manuscript and submit it to a different journal.

Rejected With Invitation to Revise and Resubmit

This decision is a mixed bag. On the one hand, the editor has rejected your manuscript for publication. On the other hand, the editor and reviewers saw enough promise in your manuscript that they believe you could possibly revise it, based on their feedback, and resubmit it for a second consideration. The good news is that the rate of acceptance for revised manuscripts is much higher (20–40%) than for initial submissions (Eichorn & VandenBos, 1985) and is probably even higher for student journals (Smith, 1998). Nevertheless, acceptance of a revised manuscript largely depends on what you do as you revise it. As Smith (1998) noted, it is important to submit a revised manuscript that is better than the original, to address substantive comments made by the editor and reviewers, and to provide reasons for ignoring any suggestions that the editor and reviewers made.

Submitting an Improved Manuscript. When you receive the editor's decision letter, you will likely receive a long list of comments and suggestions from the editor and reviewers. For example, Fiske and Fogg (1990) found a mean of 8.6 editorial comments per review (based on 402 reviews of 153 manuscripts). Also, they found that these comments often did not overlap, so you could have quite a few comments and suggestions to consider.

It is important to not get offended as you read these comments and suggestions. It is easy to take the comments as personal criticisms of you, your ideas, or your writing. However, you should see these observations as constructive criticism, not destructive. The editor and reviewers are trying to help, not harm you. In my role as editor for both student and faculty journals, I was fond of telling authors, "I want to help you write the best article that you can." *All* of us can use help with our writing and communication, so take the comments as helpful rather than critical.

Going through all the comments and suggestions is a task you should undertake with your faculty sponsor/mentor for the paper if at all possible. Faculty typically have much more experience at the publication process and may be able to help in interpreting recommendations in a positive light, rather than in a negative manner. Also, your faculty mentor can help you sort the comments and suggestions into two categories—those you need to address in the revision and those that you can possibly ignore.

Addressing Important Comments. Ideally, some of the comments and suggestions will make you wonder why you didn't think of those points in the first place. This type of recommendation will enable you to readily see how making a change will improve your manuscript. Some of these ideas will be simple to implement; others will probably take more time. Thus, even comments and suggestions with which you agree may take some time to incorporate into your manuscript.

Other comments may be more difficult for you understand. Perhaps a reviewer wants you to clarify a passage that seems totally clear to you. Maybe the editor asks for more detail about your methodology, even though you thought you included all the relevant information. Keep in mind that you are intimately acquainted with your research and manuscript because you have spent so much time on both. Even your faculty mentor is relatively familiar with your work. What seems clear to the two of you might leave other people needing more information. If these readers who are knowledgeable in your field ask for clarification, it likely means that other readers would have similar questions.

"Ignoring" Editorial Suggestions. It is quite common to receive comments and suggestions with which you disagree; you may even receive contradictory recommendations from different reviewers. Thus, you (and your research advisor) may decide *not* to implement some of the editorial suggestions when revising your manuscript. Your research advisor may be able to help you distinguish between suggested changes that are essentially mandatory and comments that are merely suggestions. For example, if the editor or the reviewers document errors in APA formatting, it is mandatory that you correct them. In contrast, a comment that begins with "I wonder if you considered …" is more likely to be a point that the reviewer would like you to think about adding or changing in your manuscript.

Please notice the quotation marks around the word "Ignoring" in this section's title. It is not a good idea to automatically cast aside issues that the editor and reviewers have raised about your manuscript. First, you *must* have a good reason for ignoring or rejecting a recommendation that someone made about your manuscript. Second, you need to communicate that good reason clearly and convincingly. To accomplish this communication, you should write a cover letter (APA, 2020, pp. 382–383) to the editor to send along with your revised manuscript. In this letter, you should detail the changes that you have made in response to ideas raised by the editor and reviewers. After documenting the changes in the revision, you should address the reviewers' suggested changes that you did not make. Here is where it is crucial to have a good reason for not making a change. If your letter makes a good case for your position, the reviewer can appreciate that you considered the issue but chose not to make a change *and* had a good reason for that decision. Editors and reviewers are people: If you simply ignore their ideas without telling them why, they may not be happy—and you want to keep your editor and reviewers happy! If you cannot come up with a good reason to ignore a suggestion, make the suggested change.

Submitting a Revised Manuscript

Typically, in submitting a revision of your manuscript, you will use the same process (email or portal) that you used to submit the original version. In the cover letter's introductory paragraph, you should inform the editor that you are submitting a revision of your original manuscript (you may have received a submission number when you first made a submission—if so, include it). As detailed in the previous section, the information in the cover letter should point out how you changed the manuscript for the better.

Once you have submitted your revision, you are back to playing the waiting game for news from the editor. Although there is no guarantee, the review process for a revised manuscript often takes less time than the corresponding process for the original submission, as the editor and reviewers may primarily look at the changes that you made.

Having Your Manuscript Accepted

Ideally, you will eventually receive a letter of acceptance from the editor. As mentioned earlier, there will likely be a few minor edits to make to your manuscript before submitting a final version. In addition, you may have some other tasks to carry out for an accepted manuscript, but these items can vary from journal to journal. For example, you may have to complete a form or forms to submit with the final manuscript, covering matters such as copyright transfer, ethics, disclosures, and permissions (APA, 2020, pp. 382–390). Alternatively, you may have submitted one or more of these forms with the original manuscript submission.

To have a manuscript published, you typically have to sign a legal form regarding copyright (APA, 2020, pp. 392–393)— that is, you have to turn over rights to the article to the journal so that the journal can distribute the work and control its reuse by other parties. You may also sign a certificate of authorship that certifies you authored the work and that each author agrees to the order of authorship.

When you submitted the manuscript, you may have been required to submit a form attesting that you followed ethical standards in conducting your research. Disclosure forms typically ask about any conflicts of interest or financial agreements that you may have; you may have had to sign such a form when you originally submitted the manuscript. As a student author, it is unlikely that you will have any conflicts of interest or financial arrangements — for example, no drug company paid you to conduct research on one of its products.

Permission forms are necessary if you used any material from another source, such as figures and tables, data, test or scale items, long quotations, or the like (APA, 2020, pp. 384–391). As the author, you are responsible for obtaining permission to include those items in your article because the publishers and authors have copyrighted them.

When you submit all the required items, you will likely receive an acknowledgment from the editor. The editor may also provide a timeline leading up to the publication date. Some journals send **page proofs** — the version of the article that the publisher is ready to publish — to authors for their review. Reading page proofs gives you one last chance to catch errors in your manuscript before publication (APA, 2020, pp. 390–392). Typically, you are limited to minor changes — this is *not* the time to rewrite large sections of the articles or make numerous wording changes. Any changes you make at the proof stage should be vital to the article.

Finally, at some point, your article will be published. It may be published online or in a print journal — some journals even publish work online versions of articles before they come out in print. With print journals, you will typically receive a complimentary copy (or copies) of the issue containing your work. This is the point at which you can celebrate and pat yourself on the back for a job well done. Be sure to make copies of your article to share with your coauthors, faculty sponsor, friends, and family (or even to wallpaper your room)! Your friends and family may not understand the article, but they will be happy for you and proud of your accomplishment. Your department may even have a location where it displays copies of articles that department members have published — you should take advantage of this recognition if it is available. You are now a published author: Congratulations!

One of my former students related to me her experience in publishing:

> *I took a class at Philadelphia College of Osteopathic Medicine several years ago that was taught by Art Freeman. He really liked a paper that I wrote for the class, and he actually asked me to turn it into a chapter for a book he was editing. My writing skills got me published in a book in which most of the other contributors were nationally recognized experts in cognitive-behavioral therapy.* (Amy Witt-Browder, MA; OBU, 1988; Licensed Professional Counselor, Tower Health System, Hamburg, PA)

Two things stand out to me about Amy's story. First, she was able to publish a chapter in a book that was composed of chapters by experts in her field. That is quite an accomplishment. Second, she attributed her accomplishment to her writing skill. You should never underestimate the importance of writing well — a point I have emphasized from the first chapter of this book.

Concluding Thoughts

This chapter has dealt with the culmination of the research process: sharing your results and your writing with others. By taking this step, you are moving toward becoming a true professional in psychology. Although few students anticipate taking this step, I strongly urge you to consider it, especially if you plan to pursue psychology as your career.

As this is the last chapter of the book, I have some salient advice for you: Keep exercising your writing skills. You may have heard that you never forget how to ride a bicycle, a belief that actually has scientific support based on neuroscience (Communications Team, 2009). Unfortunately, writing is *not* like riding a bike — it is more like working out. Although you will not completely forget how to write if you don't continue to do so, you may lose some of the gains that you have made by writing papers for classes and/or publication. I urge you to keep your skills sharp — so keep practicing writing. Research has shown that repeated practice leads to better writing (e.g., Johnstone et al., 2002). You will also probably find that, as writing becomes habitual for you, it becomes easier and easier to do. I wish you the best in your future writing!

Critical Thinking Writing Assignments

Write answers (each a paragraph or two) to the following assignment questions aimed at students who are interested in attending graduate school and are about to embark on their first research course.

Assignment 1
Why is it important to attempt to present or publish a research project you have conducted?

Assignment 2
What are the pros and cons of making a poster presentation versus an oral presentation of your research findings?

Assignment 3
What do you think are the three most important considerations in working toward publishing your research study in a journal? Justify the importance of each consideration.

Assignment 4
Imagine that you have conducted an experiment, analyzed your data, and written your research report, which you would like to publish. Select one of the undergraduate journals from Table 9.3 and visit its website. Make a written list of all the steps you would have to take to submit a manuscript for review.

References

American Psychological Association. (2010). *Publication manual of the American Psychological Association* (6th ed.).

American Psychological Association. (2019). Summary report of journal operations, 2018. *American Psychologist, 74*(5), 615–616. http://dx.doi.org/10.1037/amp0000508

American Psychological Association. (2020). *Publication manual of the American Psychological Association* (7th ed.). https://doi.org/10.1037/0000165-000

Carsrud, A. L., & Palladino, J. J. (1985). Of data and informed opinion: A reply to Furedy and McRae. *Teaching of Psychology, 12*(4), 221–222. https://doi.org/10.1207/s15328023top1204_11

Carsrud, A. L., Palladino, J. J., Tanke, E. D., Aubrecht, L., & Huber, R. J. (1984). Undergraduate psychology research conferences: Goals, policies, and procedures. *Teaching of Psychology, 11*(3), 141–145. https://doi.org/10.1177/009862838401100304

Communications Team, University of Aberdeen. (2009, July 17). *Scientists discover why we never forget how to ride a bicycle.* https://www.abdn.ac.uk/news/3275/

Eichorn, D. H., & VandenBos, G. R. (1985). Dissemination of scientific and professional knowledge: Journal publication within the APA. *American Psychologist, 40*(12), 1309–1316. https://doi.org/10.1037/0003-066x.40.12.1309

Fiske, D. W., & Fogg, L. (1990). But the reviewers are making different criticisms of my paper! Diversity and uniqueness in reviewer comments. *American Psychologist, 45*(5), 591–598. https://doi.org/10.1037/0003-066x.45.5.591

Helms, J. L., & Rogers, D. T. (2015). *Majoring in psychology: Achieving your educational and career goals* (2nd ed.). Wiley Blackwell.

Johnstone, K. M., Ashbaugh, H., & Warfield, T. D. (2002). Effects of repeated practice and contextual-writing experiences on college students' writing skills. *Journal of Educational Psychology, 94*(2), 305–315. https://doi.org/10.1037/0022-0663.94.2.305

Khersonskaya, M. Y., & Smith, R. A. (1998). Cross-cultural differences in perception of physical attractiveness. *Psi Chi Journal of Undergraduate Research, 3*(1), 39–42. https://doi.org/10.24839/1089-4136.jn3.1.39

Landrum, R. E., & Davis, S. F. (2007). *The psychology major: Career options and strategies for success* (3rd ed.). Pearson Prentice Hall.

Morgan, B. L., & Korschgen, A. J. (2006). *Majoring in psych? Career options for psychology undergraduates* (3rd ed.). Pearson Education.

Newcombe, N. S., & Bouton, M. E. (2009). Masked reviews are not fairer reviews. *Perspectives on Psychological Science, 4*(1), 62–64. https://doi.org/10.1111/j.1745-6924.2009.01102.x

Peluso, E. A. (2000). Skilled motor performance as a function of type of mental imagery. *Journal of Psychological Inquiry, 5*, 11–14.

Peters, D. P., & Ceci, S. J. (1982). Peer-review practices of psychological journals: The fate of published articles, submitted again. *Behavioral and Brain Sciences, 5*(2), 187–195. https://doi.org/10.1017/s0140525x00011183

Posey, E., & Smith, R. A. (2003). The self-serving bias in children. *Psi Chi Journal of Undergraduate Research, 8*(4), 153–156. https://doi.org/10.24839/1089-4136.jn8.4.153

Smith, R. A. (1985). Advising beginning psychology majors for graduate school. *Teaching of Psychology, 12*(4), 194–198. https://doi.org/10.1207/s15328023top1204_2

Smith, R. A. (1998). Another perspective on publishing: Keeping the editor happy. *Psi Chi Journal of Undergraduate Research, 3*(2), 51–55. https://doi.org/10.24839/1089-4136.jn3.2.51

Smith, R. A., & Davis, S. F. (2013). *The psychologist as detective: An introduction to conducting research in psychology* (6th ed.). Pearson.

Weiten, W. (2014). *Psychology: Themes and variations* (briefer version, 9th ed.). Wadsworth Cengage Learning.

Appendix A: Sample Student Journal Article

Note. Eugenio Peluso published this article in the *Journal of Psychological Inquiry* in 2000 when he was an undergraduate student at Creighton University.

Skilled Motor Performance as a Function of Types of Mental Imagery

Eugenio A. Peluso
Creighton University

This study examined the effects of mental imagery on skilled motor performance. Participants, 48 volunteers from introductory psychology classes, were assigned to either of two treatment groups or to a control group. Skilled motor performance was assessed by the number of errors and the speed with which participants performed pick-up jacks and mirror tracing tasks. Between trials, participants engaged in either relevant imagery (i.e., the tasks), irrelevant imagery (i.e., scenic environments), or no imagery. Analysis of variance was used to test for differences between groups. Following five imagery sessions, participants in the relevant imagery group committed significantly fewer errors than those in the other groups. Directions for further research include an assessment of imagery for tasks emphasizing speed versus fine motor coordination.

The use of mental imagery shifts focus from an external to an internal emphasis, allowing individuals to reevaluate and redefine their goals. Jones and Stuth (1997) reported that mental imagery enhances performance, regulates arousal levels, stimulates cognitive and affective tactics, and eases the rehabilitation process in injured athletes. By influencing the training and goals of athletes, mental imagery revolutionized the scope of athletic performance and competition.

Sports and cognitive psychologists are developing techniques to maximize athletes' potential. Lejeune, Decker, and Sanchez (1994) examined 40 novice table tennis players and found that "imagining oneself successfully completing a sports skill in the absence of the actual movement or activity increases the probability of improving one's sport performance" (p. 627). Additionally, McKenzie and Howe (1997) demonstrated that participants placed in a 15-week mental imagery training program were more consistent and recorded higher scores in dart throwing than individuals who were not in the imagery condition. DeFrancesco and Burke (1997) surveyed 115 female and male professional tennis players and found that their most common strategies during play were imagery and visualization. By using these strategies, athletes were able to construct a preparatory routine, relax during points, and focus on personal goals.

Mental imagery is not a magical cure for poor performance. Rather, it simply opens new avenues to concentration, mental control, and confidence. Concentration is an integral element in the scheme of mental imagery. There are several definitions for concentration, but many sport psychologists agree that concentration is "the ability to focus on the relevant cues in one's environment and to maintain that focus for the duration of that athletic contest" (Weinberg, 1988, p. 59). More importantly, the cues used in concentration help to promote successful mental imagery. During an event, many players will try to cue themselves in order to facilitate efficient behavior. For instance, tennis players may cue themselves by talking through a point, "racquet back, hit it hard, follow through, and anticipate the next shot." Positive and efficient thoughts in the imagery process are essential in order to reap the benefits of mental imagery. Individuals may often "leave their body" in order to understand what they are trying to do. Reportedly, Chris Evert, a well-known tennis player, described just such an experience while engaged in imagery. She said,

> I see myself hitting crisp deep shots from the baseline and coming into the net if I get a weak return. This helps me prepare mentally for a match and I felt like I had already played the match even before I walked onto the court (Weinberg, 1988, p. 99).

Many athletes believe that mental imagery involves only one sense, vision, but this conclusion is incorrect. Along with the visual sense, mental imagery encompasses one's auditory, tactile, and kinesthetic senses, and these cues act in concert to influences one's emotional condition. First, people use their visual sense to follow a tennis ball or to identify a goal in hockey. Second, they use their tactile sense to familiarize themselves with the feel of the tennis racquet or the hockey stick. Third, they use their kinesthetic sense to keep their balance on the court or in the rink. Fourth, participants use their auditory sense to listen to the tennis ball hitting the strings or a hockey puck collide off the stick. These sounds may assist a player's timing in setting up the next shot in a ten-

Mark E. Ware from Creighton University was the faculty sponsor for this research project.

nis match or assist a save by the goalie in a hockey game. Finally, one's emotional state can facilitate mental imagery. By recreating prior experiences of anger, anxiety, frustration, or joy, athletes can control or regulate these emotions during competition (Weinberg, 1988).

Mental imagery is more than relaxation. Mental imagery consists of constructing a mental routine. Research by Beauchamp, Halliwell, Fournier, and Koestner (1996) found that novice golfers who implemented a pre-putt mental routine were more accurate than golfers who simply hit the ball. As a former tennis athlete, I recall that my tennis coach often removed me from the court and advised me to visualize my play. I would replay every shot, point, and objective.

A growing body of evidence supports the conclusion that mental imagery can enhance performance. As Shane Murphy, director of the sports science institute of the U.S. Olympic team, stated, "Ultimately it is going to come down to what's between the ears" (Allman, 1992, p. 50). The present study sought to extend the results of previous mental imagery research to other skilled motor tasks using nonprofessionals. Additionally, this study sought to differentiate the effects of the types of imagery. I hypothesized that individuals who applied relevant mental imagery would commit fewer errors and perform more quickly while playing jacks or tracing a star viewed in a mirror than individuals who simply relaxed with irrelevant imagery or individuals who simply read about mental imagery techniques.

Method

Participants

Participants were 48 traditional college-age student volunteers (38 women, 10 men) from introductory psychology classes. About 80% were Euro-Americans; the remainder were Asian-Americans and African-Americans. Conditions for participation followed APA ethical standards; students were told the general nature of the study and were given an opportunity to withdraw from the study at any time without the loss of extra credit points. To maintain confidentiality, names of the participants were not placed on the data sheets.

Materials

Participants were tested using a set of jacks, consisting of six rubber jacks and one rubber ball, and a standard mirror tracing apparatus from the Lafayette Manufacturing Co., as well as a six-pointed star. The star

was inscribed with parallel lines that were .5 cm apart. A conventional stopwatch was used to time participants' performance to the nearest second.

Procedure

Participants were randomly assigned to one of three groups: a relevant imagery and relaxation group, an irrelevant imagery and relaxation group, or a no imagery and relaxation control group. Between trials for the relevant imagery group, participants mentally rehearsed either the task of dropping the ball and picking up the jacks or drawing between the lines of the star while looking at the mirror. The inclusion of two motor tasks helped evaluate the degree of generalization of findings. Between trials in the other two groups, participants either engaged in irrelevant imagery or they read printed passages describing mental imagery. Thus, the first independent variable, treatment, used an independent groups design.

A within subjects design was used for the other independent variable, trials. All of the participants in each treatment group performed the jacks and mirror tracing tasks, counterbalanced for order. Participants performed a pretest on both the jacks and the mirror tracing tasks and performed four practice trials before the subsequent posttest evaluation. Thus, I used a 3 x 2 design with repeated measures on the second variable.

The experimenter instructed the participants on how to play jacks or perform mirror tracing. Using their dominant hands, participants were instructed to drop a rubber ball, fingers pointing toward the table, pick up one jack from the table, and catch the ball after one bounce. Participants were then asked to pick up two jacks, following the same process, until they were able to pick up all six jacks at one time. For the mirror tracing task, the experimenter instructed the participants to begin at the top of the star and draw a line between the parallel lines completely around the star while looking at the mirror.

Participants were assessed for the number of errors and the speed involved in completing each task. For the jacks task, errors consisted of failing to catch the rubber ball after the bounce or picking up the wrong number of jacks. For the mirror task, an error consisted of crossing either boundary of the star.

Participants in the relevant imagery group were instructed to visualize themselves performing the jacks or the mirror tracing task before they attempted the first practice trial. They were told to construct a mental routine (i.e., drop the ball, pick up a jack, catch the ball, or look in the mirror, start at the top of the star, draw only between the lines), and to repeat the mental routine for 1 min. Participants repeated the procedure before each practice trial and before the posttest.

In the irrelevant imagery condition, participants were instructed to close their eyes, breathe deeply, and imagine a beach scene and then a mountain top scene for 1 min. They repeated this procedure before each trial.

Participants in the control group read selected passages from a book explaining the techniques of mental imagery, but they did not engage in imagery practice. The passages used in this study were taken from Weinberg's (1988) mental imagery book. Each reading session was 1 min in length. The participants read a different passage before each trial.

Results

The results of a one-way ANOVA on pretest jacks errors revealed no significant differences among treatment groups, $F(2, 45) = 2.25$, $p = .12$. The results of a two-factor ANOVA (Treatment x Trials) revealed an overall difference among treatment groups, $F(2, 45) = 7.12$, $p = .002$, and between trials, $F(1, 45) = 17.99$, $p = .0004$, but there was no significant interaction. Statistically significant differences existed among treatment groups for jacks errors on the posttest performance, $F(2, 45) = 9.79$, $p = .0003$. There were significant improvements in performance from pretest to posttest for both the relevant and the irrelevant imagery conditions, $t(15) = 6.91$, $p = .0004$ and $t(15) = 2.18$, $p = .045$, respectively. Although both groups showed improvement, the relevant imagery group had significantly fewer errors than the irrelevant imagery group at posttesting. Figure 1 illustrates these results.

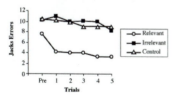

Figure 1. Jacks errors from pretest to posttest for the relevant, irrelevant, and control groups

The results of a one-way ANOVA on pretest star errors revealed no significant differences among treatment groups, $F(2, 45) = 1.32$, $p = .28$. The results of a two-factor ANOVA (Treatment x Trials) revealed an overall difference among treatment groups, $F(2, 45) = 3.68$, $p = .033$, and between trials, $F(1, 45) = 20.04$, $p < .0004$, but there was no significant interaction. Statistically significant differences existed among treatment groups for star errors on posttest performance, $F(2, 45) = 8.10$, $p = .001$. There were significant improvements in performance from pretest to posttest for the relevant imagery, irrelevant imagery, and control groups, $t(15) = 2.66$, $p = .018$, $t(15) = 2.25$, $p = .040$, and $t(15) = 2.84$, $p = .012$, respectively. Although all groups showed significant improvement, the relevant imagery group had fewer errors than the other two groups at posttesting. Figure 2 illustrates these results.

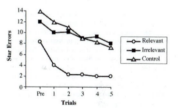

Figure 2. Star errors from pretest to posttest for the relevant, irrelevant, and control groups

The results of a one-way ANOVA on pretest time scores for both the jacks and star tasks revealed significant differences among the three treatment groups, $F(2, 45) = 3.34$, $p = .04$ and $F(2, 45) = 4.22$, $p = .02$, respectively. Despite random assignment to groups, participants in the treatment groups differed at the outset. Because of this pretest difference, no additional analyses were performed on the time data.

Discussion

The results supported the hypothesis that individuals who used relevant mental imagery committed fewer errors while playing jacks and while looking in a mirror to trace a star than individuals who relaxed with irrelevant imagery or simply read about imagery techniques. These findings were consistent with a similar study using

40 novice table tennis players (Lejeune et al., 1994), which indicated that imagining oneself completing a sports skill in the absence of the actual movement increased the probability of improving one's performance. These results were also consistent with a 15-week mental imagery program measuring dart throwing accuracy and consistency that found significant improvement for individuals who implemented relevant imagery techniques (McKenzie & Howe, 1997).

One explanation for findings in the present study may be, as DeFrancesco and Burke (1997) reported, that by using imagery and visualization, athletes were able to construct a preparatory routine, relax, and focus on personal goals. Another explanation may be Allman's (1992) contention that mental imagery is simply not relaxation. Rather, in order for athletes to attain the full benefits of mental imagery, they must construct a mental routine.

One limitation in this study was the presence of significant differences in speed among treatment groups on the pretest trial for the jacks and mirror tracing tasks, despite random assignment of participants. Replication of this study should reveal no such differences. That limitation was not crucial to this study because, in many sports, the most important activity (e.g., shooting a free throw or putting a golf ball) is the accuracy of the task, not its speed. Consider as well that baseball players are evaluated in terms of whether they hit the ball rather than how fast they swing.

Future research should examine sports or motor tasks that place a high priority on the speed of the task (e.g., short and long distance running, speed skating, and skiing). Future research should also investigate the use of relevant mental imagery on different kinds of athletic tasks. In one group of athletic tasks (e.g., field goal kicking, free throw shooting, and bowling) spectators can see the primary goal. In another group of athletic tasks (e.g., blocking schemes for interior linemen in football and set offensive and defensive formations in basketball), spectators may not notice the primary goal.

The use of relevant mental imagery in athletic performance may open the door to individuals' full potential. By implementing the techniques of mental imagery, an average athlete may become good, and a good athlete may become great.

References

Allman, W. F. (1992, August 3). The mental edge: Key to peak performance in sports and life. *U.S. News & World Report, 113*(5), 50-57.

Beauchamp, P. H., Halliwell, W. R., Fournier, J. F., & Koestner, R. (1996). Effects of cognitive-behavioral psychological training on the motivation, preparation, and putting performance of novice golfers. *Sport Psychologist, 10,* 157-170.

DeFrancesco, C., & Burke, K. L. (1997). Performance enhancement strategies used in a professional tennis tournament. *International Journal of Sport Psychology, 28,* 185-195.

Jones, L., & Stuth, G. (1997). The uses of mental imagery in athletics: An overview. *Applied and Preventative Psychology, 6,* 101-115.

Lejeune, M., Decker, C., & Sanchez, X. (1994). Mental rehearsal in table tennis performance. *Perceptual and Motor Skills, 79,* 627-641.

McKenzie, A. D., & Howe, B. L. (1997). The effects of imagery on self-efficacy for a motor skill. *International Journal of Sport Psychology, 28,* 196-210.

Weinberg, R, S. (1988). *The mental advantage: Developing your psychological skills in tennis.* Champaign, IL: Leisure Press.

Appendix B: Sample Student Journal Article With Notations for APA Style (7th ed.)

Note. APA Style evolves with each edition of the *Publication Manual. The Journal of Psychological Inquiry* published Peluso's article in 2000, which means that Peluso wrote his manuscript using the guidelines of the fourth edition of the *Publication Manual,* which was published in 1994 and is now three editions old. The comments on this version of the article do not indicate errors by Peluso or the journal—they are simply changes that would be necessary to update this article to the most recent version of APA Style (APA, 2020; see Appendix C).

> Hyphenate compound words with a participle when they modify a noun (APA, 2020, p. 163).

> Write in active voice for the Abstract (APA, 2020, pp. 73–74). There are three passive voice constructions highlighted in the Abstract and others marked throughout the article. See Chapter 3 for pointers on avoiding passive voice and Appendix C for reworded examples.

Skilled Motor Performance as a Function of Types of Mental Imagery

Eugenio A. Peluso
Creighton University

This study examined the effects of mental imagery on skilled motor performance. Participants, 48 volunteers from introductory psychology classes, were assigned to either of two treatment groups or to a control group. Skilled motor performance was assessed by the number of errors and the speed with which participants performed pick-up jacks and mirror tracing tasks. Between trials, participants engaged in either relevant imagery (i.e., the tasks), irrelevant imagery (i.e., scenic environments), or no imagery. Analysis of variance was used to test for differences between groups. Following five imagery sessions, participants in the relevant imagery group committed significantly fewer errors than those in the other groups. Directions for further research include an assessment of imagery for tasks emphasizing speed versus fine motor coordination.

The use of mental imagery shifts focus from an external to an internal emphasis, allowing individuals to reevaluate and redefine their goals. Jones and Stuth (1997) reported that mental imagery enhances performance, regulates arousal levels, stimulates cognitive and affective tactics, and eases the rehabilitation process in injured athletes. By influencing the training and goals of athletes, mental imagery revolutionized the scope of athletic performance and competition.

Sports and cognitive psychologists are developing techniques to maximize athletes' potential. Lejeune, Decker, and Sanchez (1994) examined 40 novice table tennis players and found that "imagining oneself successfully completing a sports skill in the absence of the actual movement or activity increases the probability of improving one's sport performance" (p. 627). Additionally, McKenzie and Howe (1997) demonstrated that participants placed in a 15-week mental imagery training program were more consistent and recorded higher scores in dart throwing than individuals who were not in the imagery condition. DeFrancesco and Burke (1997) surveyed 115 female and male professional tennis players and found that their most common strategies during play were imagery and visualization. By using these strategies, athletes were able to construct a preparatory routine, relax during points, and focus on personal goals.

Mental imagery is not a magical cure for poor performance. Rather, it simply opens new avenues to concentration, mental control, and confidence. Concentration is an integral element in the scheme of mental imagery. There are several definitions for concentration, but many sport psychologists agree that concentration is "the ability to focus on the relevant cues in one's environment and to maintain that focus for the duration of that athletic contest" (Weinberg, 1988, p. 59). More importantly, the cues used in concentration help to promote successful mental imagery. During an event, many players will try to cue themselves in order to facilitate efficient behavior. For instance, tennis players may cue themselves by talking through a point, "racquet back, hit it hard, follow through, and anticipate the next shot." Positive and efficient thoughts in the imagery process are essential in order to reap the benefits of mental imagery. Individuals may often "leave their body" in order to understand what they are trying to do. Reportedly, Chris Evert, a well-known tennis player, described just such an experience while engaged in imagery. She said,

> I see myself hitting crisp deep shots from the baseline and coming into the net if I get a weak return. This helps me prepare mentally for a match and I felt like I had already played the match even before I walked onto the court (Weinberg, 1988, p. 99).

Many athletes believe that mental imagery involves only one sense, vision, but this conclusion is incorrect. Along with the visual sense, mental imagery encompasses one's auditory, tactile, and kinesthetic senses, and these cues act in concert to influences one's emotional condition. First, people use their visual sense to follow a tennis ball or to identify a goal in hockey. Second, they use their tactile sense to familiarize themselves with the feel of the tennis racquet or the hockey stick. Third, they use their kinesthetic sense to keep their balance on the court or in the rink. Fourth, participants use their auditory sense to listen to the tennis ball hitting the strings or a hockey puck collide off the stick. These sounds may assist a player's timing in setting up the next shot in a ten-

> Avoid unclear referents (APA, 2020, p. 112). See Chapter 2 for clarification.

> Include statistical significance levels in the Abstract (APA, 2020, p. 74).

> This article does not contain a traditional APA-Style author note. See Chapter 5 for details about author notes and Chapter 4 for authorship considerations.

Mark E. Ware from Creighton University was the faculty sponsor for this research project.

> Use past tense for the literature review (APA, 2020, pp. 117–118).

> Cite the first author's name plus et al. in all citations of three or more authors (APA, 2020, p. 266; see also Chapter 6).

Journal of Psychological Inquiry, 2000, Vol. 5, 11–14

Avoid anthropomorphism—attributing human characteristics to objects or animals (APA, 2020, p. 117).

Use a comma to separate two independent clauses joined with a conjunction (APA, 2020, p. 155).

Do not hyphenate words with most prefixes. For a list of such prefixes, see Table 6.2 in the *APA Manual* (APA, 2020, p. 164).

This use of passive voice is acceptable because the emphasis is on the star and its lines, not on an actor (APA, 2020, p. 118).

Hyphenate adjective + noun phrase when it precedes a noun it modifies (APA, 2020, p. 163).

Use et al. (APA, 2020, p. 266; see also Chapter 6).

12

Eugenio A. Peluso

nis match or assist a save by the goalie in a hockey game. Finally, one's emotional state can facilitate mental imagery. By recreating prior experiences of anger, anxiety, frustration, or joy, athletes can control or regulate these emotions during competition (Weinberg, 1988).

Mental imagery is more than relaxation. Mental imagery consists of constructing a mental routine. Research by Beauchamp, Halliwell, Fournier, and Koestner (1996) found that novice golfers who implemented a pre-putt mental routine were more accurate than golfers who simply hit the ball. As a former tennis athlete, I recall that my tennis coach often removed me from the court and advised me to visualize my play. I would replay every shot, point, and objective.

A growing body of evidence supports the conclusion that mental imagery can enhance performance. As Shane Murphy, director of the sports science institute of the U.S. Olympic team, stated, "Ultimately it is going to come down to what's between the ears" (Allman, 1992, p. 50). The present study sought to extend the results of previous mental imagery research to other skilled motor tasks using nonprofessionals. Additionally, this study sought to differentiate the effects of the types of imagery. I hypothesized that individuals who applied relevant mental imagery would commit fewer errors and perform more quickly while playing jacks or tracing a star viewed in a mirror than individuals who simply relaxed with irrelevant imagery or individuals who simply read about mental imagery techniques.

Avoid anthropomorphism (APA, 2020, p. 117).

Method

Participants

Participants were 48 traditional college-age student volunteers (38 women, 10 men) from introductory psychology classes. About 80% were Euro-Americans; the remainder were Asian-Americans and African-Americans. Conditions for participation followed APA ethical standards; students were told the general nature of the study and were given an opportunity to withdraw from the study at any time without the loss of extra credit points. To maintain confidentiality, names of the participants were not placed on the data sheets.

Materials

Hyphenate (APA, 2020, pp. 162-163).

Participants were tested using a set of jacks, consisting of six rubber jacks and one rubber ball, and a standard mirror tracing apparatus from the Lafayette Manufacturing Co., as well as a six-pointed star. The star

was inscribed with parallel lines that were .5 cm apart. A conventional stopwatch was used to time participants' performance to the nearest second.

Procedure

Participants were randomly assigned to one of three groups: a relevant imagery and relaxation group, an irrelevant imagery and relaxation group, or a no imagery and relaxation control group. Between trials for the relevant imagery group, participants mentally rehearsed either the task of dropping the ball and picking up the jacks or drawing between the lines of the star while looking at the mirror. The inclusion of two motor tasks helped evaluate the degree of generalization of findings. Between trials in the other two groups, participants either engaged in irrelevant imagery or they read printed passages describing mental imagery. Thus, the first independent variable, treatment, used an independent groups design.

A within subjects design was used for the other independent variable, trials. All of the participants in each treatment group performed the jacks and mirror tracing tasks, counterbalanced for order. Participants performed a pretest on both the jacks and the mirror tracing tasks and performed four practice trials before the subsequent posttest evaluation. Thus, I used a 3 x 2 design with repeated measures on the second variable.

The experimenter instructed the participants on how to play jacks or perform mirror tracing. Using their dominant hands, participants were instructed to drop a rubber ball, fingers pointing toward the table, pick up one jack from the table, and catch the ball after one bounce. Participants were then asked to pick up two jacks, following the same process, until they were able to pick up all six jacks at one time. For the mirror tracing task, the experimenter instructed the participants to begin at the top of the star and draw a line between the parallel lines completely around the star while looking at the mirror.

Participants were assessed for the number of errors and the speed involved in completing each task. For the jacks task, errors consisted of failing to catch the rubber ball after the bounce or picking up the wrong number of jacks. For the mirror task, an error consisted of crossing either boundary of the star.

Participants in the relevant imagery group were instructed to visualize themselves performing the jacks or the mirror tracing task before they attempted the first practice trial. They were told to construct a mental routine (i.e., drop the ball, pick up a jack, catch the ball, or

Avoid anthropomorphism (APA, 2020, p. 117).

Provide the model number for apparatus (APA, 2020, p. 85).

Use current terms for racial groups and ethnic groups; do not hyphenate (APA, 2020, pp. 142–145; see also Chapter 2).

Remember to write in active voice as much as possible (APA, 2020, p. 118). Using passive voice is acceptable if the focus should be on "the object or recipient of the action" (APA, 2020, p. 118). See Chapter 3 for pointers on avoiding passive voice.

Do not refer to yourself in the third person (APA, 2020, p. 120). See another example later in this paragraph.

Provide measures of effect size for all statistical results (APA, 2020, p. 89). Every time there is a probability statement (*p* = .nn), it should be followed by an effect size measure. There are 15 statistical results that need effect sizes in the Results section.

Do not use a comma between the two parts of a compound predicate (APA, 2020, p. 156).

Include information about nonsignificant findings (APA, 2020, p. 86).

---

look in the mirror, start at the top of the star, draw only between the lines, and to repeat the mental routine for 1 min. Participants repeated the procedure before each practice trial and before the posttest.

In the irrelevant imagery condition, participants were instructed to close their eyes, breathe deeply, and imagine a beach scene and then a mountain top scene for 1 min. They repeated this procedure before each trial.

Participants in the control group read selected passages from a book explaining the techniques of mental imagery, but they did not engage in imagery practice. The passages used in this study were taken from Weinberg's (1988) mental imagery book. Each reading session was 1 min in length. The participants read a different passage before each trial.

Results

The results of a one-way ANOVA on pretest jacks errors revealed no significant differences among treatment groups, $F(2, 45) = 2.25$, $p = .12$. The results of a two-factor ANOVA (Treatment x Trials) revealed an overall difference among treatment groups, $F(2, 45) = 7.12$, $p = .002$, and between trials, $F(1, 45) = 17.99$, $p = .0004$, but there was no significant interaction. Statistically significant differences existed among treatment groups for jacks errors on the posttest performance, $F(2, 45) = 9.79$, $p = .0003$. There were significant improvements in performance from pretest to posttest for both the relevant and the irrelevant imagery conditions, $t(15) = 6.91$, $p = .0004$ and $t(15) = 2.18$, $p = .045$, respectively. Although both groups showed improvement, the relevant imagery group had significantly fewer errors than the irrelevant imagery group at posttesting. Figure 1 illustrates these results.

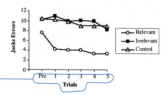

Figure 1. Jacks errors from pretest to posttest for the relevant, irrelevant, and control groups

The results of a one-way ANOVA on pretest star errors revealed no significant differences among treatment groups, $F(2, 45) = 1.32$, $p = .28$. The results of a two-factor ANOVA (Treatment x Trials) revealed an overall difference among treatment groups, $F(2, 45) = 3.68$, $p = .033$, and between trials, $F(1, 45) = 20.04$, $p < .0004$, but there was no significant interaction. Statistically significant differences existed among treatment groups for star errors on posttest performance, $F(2, 45) = 8.10$, $p = .001$. There were significant improvements in performance from pretest to posttest for the relevant imagery, irrelevant imagery, and control groups, $t(15) = 2.66$, $p = .018$, $t(15) = 2.25$, $p = .040$, and $t(15) = 2.84$, $p = .012$, respectively. Although all groups showed significant improvement, the relevant imagery group had fewer errors than the other two groups at posttesting. Figure 2 illustrates these results.

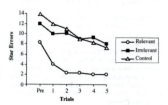

Figure 2. Star errors from pretest to posttest for the relevant, irrelevant, and control groups

The results of a one-way ANOVA on pretest time scores for both the jacks and star tasks revealed significant differences among the three treatment groups, $F(2, 45) = 3.34$, $p = .04$ and $F(2, 45) = 4.22$, $p = .02$, respectively. Despite random assignment to groups, participants in the treatment groups differed at the outset. Because of this pretest difference, no additional analyses were performed on the time data.

Discussion

The results supported the hypothesis that individuals who used relevant mental imagery committed fewer errors while playing jacks and while looking in a mirror to trace a star than individuals who relaxed with irrelevant imagery or simply read about imagery techniques. These findings were consistent with a similar study using

---

Use sans serif font when creating graphs for your manuscript (APA, 2020, p. 227). The published article may show a different font in graphs than the one you used in your manuscript (as in this case). See Chapter 8 for instructions about creating figures for your paper.

Report exact *p* values to 2 or 3 decimal places . . . round as much as possible (APA, 2020, p. 180), so the trailing 0 is not needed.

Provide DOI for journal articles that have a DOI. If no DOI exists, provide URL for the article if possible (APA, 2020, p. 294).

Provide URL for magazine articles if one exists (APA, 2020, p. 320).

14   Eugenio A. Peluso

40 novice table tennis players (Lejeune et al., 1994), which indicated that imagining oneself completing a sports skill in the absence of the actual movement increased the probability of improving one's performance. These results were also consistent with a 15-week mental imagery program measuring dart throwing accuracy and consistency that found significant improvement for individuals who implemented relevant imagery techniques (McKenzie & Howe, 1997).

One explanation for findings in the present study may be, as DeFrancesco and Burke (1997) reported, that by using imagery and visualization, athletes were able to construct a preparatory routine, relax, and focus on personal goals. Another explanation may be Allman's (1992) contention that mental imagery is simply not relaxation. Rather, in order for athletes to attain the full benefits of mental imagery, they must construct a mental routine.

One limitation in this study was the presence of significant differences in speed among treatment groups on the pretest trial for the jacks and mirror tracing tasks, despite random assignment of participants. Replication of this study should reveal no such differences. That limitation was not crucial to this study because, in many sports, the most important activity (e.g., shooting a free throw or putting a golf ball) is the accuracy of the task, not its speed. Consider as well that baseball players are evaluated in terms of whether they hit the ball rather than how fast they swing.

Future research should examine sports or motor tasks that place a high priority on the speed of the task (e.g., short and long distance running, speed skating, and skiing). Future research should also investigate the use of relevant mental imagery on different kinds of athletic tasks. In one group of athletic tasks (e.g., field goal kicking, free throw shooting, and bowling) spectators can see

the primary goal. In another group of athletic tasks (e.g., blocking schemes for interior linemen in football and set offensive and defensive formations in basketball), spectators may not notice the primary goal.

The use of relevant mental imagery in athletic performance may open the door to individuals' full potential. By implementing the techniques of mental imagery, an average athlete may become good, and a good athlete may become great.

References

Allman, W. F. (1992, August 3). The mental edge: Key to peak performance in sports and life. *U.S. News & World Report, 113*(5), 50-57.

Beauchamp, P. H., Halliwell, W. R., Fournier, J. F., & Koestner, R. (1996). Effects of cognitive-behavioral psychological training on the motivation, preparation, and putting performance of novice golfers. *Sport Psychologist, 10,* 157-170.

DeFrancesco, C., & Burke, K. L. (1997). Performance enhancement strategies used in a professional tennis tournament. *International Journal of Sport Psychology, 28,* 185-195.

Jones, L., & Stuth, G. (1997). The uses of mental imagery in athletics: An overview. *Applied and Preventative Psychology, 6,* 101-115.

Lejeune, M., Decker, C., & Sanchez, X. (1994). Mental rehearsal in table tennis performance. *Perceptual and Motor Skills, 79,* 627-641.

McKenzie, A. D., & Howe, B. L. (1997). The effects of imagery on self-efficacy for a motor skill. *International Journal of Sport Psychology, 28,* 196-210.

Weinberg, R, S. (1988). *The mental advantage: Developing your psychological skills in tennis.* Champaign, IL: Leisure Press.

Include issue number (in parentheses) from the volume if the journal has issue numbers (APA, 2020, p. 294). Do not italicize issue number or parentheses, such as *10*(2).

Provide DOI for books if one exists (APA, 2020, p. 321).

Do not include the publisher's location (APA, 2020, p. 295) as in previous editions of APA Style.

Reference: American Psychological Association. (2020). *Publication manual of the American Psychological Association* (7th ed.). https://doi.org/10.1037/0000165-000

Appendix C: Sample Student Article in Manuscript Form

Note. This manuscript version of Peluso (2000) updates the article shown in Appendix A to the current version of APA Style (APA, 2020). You can examine the APA Style discrepancies shown in Appendix B to see how the edits in this manuscript version corrected the APA Style issues. It was not possible to compute the actual effect sizes for the statistical results because the original data were not available. Instead of actual figures, each "n" would represent a number.

Skilled Motor Performance as a Function of Types of Mental Imagery

Eugenio A. Peluso

Department of Psychology, Creighton University

> Although the actual article had only one note, I included all four types of notes here—three, of course, simply list what WOULD go in that note if there was one.

Author Note

(First paragraph provides ORCID identification number if the author has one.)

(Second paragraph provides any change in institutional affiliation subsequent to the study, if applicable.)

Mark E. Ware from Creighton University was the faculty sponsor for this research project.

(Contact information for the author would typically appear in this paragraph of the author note.)

Abstract

This study examined the effects of mental imagery on skilled motor performance. Participants, 48 volunteers from introductory psychology classes, performed in either of two treatment groups or a control group. I assessed skilled motor performance by the number of errors and the speed with which participants performed pick-up jacks and mirror-tracing tasks. Between trials, participants engaged in either relevant imagery (i.e., the tasks), irrelevant imagery (i.e., scenic environments), or no imagery. I used analysis of variance to test for differences between groups. Following five imagery sessions, participants in the relevant imagery group committed significantly fewer errors (all $ps < .05$) than participants in the other groups. Directions for further research include an assessment of imagery for tasks emphasizing speed versus fine motor coordination.

Keywords: mental imagery, motor performance, sport psychology

The MARGINS on all sides of all pages should be 1 inch wide.

Skilled Motor Performance as a Function of Types of Mental Imagery

The use of mental imagery shifts focus from an external to an internal emphasis, allowing individuals to reevaluate and redefine their goals. Jones and Stuth (1997) reported that mental imagery enhanced performance, regulated arousal levels, stimulated cognitive and affective tactics, and eased the rehabilitation process in injured athletes. By influencing the training and goals of athletes, mental imagery revolutionized the scope of athletic performance and competition.

Sports and cognitive psychologists are developing techniques to maximize athletes' potential. Lejeune et al. (1994) examined 40 novice table tennis players and found that "imagining oneself successfully completing a sports skill in the absence of the actual movement or activity increases the probability of improving one's sport performance" (p. 627). Additionally, McKenzie and Howe (1997) demonstrated that participants placed in a 15-week mental imagery training program were more consistent and recorded higher scores in dart throwing than individuals who were not in the imagery condition. DeFrancesco and Burke (1997) surveyed 115 female and male professional tennis players and found that their most common strategies during play were imagery and visualization. By using these strategies, athletes were able to construct a preparatory routine, relax during points, and focus on personal goals.

Mental imagery is not a magical cure for poor performance. Rather, it simply opens new avenues to concentration, mental control, and confidence. Concentration is an integral element in the scheme of mental imagery. There are several definitions for concentration, but many sport psychologists agree that concentration is "the ability to focus on the relevant cues in one's environment and to maintain that focus for the duration of that athletic contest" (Weinberg,

MENTAL IMAGERY AND MOTOR PERFORMANCE   4

1988, p. 59). More importantly, the cues used in concentration help to promote successful

mental imagery. During an event, many players will try to cue themselves in order to facilitate

efficient behavior. For instance, tennis players may cue themselves by talking through a point,

"racquet back, hit it hard, follow through, and anticipate the next shot." Positive and efficient

thoughts in the imagery process are essential in order to reap the benefits of mental imagery.

Individuals may often "leave their body" in order to understand what they are trying to do.

Reportedly, Chris Evert, a well-known tennis player, described just such an experience while

engaged in imagery. She said,

> I see myself hitting crisp deep shots from the baseline and coming into the net if I get a
>
> weak return. This helps me prepare mentally for a match and I felt like I had already
>
> played the match even before I walked onto the court (Weinberg, 1988, p. 99).

Many athletes believe that mental imagery involves only one sense, vision, but this

conclusion is incorrect. Along with the visual sense, mental imagery encompasses one's

auditory, tactile, and kinesthetic senses, and these cues act in concert to influences one's

emotional condition. First, people use their visual sense to follow a tennis ball or to identify a

goal in hockey. Second, they use their tactile sense to familiarize themselves with the feel of the

tennis racquet or the hockey stick. Third, they use their kinesthetic sense to keep their balance on

the court or in the rink. Fourth, participants use their auditory sense to listen to the tennis ball

hitting the strings or a hockey puck collide off the stick. These sounds may assist a player's

timing in setting up the next shot in a tennis match or assist a save by the goalie in a hockey

game. Finally, one's emotional state can facilitate mental imagery. By recreating prior

experiences of anger, anxiety, frustration, or joy, athletes can control or regulate these emotions

during competition (Weinberg, 1988).

MENTAL IMAGERY AND MOTOR PERFORMANCE   5

Mental imagery is more than relaxation. Mental imagery consists of constructing a mental routine. Research by Beauchamp et al. (1996) found that novice golfers who implemented a preputt mental routine were more accurate than golfers who simply hit the ball. As a former tennis athlete, I recall that my tennis coach often removed me from the court and advised me to visualize my play. I would replay every shot, point, and objective.

A growing body of evidence supports the conclusion that mental imagery can enhance performance. As Shane Murphy, director of the sports science institute of the U.S. Olympic team, stated, "Ultimately it is going to come down to what's between the ears" (Allman, 1992, p. 50). I sought to extend the results of previous mental imagery research to other skilled motor tasks using nonprofessionals. An additional goal for this study was to differentiate the effects of the types of imagery. I hypothesized that individuals who applied relevant mental imagery would commit fewer errors and perform more quickly while playing jacks or tracing a star viewed in a mirror than individuals who simply relaxed with irrelevant imagery or individuals who simply read about mental imagery techniques.

Method

Participants

Participants were 48 traditional college-age student volunteers (38 women, 10 men) from introductory psychology classes. About 80% were European Americans; the remainder were Asian Americans and African Americans. Conditions for participation followed APA ethical standards; I informed students about the general nature of the study and gave them an opportunity to withdraw from the study at any time without the loss of extra credit points. To maintain confidentiality, participants did not place their names on the data sheets.

Materials

To test the participants, I used a set of jacks, consisting of six rubber jacks and one rubber ball, and a standard mirror-tracing apparatus from the Lafayette Manufacturing Co. (Model 31010), as well as a six-pointed star. The star was inscribed with parallel lines that were .5 cm apart. I timed participants' performance to the nearest second with a conventional stopwatch.

Procedure

I randomly assigned participants to one of three groups: a relevant imagery and relaxation group, an irrelevant imagery and relaxation group, or a no imagery and relaxation control group. Between trials for the relevant imagery group, participants mentally rehearsed either the task of dropping the ball and picking up the jacks or drawing between the lines of the star while looking at the mirror. The inclusion of two motor tasks helped evaluate the degree of generalization of findings. Between trials in the other two groups, participants either engaged in irrelevant imagery, or they read printed passages describing mental imagery. Thus, the first independent variable, treatment, used an independent-groups design.

The other independent variable, trials, used a within-subjects design. All of the participants in each treatment group performed the jacks and mirror-tracing tasks, counterbalanced for order. Participants performed a pretest on both the jacks and the mirror-tracing tasks and performed four practice trials before the subsequent posttest evaluation. Thus, I used a 3 x 2 design with repeated measures on the second variable.

I instructed the participants on how to play jacks or perform mirror tracing. Using their dominant hands, participants dropped a rubber ball, fingers pointing toward the table, picked up one jack from the table, and caught the ball after one bounce. I then had participants pick up two jacks, following the same process, until they were able to pick up all six jacks at one time.

For the mirror-tracing task, I instructed the participants to begin at the top of the star and draw a line between the parallel lines completely around the star while looking at the mirror.

Participants' assessments were the number of errors and the speed involved in completing each task. For the jacks task, errors consisted of failing to catch the rubber ball after the bounce or picking up the wrong number of jacks. For the mirror task, an error consisted of crossing either boundary of the star.

I instructed participants in the relevant imagery group to visualize themselves performing the jacks or the mirror-tracing task before they attempted the first practice trial. I told them to construct a mental routine (i.e., drop the ball, pick up a jack, catch the ball, or look in the mirror, start at the top of the star, draw only between the lines) and to repeat the mental routine for 1 min. Participants repeated the procedure before each practice trial and before the posttest.

In the irrelevant imagery condition, I instructed participants to close their eyes, breathe deeply, and imagine a beach scene and then a mountain top scene for 1 min. They repeated this procedure before each trial.

Participants in the control group read selected passages from a book explaining the techniques of mental imagery, but they did not engage in imagery practice. The passages used in this study came from Weinberg's (1988) mental imagery book. Each reading session was 1 min in length. The participants read a different passage before each trial.

Results

The results of a one-way ANOVA on pretest jacks errors revealed no significant differences among treatment groups, $F(2, 45) = 2.25$, $p = .12$, $\eta^2 = .nn$. The results of a two-factor ANOVA (Treatment x Trials) revealed an overall difference among treatment groups, $F(2, 45) = 7.12$, $p = .002$, $\eta^2 = .nn$, and between trials, $F(1, 45) = 17.99$, $p = .0004$, $\eta^2 = .nn$, but there was no significant interaction ($p > .05$). Statistically significant differences existed among treatment groups for jacks errors on the posttest performance, $F(2, 45) = 9.79$, $p = .0003$, $\eta^2 = $ .nn. There were significant improvements in performance from pretest to posttest for both the relevant and the irrelevant imagery conditions, $t(15) = 6.91$, $p = .0004$, $d = $ n.nn and $t(15) = 2.18$, $p = .045$, $d = $ n.nn, respectively. Although both groups showed improvement, the relevant imagery group had significantly fewer errors than the irrelevant imagery group at posttesting. Figure 1 illustrates these results.

The results of a one-way ANOVA on pretest star errors revealed no significant differences among treatment groups, $F(2, 45) = 1.32$, $p = .28$, $\eta^2 = $ .nn. The results of a two-factor ANOVA (Treatment x Trials) revealed an overall difference among treatment groups, $F(2, 45) = 3.68$, $p = .033$, $\eta^2 = $ .nn, and between trials, $F(1, 45) = 20.04$, $p < .0004$, $\eta^2 = $ .nn, but there was no significant interaction ($p > .05$). Statistically significant differences existed among treatment groups for star errors on posttest performance, $F(2,45) = 8.10$, $p = .001$, $\eta^2 = $ .nn. There were significant improvements in performance from pretest to posttest for the relevant imagery, irrelevant imagery, and control groups, $t(15) = 2.66$, $p = .018$, $d = $ n.nn, $t(15) = 2.25$, $p = .04$, $d = $ n.nn, and $t(15) = 2.84$, $p = .012$, $d = $ n.nn, respectively. Although all groups showed significant improvement, the relevant imagery group had fewer errors than the other two groups at posttesting. Figure 2 illustrates these results.

The results of a one-way ANOVA on pretest time scores for both the jacks and star tasks revealed significant differences among the three treatment groups, $F(2, 45) = 3.34$, $p = .04$, $\eta^2 = $ .nn and $F(2, 45) = 4.22$, $p = .02$, $\eta^2 = $ .nn, respectively. Despite random assignment to groups, participants in the treatment groups differed at the outset. Because of this pretest difference, I performed no additional analyses on the time data.

Discussion

The results supported the hypothesis that individuals who used relevant mental imagery committed fewer errors while playing jacks and while looking in a mirror to trace a star than individuals who relaxed with irrelevant imagery or simply read about imagery techniques. These findings were consistent with a similar study using 40 novice table tennis players (Lejeune et al., 1994), which indicated that imagining oneself completing a sports skill in the absence of the actual movement increased the probability of improving one's performance. These results were also consistent with a 15-week mental imagery program measuring dart throwing accuracy and consistency that found significant improvement for individuals who implemented relevant imagery techniques (McKenzie & Howe, 1997).

One explanation for findings in the present study may be, as DeFrancesco and Burke (1997) reported, that by using imagery and visualization, athletes were able to construct a preparatory routine, relax, and focus on personal goals. Another explanation may be Allman's (1992) contention that mental imagery is simply not relaxation. Rather, in order for athletes to attain the full benefits of mental imagery, they must construct a mental routine.

One limitation in this study was the presence of significant differences in speed among treatment groups on the pretest trial for the jacks and mirror-tracing tasks, despite random assignment of participants. Replication of this study should reveal no such differences. That limitation was not crucial to this study because, in many sports, the most important activity (e.g., shooting a free throw or putting a golf ball) is the accuracy of the task, not its speed. Consider as well that baseball players are evaluated in terms of whether they hit the ball rather than how fast they swing.

Future research should examine sports or motor tasks that place a high priority on the speed of the task (e.g., short and long distance running, speed skating, and skiing). Future research should also investigate the use of relevant mental imagery on different kinds of athletic tasks. In one group of athletic tasks (e.g., field goal kicking, free throw shooting, and bowling), spectators can see the primary goal. In another group of athletic tasks (e.g., blocking schemes for interior linemen in football and set offensive and defensive formations in basketball), spectators may not notice the primary goal.

The use of relevant mental imagery in athletic performance may open the door to individuals' full potential. By implementing the techniques of mental imagery, an average athlete may become good, and a good athlete may become great.

References

Allman, W. F. (1992, August 3). The mental edge: Key to peak performance in sports and life. *U.S. News & World Report, 113*(5), 50 –57.

Beauchamp, P. H., Halliwell, W. R., Fournier, J. F., & Koestner, R. (1996). Effects of cognitive-behavioral psychological training on the motivation, preparation, and putting performance of novice golfers. *Sport Psychologist, 10*(2), 157–170. https://doi.org/10.1123/tsp.10.2.157

DeFrancesco, C., & Burke, K. L. (1997). Performance enhancement strategies used in a professional tennis tournament. *International Journal of Sport Psychology, 28*(2), 185–195.

Jones, L., & Stuth, G. (1997). The uses of mental imagery in athletics: An overview. *Applied and Preventative Psychology, 6*(2), 101–115. https://doi.org/10.1016/s0962-1849(05)80016-2

Lejeune, M., Decker, C., & Sanchez, X. (1994). Mental rehearsal in table tennis performance. *Perceptual and Motor Skills, 79*(1, Pt. 2), 627–641. https://doi.org/10.2466/pms.1994.79.1.627

McKenzie, A. D., & Howe, B. L. (1997). The effects of imagery on self-efficacy for a motor skill. *International Journal of Sport Psychology, 28*(2), 196–210.

Weinberg, R, S. (1988). *The mental advantage: Developing your psychological skills in tennis.* Leisure Press.

MENTAL IMAGERY AND MOTOR PERFORMANCE   12

Figure 1

Jacks Errors From Pretest to Posttest for the Relevant, Irrelevant, and Control Groups

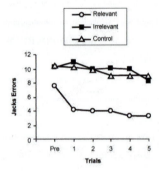

MENTAL IMAGERY AND MOTOR PERFORMANCE 13

Figure 2

Star Errors From Pretest to Posttest for the Relevant, Irrelevant, and Control Groups

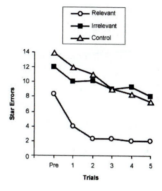

Reference: American Psychological Association. (2020). *Publication manual of the American Psychological Association* (7th ed.). https://doi.org/10.1037/0000165-000

Appendix D: Common Writing Problems, Explanations, and Solutions

A. APA Style: Common Writing Problems, Explanations, and Solutions
(Typical editing marks I use for writing issues on student papers)

My Mark(s) on Paper	Explanation/Solution
anthro (anthropomorphism)	Don't write about animals or inanimate things as if they have human characteristics (APA, 2020, p. 117). "An experiment cannot *attempt to demonstrate*, *control unwanted variables*, or *interpret findings*, nor can tables or figures *compare* (all of these can, however, *show* or *indicate*)" (*APA*, 2010, p. 69).
awk	Avoid awkward prose, wording, or constructions. Strive for clear, concise writing (APA, 2020, pp. 113–114).
bias	Avoid using biased language based on age, disability, gender, research group description, racial and/or ethnic identity, sexual orientation, socioeconomic status, or intersectionality (any combination of these factors). See the *APA Manual* (2020, pp. 131–149) for explanations and acceptable terms.
cf	Cross-reference; compare to another page — usually when you spelled a name one way in text and a different way in a reference, which indicates an error. Spelling of authors' names and dates in citations should exactly match the entries in the list of references (APA, 2020, p. 257).
font size	Do not change font size anywhere in the text of the paper — APA specifies 10–12 point fonts, depending on the specific font used (APA, 2020, p. 44).
font style	Do not change font style (i.e., font appearance or type) anywhere in the text of the paper — APA specifies serif fonts such as Times New Roman, Georgia, or Computer Modern or sans serif fonts such as Calibri, Arial, or Lucida Sans Unicode (APA, 2020, p. 44).

Continued • • •

(continued)

My Mark(s) on Paper	Explanation/Solution
informal *or* colloq	Avoid writing informally (e.g., contractions) and using colloquialisms (used in everyday speech) in your paper (APA, 2020, p. 116).
INC *or* inc	Avoid writing incomplete sentences — a complete sentence requires a subject and a verb. Beginning a thought with a subordinate conjunction (e.g., "since," "while," "because") or a relative pronoun (e.g., "who," "that," "which") may result in a phrase or a dependent clause (not a complete sentence).
indef	For clarity, make certain that the referent for a pronoun is clear (APA, 2020, p. 112). The words "this, that, these, those" are indefinite and typically need a noun to specify the referent clearly.
itals	Use italics for journal and book titles, key terms or phrases, statistical symbols, and journal volume numbers (see APA, 2020, pp. 170–172 for full list of when to use and not use italics).
lc	Use lowercase letters for minor words (three letters or fewer) in titles of books and journals and for names of conditions or groups in an experiment (see APA, 2020, pp. 165–169 for full capitalization rules).
M/F	In APA Style, "female" and "male" are adjectives, not nouns (APA, 2020, p. 139), unless the age range includes children and adults. Thus, it is OK to say "female participants," but not "females."
# mis (mismatch)	Avoid using a singular and plural referent for the same person/people (e.g., "the *participant* wrote *their* answers on a sheet of paper") or subject/verb. Often, you are trying to avoid using an awkward construction such as "he/she," which is not acceptable in APA Style (APA, 2020, p. 140). You may be able to use plural referents such as "they" to avoid this problem (APA, 2020, p. 121). **EXCEPTION:** APA Style *does* allow for the use of "they" as a singular pronoun for someone who uses "they" as their pronoun or for a person whose gender is either unknown or irrelevant (APA, 2020, pp. 120–121).

Continued • • •

(continued)

My Mark(s) on Paper	Explanation/Solution
#	Avoid leaving out spaces where they are needed (e.g., statistical results [APA, 2020, pp. 187–188], references [APA, 2020, pp. 316–352], punctuation [APA, 2020, p. 154]).
opinion *or* editorializing	Cite sources of information (ideas, theories, research) that influenced your work and for information that is not common knowledge (APA, 2020, p. 253). Avoid opinionated or editorial comments, although there is some room for conjecture about implications or applications in Discussion sections (APA, 2020, pp. 89–90).
p.? *or* p.#	Provide page numbers within citations for direct quotes (APA, 2020, p. 270).
PV	This mark indicates passive voice. In APA Style, write in active voice as much as possible. Passive voice is acceptable when you focus on an object or recipient of action rather than on the actor (APA, 2020, p. 118). APA style *does* allow use of first-person pronouns (APA, 2020, p. 120), which can help avoid passive voice, particularly in writing Method sections.
proved	Avoid using forms of the word "prove" in describing research. This point is based on statistics (rather than APA Style), which can make only probabilistic statements (remember that the probability of chance is never 0.00).
ref?	To avoid plagiarism, be sure to include citations and references for all information (even ideas) you obtain from all sources (APA, 2020, pp. 254–256). Try to paraphrase your sources rather than quoting from them (APA, 2020, pp. 269–270). If you do quote from sources, be certain to use APA Style (APA, 2020, pp. 270–278) for the quotations.
secondary	Avoid secondary sources, in which an author writes about someone else's ideas or research, as much as possible (APA, 2020, p. 258). Instead, read primary sources (the original content or source) when you can. If primary sources are unavailable, out of print, or in a language you do not understand, using secondary sources is acceptable.

Continued • • •

(continued)	
My Mark(s) on Paper	**Explanation/Solution**
temporal	"While" is always and "since" is usually a time-related word in APA Style (APA, 2020, p. 123). "While" refers to simultaneous occurrence; "since" refers to time passage after something has happened. Using "since" to mean "because" is acceptable in APA Style *if* the meaning is not ambiguous.
that/which	Use "that" for restrictive clauses and "which" for nonrestrictive clauses (APA, 2020, pp. 122–123). Restrictive clauses are necessary to the meaning of a sentence and are not set off with commas; nonrestrictive clauses add information but are not necessary for the sentence's meaning (set off with commas).
transpose	Many spelling errors occur because of simple letter transpositions (reversed order). Use Word's spell-check feature to detect many misspellings.
?	Something you wrote is unclear. Strive for clarity in your writing (APA, 2020, pp. 113–114).
wd *or* wd choice	As you write (and later edit), make certain that each word means exactly what you intend it to mean (APA, 2020, p. 113).

B. Other Important Points

Use **past tense** to refer to all aspects of the previous research that you cited (APA, 2020, pp. 117–118). Researchers conducted their research in the past, so that is the tense you should use.

***

For any **test** or **questionnaire,** you mention (by name) that some researchers have used, you must provide a reference for that instrument (APA, 2020, pp. 340–341). If you refer to it generically (e.g., an intelligence test) rather than by name (e.g., WAIS), then you do not need a reference. Although you should use secondary sources sparingly (APA, 2020, p. 253), citing a test that researchers used is a case in which a secondary citation is acceptable. For example: The researchers used the Wechsler Adult Intelligence Scale (as cited in Smith & Jones, 2008).

***

Continued • • •

(continued)

You should provide an in-text **citation** for *every* reference, and you should provide a **reference** for *every* study/article you mention in the text (APA, 2020, p. 257). The citations and references should **match**—the order of authors is very important because it reflects the relative contribution of each author to the article (APA, 2020, p. 25)! If authors' middle initials appear on the article, include them in your references (APA, 2020, p. 286).

***

Writing in a research report should be informative, not flowery or dramatic. You are simply trying to communicate basic information to the reader. Strive for **conciseness** and **clarity**. In other words, be as specific and direct and brief as you can in your writing (APA, 2020, pp. 111–117). One particular example occurs frequently in many student papers:

"In a study by Smith and Jones (1984), the researchers found. . . ." *(This construction is Indirect and more wordy than necessary.)*

"Smith and Jones (1984) found ..." *(This construction is much more direct and less wordy.)*

***

Avoid redundancy (APA, 2020, pp. 114–115). Examples: whether (or not); their (own)—*the parenthetical words are typically redundant*

***

Read the "Strategies to Improve Your Writing" section of the *APA Manual* (APA, 2020, pp. 125–127) and implement those strategies.

***

AFFECT vs. EFFECT
These words are often confused with each other—probably because both can be a noun and both can be a verb. However, in the vast majority of cases, you will probably use "affect" as a verb ("The IV affected the DV.") and use "effect" as a noun ("The IV had a large effect on the DV.").

In case you are interested, when you use "affect" as a noun, it is synonymous with "emotion" ("The patient showed flat affect.").

When you use "effect" as a verb, it means "to bring about" ("The presidential candidates hope to effect a change in U.S. policy.").

Reference: American Psychological Association. (2010). *Publication manual of the American Psychological Association* (6th ed.).

American Psychological Association. (2020). *Publication manual of the American Psychological Association* (7th ed.). https://doi.org/10.1037/0000165-000

Glossary

2 × 2 factorial design—An experimental design with two independent variables, each of which has two levels or groups

2 × 2 × 2 factorial design—An experimental design with three independent variables, each of which has two levels or groups

3 × 2 factorial design—An experimental design with two independent variables, with one independent variable having three levels or groups and the other independent variable having two levels or groups

abstract—A brief summary of an article printed on the first page of the article

acceptance rate—The percentage of journal manuscripts submitted that are accepted for publication

active voice—A verb construction in which the verb represents an action performed by the subject of a sentence; preferred in APA Style

American Psychological Association's ethics code—A set of standards compiled to describe rules of conduct for psychologists in scientific, educational, and professional roles

analysis of variance (ANOVA)—An inferential statistical test used to compare (a) the means from three or more samples or (b) the means from two or more independent variables

annotated bibliography—A list of references to sources with a brief description of the information contained in each source

annotation—A descriptive note about a cited source; may include summary information about and/or evaluation of the source

APA (American Psychological Association) Style—Style mandated by the American Psychological Association for writing psychological papers; it addresses both writing style and formatting

APA Manual—(see *Publication Manual of the American Psychological Association*)

APA Publication Manual—(see *Publication Manual of the American Psychological Association*)

Apparatus/Materials/Testing Instruments/Measures subsection—Typically the second subsection within the Method section; describes the equipment (apparatus), stimuli (materials), standardized inventories (testing instruments), or experimenter-devised instruments (measures) that the experimenter used in the study

appendix—Supplementary material that appears at the end of a journal article or paper; in APA Style, used for material that is brief and easily presented in print

author information—Name(s) and institutional affiliation(s) of author(s) of article; includes contact information such as email address

author search—A search in an electronic database focused on one particular author

Boolean operators—Words that connect search terms to broaden or narrow a bibliographic search; AND, OR, NOT

central tendency—One score used to describe a set of data; a typical or representative score

chi-square test (χ^2)—A statistical test that compares frequency counts or percentages/proportions by comparing observed frequencies to expected frequencies

Chicago style—Writing style developed by the University of Chicago in the early 1900s; used in the humanities and some social sciences (also known as **Turabian style**)

citation—A text notation to a publication signifying that the author used information from that reference; includes the name(s) of the author(s) and the date of publication

confederates—People who appear to be research participants but who actually work for the experimenter; they often attempt to influence actual research participants during an experiment

continuous pagination—The page numbering system for a journal that begins at page 1 for the first issue of the year and uses consecutive numbering throughout the entire year

cross-cultural research—Research conducted with participants from or in a different culture; seeks to determine whether results hold across cultures

d—A measure of effect size used for a difference between two means

degrees of freedom—The number of values that are free to vary in the calculation of a statistic; used with inferential statistics to help determine the probability of chance

dependent variable—A behavior that the experimenter measures to determine the effect of the independent variable

descriptive statistics—Statistics used to summarize and describe data

descriptor search—A bibliographic search of records performed by entering a word or term from the PsycINFO Thesaurus into the DE Subjects search field; allows for the most precise bibliographic searching

descriptor term (subject term)—A single word or brief phrase used to describe the content of a source; a record typically has about six such terms; also known as *index term*

digital object identifier (DOI or **doi)**—A unique alphanumeric string used to identify particular content such as a journal article; it is permanent and will not change, unlike many URLs

Discussion section—The fourth major section of an APA-Style research report; often summarizes the results of an experiment, contrasts those results with the results of previous research, and draws a conclusion about the experiment

dissertation—A long paper written as part of the requirements for a doctoral degree; in psychology, most often a write-up of an experimental study

DOI (or doi)—(see digital object identifier)

editing/revising—Reworking a paper after it has been written to make it a better paper—focusing on elements such as clarity, focus, communication, conciseness, and so on

effect size—The magnitude or size of an experimental treatment or independent variable

electronic literature search (online search)—A process of searching for relevant publications through an online database (e.g., PsycINFO)

et al.—Latin abbreviation for "and others"; used to take the place of authors' names in certain types of text or parenthetical citations

eta squared (η^2)—A measure of effect size used to measure the proportion of the total variance that can be attributed to an effect; preferred effect size measure for ANOVA

F test—An inferential statistical test used to compare (a) the means from three or more samples or (b) the means from two or more independent variables

factorial ANOVA—A version of ANOVA used for experimental designs with two or more independent variables (see 2×2, $2 \times 2 \times 2$, and 3×2 factorial designs at beginning of Glossary for specific examples)

figure—A graphical display of statistical results

font—A specific style of typeface such as Times New Roman or Arial; Word allows the writer to change typefaces through a pull-down menu

footnote—A note documenting or explaining some text material (not important enough to put in the actual text) that usually appears at the bottom of a page; reserved in APA Style for additional content or copyright permission

free-text search—A bibliographic search of all record fields conducted by entering any word in a search box

goodness of fit test—A version of the chi-square test that compares actual observations to observations predicted from a hypothesis or theory

hit—A source matching the criteria set in a bibliographic search

independent variable—In a true experiment, a stimulus that the experimenter directly manipulates to determine its effect on a behavior

industrial/organizational (I/O) psychology—A branch of psychology that focuses on the application of psychological research and theory in business and industrial settings

inferential statistics—Statistics used to draw conclusions (inferences) about samples; used to determine whether an independent variable has a significant effect on a dependent variable

informed consent—Written agreement from research participants indicating that they are willing to participate in an experiment after having the research and any factors that might affect their participation in the experiment explained to them

Institutional Review Board (IRB)—A college or university committee that reads research proposals to determine whether the research is ethically acceptable

interaction—The joint statistical effect of two (or more) independent variables on a dependent variable in a factorial design

interlibrary loan—A system in which one library obtains material from another library for a patron's use

introduction section—The introduction to an article, which is the first major section of an APA-Style research report; typically contains a review of relevant research and hypothesis(-es)

journal—In psychology, a scholarly academic publication that includes scientific articles, usually reporting the results of scientific experiments

journal issue—A single copy of a scholarly journal that is published on a preset calendar basis; a journal that publishes quarterly would have four issues per year

linked full text—The full text of a hyperlinked journal article, usually in PDF form

literature review—A summary of previous research that is relevant to a particular topic area; in an introduction, typically leads up to the experiment being reported

M—Symbol for a mean; an alternative to $\overline{X}$ or μ that is acceptable in documents written in APA Style

main effect—The statistical effect of a single independent variable on a dependent variable in a factorial design

Manual—(see *Publication Manual of the American Psychological Association*)

margins—The area of "white space" on a typed page at the top, bottom, and both sides of the page

mean—The arithmetic average of a set of scores; symbolized by $\overline{X}$ for a sample of scores or μ for a population of scores

median—The number exactly in the middle of a distribution of scores

meta-analysis—A statistical method of summarizing the results of multiple research findings to provide a clearer overall picture of those findings

Method section—The second major section of an APA-Style research report; contains detailed information about the research conducted

minimal risk—A federal government term applied to research participants, meaning that they are at no more risk from research participation than they would be in routine life or physical/mental examinations

MLA style—Writing style developed by the Modern Language Association; used in literature and the humanities

mode—The most frequently occurring score in a distribution of scores

nonrestrictive clause—A clause serving as an adjective to modify a word; not essential to the meaning of a sentence (the meaning would not change if the clause was deleted); set off with commas

nonsignificant effect—A difference between two or more groups that is small and likely due to chance

one-way ANOVA—A version of ANOVA comparing means from three or more samples from one independent variable

operational definition—Defining a variable in terms of the action needed to produce it (e.g., thirst = 3 hours of water deprivation)

original study—A research study conducted on a new topic and that asks a new research question

Oxford comma—In a list of three or more items, the comma coming after the penultimate item in the list, immediately before "and" or "or."

p value (probability value or **probability of chance)**—In general, a probability value; more specifically, the probability of a statistical result occurring by chance (if the null hypothesis is true)

page proofs—A sample of a journal article (or book chapter) ready to be published; authors can examine them for errors to be corrected before publication

Participants/Subjects subsection—Typically the first subsection within the Method section; describes the participants or subjects who took part in the study

passive voice—A verb construction in which a noun (or noun phrase) that would be an object in an active-voice construction becomes the subject of a sentence; not preferred in APA Style

past tense—A verb tense indicating that an action has already taken place; typically used to write about past research results

Pearson product–moment correlation (r)—A measure of linear correlation—the degree of relationship between two variables

plagiarism—Use of another person's ideas, information, or words without giving credit to that person

post hoc test—Statistical comparisons between pairs of means when there is a significant F-test finding

prepositional phrase—A group of words containing a preposition and a noun, pronoun, or words used as a noun; because it is a phrase, it cannot stand alone as a sentence

primary source—A source such as a journal article or book that reports original research or content

Procedure subsection—Typically the third subsection within the Method section; provides a step-by-step description of what the participants and experimenter did during the experiment

programmatic research—A series of research experiments focused on the same narrow topic

proofreading—Reading a paper after it has been written, looking for errors in grammar, spelling, punctuation, and other problems

Psi Chi—The national honor society for psychology (www.psichi.org/)

PsycINFO—An electronic database that compiles journal articles, books, and dissertations related to psychology and social sciences

PsycINFO record—Complete bibliographic and summary information about any source obtained by searching PsycINFO

PsycINFO Thesaurus—A PsycINFO resource that provides a listing of descriptor terms related to the content of the database; allows the user to determine technical psychological terms used in the discipline

Publication Manual of the American Psychological Association (APA Publication Manual, APA Manual, Manual)—The official style guidebook for APA-Style writing; published by the American Psychological Association

Purdue Online Writing Laboratory (OWL)—An online resource for writing resources and instructional material; in addition to information about writing in general, it contains information specific to disciplines and writing styles (e.g., APA Style)

r—Symbol for a Pearson product–moment correlation

record—Complete bibliographic and summary information about any source obtained by searching an electronic database

reference—A complete bibliographic record of a source cited in a journal article or paper

reference list—A comprehensive list of complete bibliographic material for each source cited in a paper

rejection rate—The percentage of journal manuscripts submitted for publication that are rejected

relative pronoun—A pronoun that connects a clause or a phrase to a noun; the clause or phrase describes or modifies the noun (e.g., "This is the team *that* no one wants to play.")

repaginate by issue—The page numbering system for a journal that begins each issue with page 1

replication study—A research study conducted exactly as a previous study; seeks to confirm (replicate) the previous findings

replication-with-extension study—A research study that seeks to confirm (replicate) the results of a previous study but conducted in a different setting, under differing conditions, or with a different participant population

restrictive clause—A clause serving as an adjective to modify a word; essential to the meaning of a sentence; not set off with commas

Results section—The third major section of an APA-Style research report; contains statistical information related to the findings of the experiment

revising—(see editing/revising)

running head—A shortened version of an article's title printed on the top left of each page of a manuscript; also appears at the top of alternate pages of a journal article (required for papers submitted for publication; may not be required for student papers)

s—Symbol for the standard deviation of a sample of scores

SD—Symbol for standard deviation; an alternative to s or σ that is acceptable in documents written in APA Style

secondary source—A source such as a journal article or book that summarizes research or content from another source (e.g., Jones summarizes Smith's research, so Jones is a secondary source)

skewed data—A distribution of scores in which the majority of scores fall near the high or low end of the distribution rather than in the middle

standard deviation—A measure of variability; the square root of the variance; symbolized by s for a sample of scores or σ for a population of score

statistically significant—A difference between two or more groups that is unlikely to have occurred by chance

statistics—A branch of mathematics that involves analysis of data

subordinate clause—A clause that begins with a subordinate conjunction or a relative pronoun; it does not express a complete thought, so it cannot stand alone as a sentence (e.g., "After the subjects heard the stimuli"—the reader is left wondering what happened after the subjects heard the stimuli)

supplemental materials—Supplementary material relevant to an article that is available online; in APA Style, used for material that is more useful as a download or not easily shown in print

t **test**—An inferential statistical test used to compare the means from two samples

table—A chart in an article or paper that shows an array of descriptive statistics (or, sometimes, text)

term paper—A paper written by a student as a class assignment, usually summarizing a number of research studies in a focused area of research; might also be referred to as a literature review

test of independence—A version of the chi-square test that determines whether two variables are independent of each other

thesis—The main point or subject of a paper, article, or other piece of writing

title—Descriptive name for an article; summarizes the main idea of the article (no prescribed word limit in APA Style, but should be concise)

title search—A bibliographic search of the Title field of journal or book records by entering a word in a search box

Tukey post hoc test—A specific type of post hoc test used for significant *F*-test results with three or more groups; allows for comparisons between all pairs of means without inflating error rate

Turabian style—(see Chicago style)

variability—The degree to which scores are distributed around the mean

vita (curriculum vitae)—A detailed listing of a person's academic educational history and accomplishments; an academic version of a resume

References

Alcott, A. B. (1872). *Concord days*. Roberts Brothers.

Alley, M. (1987). *The craft of scientific writing*. Prentice-Hall.

American Psychiatric Association. (2013). *Diagnostic and statistical manual of mental disorders: DSM-5* (5th ed.). https://doi.org/10.1176/appi.books.9780890425596

American Psychological Association. (1994). *Publication manual of the American Psychological Association* (4th ed.).

American Psychological Association. (2001). *Publication manual of the American Psychological Association* (5th ed.).

American Psychological Association. (2002). Ethical principles of psychologists and code of conduct. *American Psychologist, 57*(12), 1060–1073. https://doi.org/10.1037//0003-066x.57.12.1060

American Psychological Association. (2010). *Publication manual of the American Psychological Association* (6th ed.).

American Psychological Association. (2019). Summary report of journal operations, 2018. *American Psychologist, 74*(5), 615–616. http://dx.doi.org/10.1037/amp0000508

American Psychological Association. (2020). *Publication manual of the American Psychological Association* (7th ed.). https://doi.org/10.1037/0000165-000

Aronson, E., & Carlsmith, J. M. (1968). Experimentation in social psychology. In G. Lindzey & E. Aronson (Eds.), *The handbook of social psychology* (2nd ed., Vol. 2, pp. 1–79). Addison-Wesley.

Becker, L. A. (1999). *Measures of effect size (Strength of association)* University of Colorado, Colorado Springs. https://www.uccs.edu/lbecker/glm_effectsize.html

Beins, B. C. (2008). Why we believe: Fostering critical thought and scientific literacy in research methods. In D. S. Dunn, J. S. Halonen, & R. A. Smith (Eds.), *Teaching critical thinking in psychology: A handbook of best practices* (pp. 199–210). Wiley-Blackwell. https://doi:10.1002/9781444305173.ch17

Bellquist, J. E. (1993). *A guide to grammar and usage for psychology and related fields.* Lawrence Erlbaum Associates. https://doi.org/10.4324/9781315806655.

Bem, D. J. (1995). Writing a review article for *Psychological Bulletin. Psychological Bulletin, 118*(2), 172–177. https://doi.org/10.1037/0033-2909.118.2.172

Bennett, C., & Blissett, J. (2014). Measuring hunger and satiety in primary children: Validation of a new picture rating scale. *Appetite, 78,* 40–48. https://doi.org/10.1016/j.appet.2014.03.011

Bentley, M., Peerenboom, C. A., Hodge, F. W., Passano, E. B., Warren, H. C., & Washburn, M. F. (1929). Instructions in regard to preparation of manuscript. *Psychological Bulletin, 26*(2), 57–63. https://doi.org/10.1037/h0071487

Bjork, D. W. (1997). *B. F. Skinner: A life.* American Psychological Association. https://doi.org/10.1037/10130-000.

Blumenthal, A. L. (1991). The intrepid Joseph Jastrow. In G. A. Kimble, M. Wertheimer, & C. L. White (Eds.), *Portraits of pioneers in psychology* (pp. 74–87). American Psychological Association. https://doi.org/10.4324/9781315799568

Brewer, C. L., Hopkins, J. R., Kimble, G. A., Matlin, M. W., McCann, L. I., McNeil, O. V., Nodine, B.F., Quinn, V.N., & Saundra. (1993). Curriculum. In T. V. McGovern (Ed.), *Handbook for enhancing undergraduate education in psychology* (pp. 161–182). American Psychological Association. https://doi.org/10.1037/10126-000

Bruner, K. F. (1942). Of psychological writing: Being some valedictory remarks on style. *Journal of Abnormal and Social Psychology, 37*(1), 52–70. https://doi.org/10.1037/h0062165

Calkins, L. M. (1994). *The art of teaching writing* (2nd ed.). Heinemann.

Carlston, D. (2010). Social cognition. In R. F. Baumeister & E. J. Finkel (Eds.), *Advanced social psychology: The state of the science* (pp. 63–99). Oxford University Press.

Carsrud, A. L., & Palladino, J. J. (1985). Of data and informed opinion: A reply to Furedy and McRae. *Teaching of Psychology, 12*(4), 221–222. https://doi.org/10.1207/s15328023top1204_11

Carsrud, A. L., Palladino, J. J., Tanke, E. D., Aubrecht, L., & Huber, R. J. (1984). Undergraduate psychology research conferences: Goals, policies, and procedures. *Teaching of Psychology, 11*(3), 141–145. https://doi.org/10.1177/009862838401100304

Cash, T. F. (2009). Caveats in the proficient production of an APA-Style research manuscript for publication. *Body Image, 6*(1), 1–6. https://doi.org/10.1016/j.bodyim.2008.10.003

Cathey, C. (2007). Power of peer review: An online collaborative learning assignment in social psychology. *Teaching of Psychology, 34*(2), 97–99. https://doi.org/10.1177/009862830703400205

Chen, S. C. (1937). Social modification of the activity of ants in nest-building. *Physiological Zoology, 10*(4), 420–436. https://doi.org/10.1086/physzool.10.4.30151428

Christiansen, M. (1990). The importance of revision in writing composition. *Education Digest, 56*(2), 70–72.

Cingel, D. P., & Sundar, S. S. (2012). Texting, techspeak, and tweens: The relationship between text messaging and English grammar skills. *New Media & Society, 14*(8), 1304–1320. https://doi.org/10.1177/1461444812442927

Cohen, J. (1988). *Statistical power analysis for the behavioral sciences* (2nd ed.). Erlbaum. https://doi.org/10.4324/9780203771587

Communications Team, University of Aberdeen. (2009, July 17). *Scientists discover why we never forget how to ride a bicycle.* https://www.abdn.ac.uk/news/3275/

Cunningham, M. R. (1986). Measuring the physical in physical attractiveness: Quasi-experiments on the sociobiology of female facial beauty. *Journal of Personality and Social Psychology, 50*(5), 925–935. https://doi.org/10.1037/0022-3514.50.5.925

Cunningham, M. R., Barbee, A. P., & Pike, C. L. (1990). What do women want? Facialmetric assessment of multiple motives in the perception of male facial physical attractiveness. *Journal of Personality and Social Psychology, 59*(1), 61–72. https://doi.org/10.1037/0022-3514.59.1.61

Cunningham, M. R., Roberts, A. R., Barbee, A. P., Druen, P. B., & Wu, C.-W. (1995). "Their ideas of beauty are, on the whole, the same as ours": Consistency and variability in the cross-cultural perception of female physical attractiveness. *Journal of Personality and Social Psychology, 68*(2), 261–279. https://doi.org/10.1037/0022-3514.68.2.261

Data is or data are? (2012, July 8). *The Guardian.* https://www.theguardian.com/news/datablog/2010/jul/16/data-plural-singular

Davis, S. F. (2010, April). Conduct a personal writing habits inventory. In R. A. Smith (Chair), *How to publish your manuscript.* [Symposium]. Southwestern Psychological Association 56th Meeting, Dallas, TX, United States.

Davis, S. F., & Smith, R. A. (2005). *An introduction to statistics and research methods: Becoming a psychological detective.* Pearson Prentice Hall.

Drabick, D. A. G., Weisberg, R., Paul, L., & Bubier, J. L. (2007). Keeping it short and sweet: Brief, ungraded writing assignments facilitate learning. *Teaching of Psychology, 34*(3), 172–176. https://doi.org/10.1080/00986280701498558

Dunn, D. S. (2013). *Research methods for social psychology* (2nd ed.). Wiley.

Dunn, D. S., Brewer, C. L., Cautin, R. L., Gurung, R. A. R., Keith, K. D., McGregor, L. N., Nida, S.A., Puccio, P., & Voigt, M. J. (2010). The undergraduate psychology curriculum: Call for a core. In D. F. Halpern (Ed.), *Undergraduate education in psychology: A blueprint for the future of the discipline* (pp. 47–61). American Psychological Association. https://doi.org/10.1037/12063-000

Eagly, A. H., Ashmore, R. D., Makhijani, M. G., & Longo, L. C. (1991). What is beautiful is good, but …: A meta-analytic review of research on the physical attractiveness stereotype. *Psychological Bulletin, 110*(1), 109–128. https://doi.org/10.1037//0033-2909.110.1.109

Eichorn, D. H., & VandenBos, G. R. (1985). Dissemination of scientific and professional knowledge: Journal publication within the APA. *American Psychologist, 40*(12), 1309–1316. https://doi.org/10.1037/0003-066x.40.12.1309

Farris, C., & Smith, R. (1992). Writing-intensive courses: Tools for curricular change. In S. H. McLeod & M. Soven (Eds.), *Writing across the curriculum: A guide to developing programs* (pp. 52–62). Sage.

Feinman, S., & Gill, G. W. (1978). Sex differences in physical attractiveness preferences. *Journal of Social Psychology, 105*(1), 43–52. https://doi.org/10.1080/00224545.1978.9924089

Fernberger, S. W. (1932). The American Psychological Association: A historical summary, 1892–1930. *Psychological Bulletin, 29*(1), 1–89. https://doi.org/10.1037/h0075733

Fiske, D. W., & Fogg, L. (1990). But the reviewers are making different criticisms of my paper! Diversity and uniqueness in reviewer comments. *American Psychologist, 45*(5), 591–598. https://doi.org/10.1037/0003-066x.45.5.591

Flower, L., Hayes, J. R., Carey, L., Schriver, K., & Stratman, J. (1986). Detection, diagnosis, and the strategies of revision. *College Composition and Communication, 37*(1), 16–55. https://doi.org/10.2307/357381

Garrett, N., Bridgewater, M., & Feinstein, B. (2017). How student performance in first-year composition predicts retention and overall student success. In T. Ruecker, D. Shepherd, H. Estrem, & B. Brunk-Chavez (Eds.), *Retention, persistence, and writing programs* (pp. 93–113). Utah State University Press. https://doi.org/10.7330/9781607326021.c006

Gitter, A. G., Lomranz, J., Saxe, L., & Bar-Tal, Y. (1983). Perceptions of female physique characteristics by American and Israeli students. *Journal of Social Psychology, 121*(1), 7–13. https://doi.org/10.1080/00224545.1983.9924460

Godden, D. R., & Baddeley, A. D. (1975). Context-dependent memory in two natural environments: On land and underwater. *British Journal of Psychology, 66*(3), 325–331. https://doi.org10.1111/j.2044-8295.1975.tb01468.x

Haaga, D. A. F. (1993). Peer review of term papers in graduate psychology courses. *Teaching of Psychology, 20*(1), 28–32. https://doi.org/10.1207/s15328023top2001_5

Harner, J. L. (2000). *On compiling an annotated bibliography* (2nd ed.). Modern Language Association of America.

Helms, J. L., & Rogers, D. T. (2015). *Majoring in psychology: Achieving your educational and career goals* (2nd ed.). Wiley Blackwell.

Hofer, B. K. (2002). Personal epistemology as a psychological and educational construct: An introduction. In B. K. Hofer & P. R. Pintrich (Eds.), *Personal epistemology: The psychology of beliefs about knowledge and knowing* (pp. 3–14). Lawrence Erlbaum Associates.

Hurford, J. R. (1994). *Grammar: A student's guide.* Cambridge University Press.

Johnstone, K. M., Ashbaugh, H., & Warfield, T. D. (2002). Effects of repeated practice and contextual-writing experiences on college students' writing skills. *Journal of Educational Psychology, 94*(2), 305–315. https://doi.org/10.1037/0022-0663.94.2.305

Kay, A. (2011, May 30). What employers want: 5 more skills to cultivate. *USA Today.* http://usatoday30.usatoday.com/money/jobcenter/workplace/kay/2011-05-30-skills-employers-want-part-ii_n.htm

Keith, K. D., & Beins, B. C. (2017). *The Worth expert guide to scientific literacy: Thinking like a psychological scientist.* Worth Publishers.

Kennette, L. N., & Frank, N. M. (2013). The value of peer feedback opportunities for students in writing intensive classes. *Psychology Teaching Review, 19*(2), 106–111. https://files.eric.ed.gov/fulltext/EJ1149732.pdf

Khersonskaya, M. Y., & Smith, R. A. (1998). Cross-cultural differences in perception of physical attractiveness. *Psi Chi Journal of Undergraduate Research, 3*(1), 39–42. https://doi.org/10.24839/1089-4136.jn3.1.39

Kirk, R. E. (1968). *Experimental design: Procedures for the behavioral sciences.* Brooks/Cole.

Kobrin, J. L., Patterson, B. F., Shaw, E. J., Mattern, K. D., & Barbuti, S. M. (2008). *Validity of the SAT for predicting first-year college grade point average* (College Board Research Report No. 2008-5). College Board. https://www.researchgate.net/publication/267954770

Kubista, A. (2010, September 15). *What is the point?* Walden University Writing Center. http://waldenwritingcenter.blogspot.com/2010/09/what-is-point.html

Lakens, D. (2013). Calculating and reporting effect sizes to facilitate cumulative science: A practical primer for *t*-tests and ANOVAs. *Frontiers in Psychology, 4.* https://doi.org/10.3389/fpsyg.2013.00863

Landrum, R. E., & Davis, S. F. (2007). *The psychology major: Career options and strategies for success* (3rd ed.). Pearson Prentice Hall.

Langlois, J. H., Ritter, J. M., Roggman, L. A., & Vaughn, L. S. (1991). Facial diversity and infant preferences for attractive faces. *Developmental Psychology, 27*(1), 79–84. https://doi.org/10.1037//0012-1649.27.1.79

MacPherson, J., Sternhagen, S., Miller, T., Devitt, M., Petros, T. V., & Beckwith, B. (1996). Effect of caffeine, impulsivity, and gender on the components of text processing and recall. *Experimental and Clinical Psychopharmacology, 4*(4), 438–444. https://doi.org/10.1037/1064-1297.4.4.438

Madigan, R., Johnson, S., & Linton, P. (1995). The language of psychology: APA Style as epistemology. *American Psychologist, 50*(6), 428–436. https://doi.org/10.1037//0003-066x.50.6.428

Mahrer, K. D. (2004). Proofreading your own writing? Forget it! *The Leading Edge, 23*(11), 1130–1131. https://doi.org/10.1190/1.1825945

Markow, D., & Pieters, A. (2011). *The MetLife survey of the American teacher: Preparing students for college and careers. A survey of teachers, students, parents, and* Fortune *1000 executives.* MetLife. https://files.eric.ed.gov/fulltext/ED519278.pdf

McLeod, S. H. (1992). Writing across the curriculum. In S. H. McLeod & M. Soven (Eds.), *Writing across the curriculum: A guide to developing programs* (pp. 1–8). Sage.

Modern Language Association. (2016). *MLA handbook* (8th ed.).

Morgan, B. L., & Korschgen, A. J. (2006). *Majoring in psych? Career options for psychology undergraduates* (3rd ed.). Pearson Education.

Morton, E. (2016). *The effects of caffeine on memory and recall* [Unpublished manuscript]. Department of Psychology, Moravian College.

National Center for Education Statistics. (2012). *The nation's report card: Writing 2011* (NCES 2012-470). Institute of Education Sciences, U.S. Department of Education. https://nces.ed.gov/nationsreportcard/pdf/main2011/2012470.pdf

National Commission on Writing for America's Families, Schools, and Colleges. (2004). *Writing: A ticket to work ... or a ticket out: A survey of business leaders.* College Entrance Examination Board. https://www.nwp.org/cs/public/print/resource/2540

Nevid, J. S., Pastva, A., & McClelland, N. 2012). Writing-to-learn assignments in introductory psychology: Is there a learning benefit? *Teaching of Psychology, 39*(4), 272–275. https://doi.org/10.1177/0098628312456622

Newcombe, N. S., & Bouton, M. E. (2009). Masked reviews are not fairer reviews. *Perspectives on Psychological Science, 4*(1), 62–64. https://doi.org/10.1111/j.1745-6924.2009.01102.x

Nichol, M. (2011). How to avoid bias in your writing. *Daily Writing Tips.* https://www.dailywritingtips.com/how-to-avoid-bias-in-your-writing/

Norcross, J. C., Hailstorks, R., Aiken, L. S., Pfund, R. A., Stamm, K. E., & Christidis, P. (2016). Undergraduate study in psychology: Curriculum and assessment. *American Psychologist, 71*(2), 89–101. https://doi.org/10.1037/a0040095

Ondrusek, A. L. (2012). What the research reveals about graduate students' writing skills: A literature review. *Journal of Education for Library and Information Science, 53*(3), 176–188.

Orcher, L. T. (2014). *Conducting research: Social and behavioral science methods* (2nd ed.). Pyrczak. https://doi.org/10.4324/9781315266626

Peluso, E. A. (2000). Skilled motor performance as a function of type of mental imagery. *Journal of Psychological Inquiry, 5,* 11–14.

Perlman, B., & McCann, L. I. (2005). Undergraduate research experiences in psychology: A national study of courses and curricula. *Teaching of Psychology, 32*(1), 5–14. https://doi.org/10.1207/s15328023top3201_2

Perrett, D. I., May, K. A., & Yoshikawa, S. (1994). Facial shape and judgements of female attractiveness. *Nature, 368*(6468), 239–242. https://doi.org/10.1038/368239a0

Peters, D. P., & Ceci, S. J. (1982). Peer-review practices of psychological journals: The fate of published articles, submitted again. *Behavioral and Brain Sciences, 5*(2), 187–195. https://doi.org10.1017/s0140525x00011183

Pew Research Center. (2016, September 13). *The parties on the eve of the 2016 election: Two coalitions, moving further apart.* http://assets.pewresearch.org/wp-content/uploads/sites/5/2016/09/09-13-2016-Party-ID-release-final.pdf

Posey, E., & Smith, R. A. (2003). The self-serving bias in children. *Psi Chi Journal of Undergraduate Research, 8*(4), 153–156. https://doi.org/10.24839/1089-4136.jn8.4.153

Purcell, K., Buchanan, J., & Friedrich, L. (2013). *The impact of digital tools on student writing and how writing is taught in schools* (National Writing Project/Pew Research Center). https://www.nwp.org/afnews/PIP_NWP_Writing_and_Tech.pdf

Robinson, E. S., & Brown, M. A. (1926). Effect of serial position upon memorization. *American Journal of Psychology, 37*(4), 538–552. https://doi.org/10.2307/1414914

Rundus, D. (1971). Analysis of rehearsal processes in free recall. *Journal of Experimental Psychology, 89*(1), 63–77. https://doi.org/10.1037/h0031185

Saville, B. K., Zinn, T. E., Lawrence, N. K., Barron, K. E., & Andre, J. (2008). Teaching critical thinking in statistics and research methods. In D. S. Dunn, J. S. Halonen, & R. A. Smith (Eds.), *Teaching critical thinking in psychology: A handbook of best practices* (pp. 149–160). Wiley-Blackwell. https://doi.org/10.1002/9781444305173.ch13

Sego, A. S., & Stuart, A. E. (2016). Learning to read empirical articles in General Psychology. *Teaching of Psychology, 43*(1), 38–42. https://doi.org/10.1177/0098628315620875

Sigal, M. J., & Pettit, M. (2012). Information overload, professionalization, and the origins of the *Publication Manual of the American Psychological Association*. *Review of General Psychology, 16*(4), 357–363. https://doi.org/10.1037/a0028531

Sinclair, C. (2010). *Grammar: A friendly approach* (2nd ed.). Open University Press/McGraw-Hill.

Singular "they." (2020, October 22). *APA Style*. https://apastyle.apa.org/style-grammar-guidelines/grammar/singular-they

Smith, A. P., Maben, A., & Brockman, P. (1994). Effects of evening meals and caffeine on cognitive performance, mood and cardiovascular functioning. *Appetite, 22*(1), 57–65. https://doi.org/10.1006/appe.1994.1005

Smith, R. A. (1985). Advising beginning psychology majors for graduate school. *Teaching of Psychology, 12*(4), 194–198. https://doi.org/10.1207/s15328023top1204_2

Smith, R. A. (1998). Another perspective on publishing: Keeping the editor happy. *Psi Chi Journal of Undergraduate Research, 3*(2), 51–55. https://doi.org/10.24839/1089-4136.jn3.2.51

Smith, R. A. (2008). A tasty sample(r): Teaching about sampling using M&M's. In L. T. Benjamin, Jr. (Ed.), *Favorite activities for the teaching of psychology* (pp. 8–10). American Psychological Association.

Smith, R. A., & Davis, S. F. (2013). *The psychologist as detective: An introduction to conducting research in psychology* (6th ed.). Pearson.

Spatz, C. (2019). *Basic statistics: Tales of distributions* (12th ed.). Outcrop.

Sternberg, R. J. (2003). *The psychologist's companion: A guide to scientific writing for students and researchers* (4th ed.). Cambridge University Press. https://doi.org/10.1017/CBO9780511819261.

Stroop, J. R. (1935). Studies of interference in serial verbal reactions. *Journal of Experimental Psychology, 18*(6), 643–663. https://doi.org/10.1037/h0054651

Strunk, W., Jr., & White, E. B. (2000). *The elements of style* (4th ed.). Pearson Education.

Swensen, D. (2011, November 9). Writing when you're sick, tired, or just hate the world. *Surlymuse*. http://surlymuse.com/writing-when-youre-sick-tired-or-just-hate-the-world/

Thakerar, J. N., & Iwaki, S. (1979). Cross-cultural comparisons in interpersonal attraction of females toward males. *Journal of Social Psychology, 108*(1), 121–122. https://doi.org/10.1080/00224545.1979.9711969

Turabian, K. L. (with Booth, W. C., Colomb, G. G., Williams, J. M., & University of Chicago Press Editorial Staff). (2013). *A manual for writers of research papers, theses, and dissertations: Chicago style for students and researchers* (8th ed.). University of Chicago Press.

Turabian, K. L. (2018). *A manual for writers of research papers, theses, and dissertations* (9th ed.; revised by W. C. Booth, G. C. Colomb, J. M. Williams, J. Bizup, W.T. Fitzgerald, & University of Chicago Press Editorial Staff). University of Chicago Press.

University of Chicago Press. (2017). *The Chicago manual of style* (17th ed.). https://doi.org/10.7208/cmos17

University of Warwick. (2014, September 9). Students take note: Evidence that leaving essays to the last minute ruins your grades. *ScienceDaily*. www.sciencedaily.com/releases/2014/09/140909144542.htm

Victor, D. (2018, February 9). Oxford comma dispute is settled as Maine drivers get $5 million. *The New York Times*. https://www.nytimes.com

Wadsworth, J., Halfman, A. H., & Upton, T. (2002). Strategies to improve the writing of graduate students. *Rehabilitation Education, 16*(3), 295–305.

Walsh, B. (2015, April 7). Grammar geekery with Bill Walsh (April) [Web log post]. *The Washington Post*. https://live.washingtonpost.com/grammar-geekery-with-bill-walsh-20150407.html

Weiten, W. (2014). *Psychology: Themes and variations* (briefer version, 9th ed.). Wadsworth Cengage Learning.

Whitley, B. E., Jr., & Frieze, I. H. (1985). Children's causal attributions for success and failure in achievement settings: A meta-analysis. *Journal of Educational Psychology, 77*(5), 608–616. https://doi.org/10.1037/0022-0663.77.5.608

Wuensch, K. L. (2015). *Standardized effect size estimation: Why and how?* East Carolina University. http://core.ecu.edu/psyc/wuenschk/StatHelp/Effect%20Size%20Estimation.pdf

York University. (n.d.). *SPARK: Student papers & academic research kit.* https://spark.library.yorku.ca/

Zajonc, R. B. (1965). Social facilitation. *Science, 149*(3681), 269–274. https://doi.org/10.1126/science.149.3681.269

Zajonc, R. B., Heingartner, A., & Herman, E. M. (1969). Social enhancement and impairment of performance in the cockroach. *Journal of Personality and Social Psychology, 13*(2), 83–92. https://doi.org/10.1037/h0028063

Name Index

Subject Index